Creative Teaching of the Language Arts in the Elementary School

2nd edition

JAMES A. SMITH

State University of New York at Oswego

Allyn and Bacon, Inc.
Boston · London · Sydney

To
Mrs. Elizabeth Dunster Radley
who once had such an effect on
my life that everything became
possible

CONTENTS

077224

FOREWORD

In the Foreword of the first editions of the Creative Teaching series E. Paul Torrance expressed a concern that many exciting, meaningful and potentially important ideas have died because no one has translated them into practical methods and that this could be the fate of the creative movement. Fortunately, this concern has not been realized. In the past ten years educational literature has been flooded with reports of research studies, theories and experimental programs which focus on the creative development of each child as a goal in modern education.

Including the development of creativity in each child as an educational objective is a staggering challenge for all school personnel. It calls for the invention of new materials and tools, the development of new time schedules and new patterns of organization, a new approach to child study, the invention of new testing methods, the devising of unique evaluation processes and the creation of new textbooks and teaching procedures. And most of all the task calls for a commitment and dedication on the part of many people to take risks, to make choices and decisions, to push their own creative potential to new limits.

This has been done! In the past ten years the creative spark has caught fire. Thousands of people in all walks of life have found in the creative movement, self-realization and the challenge of making life meaningful for others. The educational scene in America has become peppered with experimental projects in the development of creative thinking.

No movement in education has swept the world as the creative movement has. The need for creative people across the globe today is tremendous. Developing the creative potential of each child has become an educational objective even unto the far corners of the world. The authors of the Creative Teaching series hope these volumes will contribute in some bold measure to producing the changes in teaching methods in the elementary school necessary to realize this objective.

James A. Smith
Oswego, New York

PREFACE

The Creative Teaching series was released by Allyn and Bacon in 1966 and 1967. At once, the language arts volume became the best seller. This author was overwhelmed by a flood of letters expressing the enthusiastic response. Teachers felt that it supported their need for a more humane way of teaching and it triggered their imaginations in getting the curriculum back to the child. Psychologists felt that the material in it better fulfilled the personality needs of children and various learning theories than the noncreative, more traditional manner of teaching. Linguists and students of language wrote to express their gratitude that someone was translating into practice the facts research was telling us about English.

In the first edition of *Creative Teaching in the Language Arts in the Elementary School,* the author drew heavily from the Book I of the series, *Setting Conditions for Creative Teaching in the Elementary School* (which reported research in the area of creativity up to 1967), to formulate a set of principles on which creative teaching in the language arts could be founded. The remainder of the book drew from the accepted knowledge and practices in the area of the language arts, combined it with knowledge in the area of creativity and translated this combination into strategies for the teacher in teaching for creativity or simply for creative teaching.

The current volume re-enforces the concept that to develop creativity in children or to teach creativity the teacher should operate from a basic set of principles and behaviors. Over the period of years between the first and second editions, the principles of creative teaching as they appeared in Book I have withstood the test of time.

The present volume also re-enforces the concept that one of the greatest needs of mankind is the development of creative means of communication. Creative communication implies communication that is effective as well as correct, and the ability to choose the proper time to use both or either.

A great deal of the material in this book has been borrowed

from the first edition but much of the material is new, especially the examples of children's work. The author has added to the text to bring the reader up to date. Some worthwhile and helpful material has come from students of the English language which should give the teacher greater insights and support for teaching creativity.

This volume will be most effective when combined with Book I although the author has attempted to summarize that volume in Chapter I. The book was written with two groups of teachers in mind, the college student in teacher education and the teacher in service.

The author is indebted to many people for the materials presented in this volume. Among them are the many children who granted him permission to use their writings and drawings, his creative teacher-colleagues in education who tried out many ideas in their classrooms and sent him the results, his own students in his courses at Syracuse University, and at State University College at Oswego and the hundreds of teachers who allowed him to visit their classrooms to work with children.

He is indebted especially to to the following people: Mrs. Susan Harmon, Niagara Falls, New York, Public Schools; Mr. Paul Bell, Auburn, New York, Public Schools; Miss Janice Wolek, Nichols School, Syracuse, New York; Mrs. Kathy Brown, Craven Crawford School, Liverpool, New York; Mrs. June Anderson, Norfolk Public Schools, Virginia; Miss Margaret Kalette, Syracuse, New York, Public Schools; Miss Norene Bigelow, Norwich, New York, Public Schools; Mrs. Ruth Baxter, Utica Public Schools, New York; Miss Connie O'Connor and Miss Donna Pinkney, student teachers, State University College of Oswego, New York; Mr. Peter Moses, Lakeshore, New York, Public School; Miss Patricia Harrington and Mrs. Leslie Maturano, St. Mary's School, Oswego, New York; Mrs. Sheryl Nash, Baldwinsville, New York, Public Schools; Mrs. Dorothy Clark and Mrs. Helen Benjamin, State University College Campus School, Oswego, New York; Mrs. Carol Shamon, Liverpool Public Schools, New York.

J.A.S.

PART 1

The Nature of Communication

Fourth graders prepare for a puppet show based on Where the Wild Things Are *by Maurice Sendak.*

CHAPTER I

The Nature of
Creative Teaching

A New Beginning

Now's the time to forget your worries.
Forget the wind and winter flurries.

Plant your new seed and grow your roots.
Throw away sloshy old rubbers and boots.

Grow yourself new. Grow yourself tall.
Grow yourself happy, not bitter at all.

Grow yourself friendly. Grow yourself high.
Grow yourself helpful. Your limit's the sky.

KAREN M.
Grade 5

TO THE READER

The poem above was written by a fifth grade child. It is almost as though she wrote it especially for me for the beginning of this book. "Your limit's the sky," she says, and "Grow yourself new." To be creative this is exactly what you must do: approach teaching with an entirely new viewpoint and realize that every thought or idea you have is worth considering. What *you* think is important, and the sky's the limit!

3

In Chapter I we explore this concept: how to approach teaching in a new and different way. As a result of reading this chapter the reader will become acquainted with the following: (1) a workable definition of creativity; (2) the basic principles of creativity as revealed by research over the last ten years and (3) the principles, culled from that research, which distinguish creative teaching from "traditional" teaching.

THREE CHALLENGES

In my files I have folder after folder on children whom I have taught. I would like to share notes from the files of three of them with you.

David: A Challenge

From the slums he came
To the University school
And his heart was stone!
Hate!
Hostility!
Faithlessness!
He had been hurt!
Hurt at four so his life was bitter.
Loving no one.
Caring for nothing!
Oh, David!

IT MEANT: *A whirlwind of energy released in our Nursery School*
Dishes broken, clay thrown, paint everywhere.
A cyclone which breezed by the teachers, leaving them spinning
Children crying, mothers complaining, teachers wringing hands in despair.

IT MEANT: *Lies, missing toys, stolen crackers, mischief, vandalism.*

A different set of values.
A different type of concepts.
A different kind of language.

No way to communicate except by words but
No understanding behind the words.
David, Ah, David—a miniature well of loneliness.
Child of God—our greatest challenge. Could he be saved?

Missy: Another Challenge

Next I would speak of Missy

"Missy, Missy
Pretty and Prissy" the children sang.
She was!
Pretty as a doll
Dressed like a princess—
First Grade Queen!
Prim, proper, golden
Loved by all
Spoiled by all—
A picture-book child.
What did it mean?

IT MEANT: *Healthy, robust body*
Happy bright eyes, blue and sparkling and alive with de-
lights furnished for her in a friendly world.

IT MEANT: *Hours of happiness—*
Circles of friends, loving relatives, doting parents.
Everyone to love her. Everyone to care.
Everyone.

IT MEANT: *Docility in the first grade room.*
Good manners, everything in its proper place.
Sweet gentleness, envy on the part of others. Loving dot-
ing teachers.

IT MEANT: *Too much in too little time*
Tears at being refused anything—
"No," said Father. "You cannot have a new doll this
Saturday—you just got a new one for your birthday!"
Tears, shrieks, kicking of feet—
"My father is a rotten old stinker!"
A different set of values
A different type of concept.
"Missy, Missy
Pretty and Prissy"
Well, maybe not so much as we thought;
Missy—needs help—Missy, too, a challenge.

Jack: Another Challenge

Then, there is Jack
He came to the fifth grade in our slums not long ago—
He walked with a few others.
"Underprivileged" they said of him.
What did it mean?

IT MEANT: *Skinny, big-eared kid with a generous*
mouth and a splash of freckles.

Wise eyes, deep and sad but blue and alive—questioning
yet gallant.

IT MEANT: *An aggressiveness to remain an entity.*
Flight of the imagination above the humdrum.
A world of rainbow make-believe to blot out the ugly
world of real.

IT MEANT: *An uninhibited naturalness.*
A charming smile.
A burst of enthusiasm
A fountain of energy
A scrawny pillar of strength
Creativity!

Jack stood by the window of the fifth grade room one fall
day watching the maple tree on our playground shed its
red leaves in the golden sunlight—
He said, "Drop by drop, the tree bleeds to death."
He stood there again—
Another day—a winter day
Looking at the squalor across the street
And I looked at him.
He smiled—and his eyes shone as he looked at mine—
"Gee," he said, "livin' is lots of good stuff."
Jack!
How did his soul stay bright like the tinsel in the stars?

THE CHALLENGE OF THE INDIVIDUAL

Three cases; three challenges. Every classroom is full of them
and the problems which they pose for the classroom teacher. How
can each child develop to his fullest potential? It is part of the
the great American dream. Our schools are construed so it might
happen. Smith says, "In a democracy, individuals count but they
don't count for much unless they remain individual." How can we
develop the greatest natural resource this nation has, the individual differences in its children?

One way which seems to be popular in this country today is
through various plans of grouping. Our schools have grouped
homogeneously and heterogeneously. We have had mass-graded,
ungraded and multi-graded plans. To get to each individual child
we have devised plans of team teaching, tandem teaching and re-
medial teaching. We have experimented with new organizational
plans from the Joplin plan through the Amedon plan to the currently popular open school. We have altered curriculum concepts
and initiated new math, individual progress plans, continuous
progress plans and individualized instruction.

THE CHALLENGE MET: CREATIVE DEVELOPMENT

All of these plans involve the manipulation of children; management, as it were, imposed from without. The best solution, however, to helping an individual is to help him to help himself: to bring out those qualities within him which will help him become what he can be, help him become self-realized. Creative approaches to teaching can do this and, combined with other approaches such as those mentioned above, may prove to be the answer for much of the struggle to make education relevant and to set the powers of the individual free.

Through creative teaching David, Missy and Jack were helped to adapt to the life-style of others without losing their own personalities. In creative teaching the teacher is not always concerned about working alone with the individual in a group: she realizes that a child may need the rest of the children to meet his particular needs. David, Missy and Jack could not have their problems solved in isolation from other children; often instruction for individuals can take place in a large group. We will explore this concept later.

What then is creative teaching? To understand it we must first of all understand creativity. This we will do by defining it, by taking a look at the creative child and by reviewing the principles which distinguish creative teaching.

A DEFINITION

Creativity is defined in the Creative Teaching series as the ability to tap past experiences and come up with something new. This product need not necessarily be new to the world, but new to the individual. Creative products take on many forms. In this volume we are concerned with developing creativity through the use of speech, reading and writing. We are also interested in creative ways of going about this task.

PRINCIPLES OF CREATIVITY[1]

Research in the past ten years has helped educators to arrive at some basic conclusions on creativity. It will help us to better understand what creative teaching is if we review these principles:

---

1. Taken from James A. Smith, *Setting Conditions for Creative Teaching in the Elementary School* (Boston: Allyn and Bacon, 1966), pp. 1–21.

1. All children are born creative and have creative powers.
2. There is a relationshp between creativity and intelligence; highly creative people are always highly intelligent, though highly intelligent people are not always creative. All children can create to some degree. There is very little relationship between intelligence and creativity other than the fact that a degree of intelligence is necessary for the creative process to take place.
3. Creativity is a form of giftedness which is not measured by current intelligence tests.
4. All areas of the curriculum may be used to develop creativity. It is not confined solely to the creative arts.
5. Creativity is a process and a product.
6. Creativity is developed by focusing on those processes of the intellect which fall under the general area of divergent thinking. This area of the intellect has been greatly neglected in our teaching up to this point.
7. All creative processes cannot always be developed at one time, or in one lesson. Lessons must be planned to focus on each process.
8. Creativity cannot be taught; we can only set conditions for it to happen and insure its reappearance through re-enforcement.
9. More knowledge, more skills and more facts than ever before are required for creativity to be developed.
10. The sequence of creative development leads us to believe that children must be able to tap all of life's experiences in order to become truly creative; unnecessary rules and actions may force much of their experience into the preconscious or subconscious mind where it cannot be readily used.
11. Excessive conformity and rigidity are true enemies of creativity.
12. Children go through certain steps in the creative process.
13. Creative teaching and creative learning have been more effective than other types of teaching and learning.
14. Children who have lost much of their creativity may be helped to regain it by special methods of teaching.
15. Creativity is developmental; children begin at a simple stage and progress to more difficult stages of productivity.

CHARACTERISTICS OF CREATIVE CHILDREN[2]

The characteristics of creative children have been identified through research. Those behavior patterns which identify the creative child are often apparent in their creative oral and written expression. Because the creative child is not always well accepted by his peers (and his teacher), his teacher can understand him better if she is aware of these characteristics. I have selected from my files and notes some language material which I feel demonstrates each particular characteristic in a creative child.

1. *Creative children tend to be more sensitive to life experiences than other children.* One ten-year-old writes the following thoughts about spring.

Spring

Feeling

Spring feels cool and warm and you have a gay feeling. When going barefoot you can feel the grass. The roses feel very soft and smooth. The rain feels cool and sometimes makes you unhappy.

Smelling

The air smells fresh and clean. The roses have a beautiful scent.

Seeing

The beautiful sun beats down on your skin. You can see the colorful flowers, the raindrops falling, the green, green grass. The green world is spring.

Tasting

You can taste the rain. The wind can be tasted if you have an imagination.

Hearing

The birds are calling in the morning. The wind can be heard. While having showers the rain can be heard beating on life.

LESLIE DALTON
Grade 5

---

2. See Donald W. MacKinnon, "What Makes a Person Creative?" *Saturday Review* (February 1962): 15–17+, and E. Paul Torrance, *Guiding Creative Talent* (Englewood Cliffs, N.J.: Prentice-Hall, 1962), pp. 66–67.

2. *Creative children react more fully with emotions than non-creative children.*

Helen, grade 3, an uncreative child in my classroom, writes:

Strawberries

Strawberries are red. They are good. I like to eat them. I like them in strawberry shortcake.

Terry, a creative child, writes about the same topic in a haiku poem:

Strawberries

Strawberries are red
With little dimples on them
And so good to eat.

TERRY C.
Grade 3

3. *Creative children tend to have superior verbal fluency.* Two sixth grade groups were asked to brainstorm all the uses they could for: (1) a bath tub and (2) a paper cup. One group had been labeled as highly creative by the teachers who were currently involved in a creativity course at a neighboring college. In the resulting lists, the creative group came up with 28 ideas for the bathtub in ten minutes and 27 ideas for the paper cup. The creative group excelled the less creative group by 10 ideas. The ideas were also much more unusual. Following is a list of some of the unusual ideas suggested by the creative group showing their fluency of thinking.

Bathtub

Punch bowl
Flower pot
Bird bath
Storage chest
Aquarium
Barbeque pit
Sunk in the ground for a kiddy pool
Cover with glass and use for ant farm
Litter box
Put wheels on it and use it as a go-cart
Cover top and use it for animal cage

Paper Cup

A walkie-talkie
Cover and use for ornament
Spice holders
Eye shades
Party hats for kids
Mini-lampshade
Urine specimen holder
Darn socks on it
Muzzle for dog

4. *Creative children tend to have superior verbal flexibility.* When Mark was asked what the big fat snowflakes falling outside the window made him think of, he replied, "little ants coming down on parachutes!" Such is the language of children.

Pegianne is at no loss of words in expressing herself in the following poem:

At Highland Forest

There are falls at Highland Forest.
There are tall evergreens.
There are hills on which to climb,
To see beautiful scenes.

There are places to have picnics,
And to have a lot of fun.
Under lovely shady trees
Or in the burning sun.

There is snow upon the mountains,
Birds sing gaily in the trees.
There are pools and pools of water,
And grass that is so green.

It's the place I visit often,
With my family and my friends.
Up the steep mad hills and,
Around the curvey bends.

PEGIANNE LOOMIS

5. *Creative children are more original than other children.* Lynn uses many of her original ideas in this poem:

Flowers

When a bee goes into a flower,
It has a small pollen shower,
The bee stays mainly in the center of the flower,

Where the pollen has all its power,
If you should ever see,
In the center, a bee,
You should think about it in advance,
Because you might see pollenation by chance,
This is so significant to watch,
You might want to take a small snapshot,

When flowers are from the wilderness,
They have a great prettiness,
And if you should ever wear one,
You would always have the most fun!

LYNN
Grade 6

6. *Creative children can perceive and can pass judgments, but they prefer perceiving to judging.*

Madelyn writes me a poem passing judgment on herself and her day.

Such A Fool

Did you ever hear the wind blow
  Beneath the trees? In and out it goes.
For the deer and her baby does
  The breeze is so cool,
The day is bright and beautiful
  And me—such a fool
For staying in the city
  Sitting on a stool!
For I could be out in the forest
  Where it is bright and beautiful.

MADELYN
Grade 5

7. *Creative children tend to be more self-sufficient than other children.*

A group of junior high students were brought into the kindergarten to learn to assist the kindergarten teacher. When they returned to their English classes their teacher asked them to write about their experiences. All the students wrote about how it felt to be a teacher, but Susan did not. She submitted this poem:

When I am with a child—
  I think as a child
  I act as a child
  I love as a child.

When I am with those who are older—
I think as an adult
I behave as an adult
I believe as an adult.
When I am with those who are older—
I somehow wish I were a child again.

SUSAN
Grade 8

8. *Creative children tend to be more independent in their judgments.* After I visited a sixth grade class where I had some pleasant, profitable experiences, the children wrote letters of thanks. Each was different; some wrote prose, some wrote poems and some illustrated their work. The teacher had simply stated, "It is up to you to decide how you will thank Mr. Smith." The creative children decided very quickly what to do. Their letters were charming.

Heman Street School
East Syracuse, New York
March 2, 1961

Dear Dr. Smith,

We liked your visit very much.
You showed us how to write and such.
And because you were so much fun,
We were sorry you had to run.

We have an idea for our play.
We hope you will come and see it someday.
We hope you like it because we do,
And we hope the other classes will like it too.

Yours truly,
Gail Sterling

9. *Creative children tend to be more stable than other children.* Their writing shows their ability to face adventure and catastrophe in life.

The Wolf Dog

Up in the mountains lived Jim Turner and his daughter Vicky. Jim was reading a book and Vicky was lying on the floor staring at the fire. He could tell something was on her mind. He put down his book and asked "What's on your mind, Vicky?" She hesitated. "Today when I was outside I found a beautiful dog," said Vicky. "The most beautiful dog in the world," she said. "Where is the dog?" he asked. She said, "He's outside of the door. I tied him up." "I wondered what was howling so loud and close," he said laughingly.

13

*"Bring him in," he said. "I'd like to see this beautiful dog."
She went out and brought the dog in. After Jim had looked
the dog over, she said, "Can I keep him? I'll take good care of
him." "Well I . . ." "Please, please," exclaimed Vicky. "All
right," said Jim. "Thank you Dad," she said. "Do you have a
name for him?" asked Jim. "I thought of one in the afternoon," she said. "Good, what is the name?" asked Jim. "Wolf
Dog," Vicky said. "Well it's time for bed," said Jim. "Can I
keep him in the house?" "Sure you can," said Jim. "Good
night Dad," she said. "Good night Wolf Dog," she said. "Good
night Vicky," Jim said.*

*Two months later, Vicky, Jim and the Wolf Dog were get-
ting along together fine. One night they forgot to lock the
door. They left it open a little. When they were asleep, Wolf
Dog snuck out of the door. When he got out he ran as fast as
he could. That morning when Vicky and Jim got up they
looked and hunted in the woods but gave up. Vicky was
very sad.*

*He ran and ran and he found himself a hole he could
sleep in for the night. Meanwhile a wolf had caught his scent
and was coming toward him. The Wolf Dog saw him coming
and got ready to fight. With mighty force they started fighting. In a few minutes the struggle was over.*

*The Wolf Dog had won with a few cuts and bruises. But
he had a painful cut in the throat.*

*A few months later his throat healed. He now had a mate
and a family of five children. He was very happy with his
family. The children were strong and good looking.*

*About one month later a wolf attacked the den. The Wolf
Dog struggled but finally the wolf fell to the earth. But the
Wolf Dog got cut in the throat like the last time. The family
was safe and that was what was important. He dragged his
body to the cave but didn't make it because he died.*

The End

DIANE BOMBARDIERI
Grade 6

10. *Creative children have a sense of humor, a playfulness
with words not witnessed in noncreative children.* Diana even
creates a word to express her feelings:

Arithmetic

*Arithmetic is very queer
It makes you think all the year.
Problems, problems—oh what problems!
They give me a case of soblems.*

DIANA
Grade 5

11. *Creative children are more interested in nonconventional roles than other children.*

What Will I Be When I Grow Up

Nurses are great
    And so are doctors,
Lawyers, teachers, actors
    I like stewardesses
And farmer's kids
    Who sit and ride big tractors
An actress? No
    Playwright? Perhaps
A census-taker-rater?
    I'd rather be a clerk
A telephone operator
    What will I be
When I grow up?
    I know it is a panic
But of all the jobs
    I'll choose just one
An automobile mechanic!

KAREN
Grade 5

12. *Creative boys seem to be more feminine in their interests than noncreative boys (and creative girls more masculine).*

Donald writes of nature (his impressions of a snow fight) in a manner that shows his wide interests and Sharon writes about a topic often reserved for boys.

Wandering Things

Lowsome things coming to warm the earth
Coming to cover the emerald ground with crystal.
Children take and make trouble out of it.
It is innocent but still goes on trial.

DONALD
Grade 4

Cars

They whirr and spit
And sputter and wheeze,
They growl and groan
And spat and sneeze
They shout and holler

They hack and cough
These cars at the races:
They're off! They're off!

SHARON
Grade 4

13. *Creative children tend to be more dominant and self-assertive.*

Mrs. Lomax set conditions each day for the children to write some poetry or prose. One day Peter rebelled but did it in a delightful manner.

I Cannot!

I cannot write a poem
I cannot write a story
I cannot say nice things
I do not have ideas
So I will not write
I feel unhappy.
Maybe tomorrow I will write
Maybe tomorrow—
I will be happy!

PETER
Age 8

14. *Creative children are apt to be estranged from their peers.*

Victor said to me, "Loneliness is like being all by yourself even when you are in a crowd."

15. *Creative children are more adventurous and resourceful than other children.*

An Adventure

My name is Ronald Kempster. I am the guard at a Drug Factory. I must see that all workers that enter the building have a pass card. My job is pretty boring, so I spend most of my time watching the workers wives that come to pick them up at 6:00. All the workers are men. I would like to tell you about the time some men got into our factory and took out some of the drugs illegally. It was a very hot June day. All the other guards had gone on vacation and I had to work all day everyday. The heat made me drowsy and I had to fight from going to sleep. Just as I was weakening in my fight I saw a man climbing over the fence into the factory grounds. I thought that if I yelled at him he would get away before

I had a chance to talk to him, so I ran towards the building and looked around the corner. The man had his back against the wall sliding up towards the corner where I was. I got back against the wall hardly daring to breathe. I had a stick to hit him with when he got to the corner. After about 5 minutes of nothing, I peeked around the corner. The man was gone. I walked along the side of the building. I was not alert so I did not see a foot that was stuck out in front of me just as I got to the corner. I tripped over it and sprawled out on my stomach. I twisted my head around just in time to see the man I had seen before running around the corner which I had been guarding. I jumped up and dashed after him. As I drew nearer I sprang. Where I landed I can't tell you because I fainted in mid air, but when I woke up I was in the manager's office. "Kempster," he said "that man that you caught . . ." "I caught him?" I interrupted. "Yes he's beside you." "Oh." "That man was sent here on purpose to see how good our guarding system is. Unfortunately it is not very good."

"But I caught him."

"I know but while you were chasing him 5 other thieves got in and took 5 lbs. of drugs in the form of liquid and dis solving powder."

"Don't worry I'll get the drugs back."

"But Kempster, each man left in a different direction."

"Oh."

"You are dismissed now Kempster. Oh, and Kempster, you are off duty. We have some new guards." I left the office and walked out on to the street. What was I going to do? Then i struck me. The old deserted warehouse down by the wharf That was a perfect place to hide drugs. I got into my car and went down there.

It was growing darker. I snuck up to the front door and put my ear against it. This is what I heard.

"Tonight we will put these drugs into the city water supply and soon all the people will be going crazy." I left the door and walked around the warehouse. Across the street was a phone booth. I walked over and phoned the police. On my way out I noticed a gun on the ground. I picked it up and walked back to the warehouse. Then with gun in hand I threw back the door and walked in. There were six men inside, all unarmed.

"Well it looks as though you're caught," I said bravely.

"Please don't shoot us," one begged.

"I won't shoot you if there's no funny business," I said.

Just then I heard sirens and the screeching of brakes. Eight armed policemen came in.

"Nice job," one said. I walked outside and got in my car. On my way home I thought, maybe I'm not such a good guard but those men weren't so smart either. They hadn't even noticed that the gun I had threatened them with was a child's water pistol.

RONALD
Age 11

16. *Creative children have a great deal of energy, a great zest for living, a high degree of effectiveness, and are industrious.*

Nan Sue's poem reflects the curious mind of the creative child that drives them to action and thought.

I Wonder

I wonder, I wonder why the sky is blue,
I wonder, I wonder why we do things that we do.
I wonder, I wonder why the sea is deep,
I wonder, I wonder why do people weep.
I wonder, I wonder why little dogs bark,
I wonder, I wonder what makes the dark.
I wonder, I wonder what makes us think,
I wonder, I wonder why boats don't sink.
I wonder, I wonder what makes the sun shine,
I wonder, I wonder what good friend is mine.

NAN SUE TEITELBAUM
Grade 6

17. *Creative children are often challenged by disorder.*

From a pile of junk, some of my third graders invented a Christmas tree ornament. We listed words to describe it. Then, each wrote to me about it:

This beautiful glowing glass,
Looks much like golden brass.
With its beautiful little ring,
It's fit for a king.
With its little balls a glowing.
It is really worth a showing.

JEFF
Grade 3

The Ornament

Inside the two crystal glasses were colorful balls, golden beads, silver and bright red flowers strung together and shin-

FIGURE 1-1.   *Christmas ornaments created by an eight-year-old.*

ing ribbon on the outside. A gleaming ball crowned the top
of the ornament.

DOUG MCRAE
Grade 3

18. *Creative children seem always to be baffled by something.*

Tell Me

What makes stars shine in the night?
How does the sun make colored light?
What makes things taste? What is a feeling?
How come the flies stay on the ceiling?

JACK WESLEY
Grade 4

19. *Creative children seem to be introversive.*

A Hurt

Did you ever want to go somewhere or do something very badly? I did. I wanted very much to go to the new Pre-Teen Canteen dance. I wanted to go so badly it hurt.

The committee in charge of the dance decided it was to be a "date" dance. Every day I waited for some boy to ask me to go. I even batted my eyelashes at a few. As the days wore on I became more and more miserable. I felt like crying all the time. I had a lump in my throat as big as a ball. I didn't want to talk to anyone. My feet felt like lead. I dragged around the halls at school and around the house. I avoided the groups of girls talking about the dance. My mother wanted to get a doctor; she thought I was sick.

I grew more miserable with each passing day, but no one asked me to the dance. That was my greatest hurt!

Ellen
Grade 6

20. *Creative children are attracted to the unknown and the mysterious.*

The Mysterious Room

About 50 years ago some one by the name of Philip Forlonso built a very large house.

He lived in it until one day some one said he had died. But some one kidnapped him and took him away and he was never seen again. Then the house was said to be haunted and no one went near that house again.

Then one day a David Carcini came to town to visit. And about a week after he came, he was told about this house and about who built it. And then he said, "That man was my grandfather and left me that house to me in his will!" So the next day he asked where it was and they said on that dirt road. So after that he found the house and went up the worn-down stone walk onto the old porch with creaky steps leading up to it and opened the creaky door. He was astonished when he looked in because it looked like some one had been living there which was said to be not true.

After looking around the downstairs he went up the creaky stairs onto the next floor. Which looked just like the down-stairs rooms all messed up. But the hall looked like the hall downstairs which was nice and neat.

After looking around the hall and finding nobody, he found another flight of stairs and said "It is getting late so I think

I'll go back to my hotel room." After going downstairs he opened the creaky door and he found a note saying:

Dear David,

I was said to be dead but I am really not. Please stay here for dinner.

Your Grandfather

"That is ridiculous. I think some one is playing a joke on me," he thought. Suddenly he heard running footsteps. And when he looked up he saw the man that showed him where the road was to the house. Then David went back to his hotel room. And just as he started to lie down on his bed a knock came on the door so he answered it unwillingly. A young man with a blue suit stood there and said "Telegram for Mr. David Carcini" and David took the telegram. And it said:

Dear David,

I did not see you at dinner tonight.

Your Grandfather

and now he knew it was a joke.

After a good night's sleep, he went over to the house very early. He decided to go to the third floor today. When he got up to the third floor the hall was very neat. So he went in every room except the last and they were all very messy. When he opened the last door, there was a man sitting in a big black leather chair turning around and saying "Well young David how have you been? I hope you've been fine. Well tonight I'd like you to stay for dinner." David said "No I have other plans tonight." "Well I am sorry to hear that, maybe some other time."

So David left and said to himself, "That man looks familiar but not like my grandfather." Then he heard two people laughing and it was coming from the room he was just in.

He went over and looked through the keyhole. And saw a man getting out of an outfit; there was a woman and they were both laughing.

After David had gone down two flights of stairs he opened the door, went down the old walk got in his car and drove straight to the man's house. When he got there he asked the maid where the man of the house was. She said "They went up to that old haunted house."

"They? Who's they?" he replied.

"Him and the Mrs.," she said

"Thank you very much," he said.

"I think that I should give him a good scare," he said get-

ting into his car. *"I think I'll go back up to the house and when he comes out I'll chat with him for a while."*

When he got to the car, he saw some one lying all tied up and after a second he realized it was his grandfather. After his grandfather told him what had happened, David went up to the room with his grandfather. And the room had changed to become dark and messy. So David flicked the light switch and the whole room had changed to the same room that he was in before. They saw the woman and the man who confessed about telling people that the house was haunted and they didn't want anybody trying to sell it or buy it because they wanted peace and quiet out there. And, they said that they kidnapped the grandfather.

After they had gotten all straightened out, they all pitched in and cleaned up the place and lived there for a very long time.

The End

NEIL SPRAGUE
Grade 5

21. *Creative children are self-starters and are persistent.*

I wrote six titles on the chalkboard one day, all about spring. Before I could get to the time in the day when we were going to discuss the topics and use them for creative writing, six children in the class had already selected one and had composed a story or poem about it. This is Todd's.

Spring Awakes

Green grass is growing
Green grows the hills
Soft winds are blowing
Golden daffodils

My heart is singing
Melodies fill the air
Birds now are winging
Spring's everywhere!

TODD
Grade 6

PRINCIPLES BASIC TO CREATIVE TEACHING

An understanding of creativity combined with an understanding of the behaviors of the creative child leads us to conclude that the following set of statements may serve as a set of principles and a foundation for creative teaching. Some of these principles apply to all good teaching, but a composite of all the principles over a period of time leads to creative teaching.

1. *In creative teaching, something new, different or unique results.* The first criterion for creative teaching is that the product or the process must be new. In the creative teaching of the language arts children invent new poems, stories, patterns of poetry, word combinations and even words.

2. *In creative teaching, divergent thinking processes are stressed.* Divergent thinking processes are not concerned with an absolute or correct answer. In divergent thinking, knowledges, facts, concepts, understandings and skills learned through convergent thinking processes are put to new uses and new answers result rather than one absolute or correct answer. Divergent thinking processes develop such qualities as flexibility of thinking, originality, fluency of ideas, spontaneity and uniqueness and are the basis of creative thinking. Creativity is a kind of giftedness.

The training of the divergent thinking processes in the elementary schools has been grossly neglected because little was known of the nature of creativity and how it develops. Research in the area of creativity has added substantial understanding of our thought processes. Neglect of training of this area of the intellect is no longer justifiable.

In teaching the language arts, the teacher has many opportunities to develop the convergent and divergent functions of the intellect. Learning the uses of a comma is an example of the memorization of absolute facts which are constantly applied in practical writing as a social courtesy. This is convergent thinking.

To develop divergency of thinking in children is to develop creativity. Every aspect of the language arts curriculum may be utilized to do this, even handwriting and spelling, as developed in Chapters VII and IX.

3. *In creative teaching, motivational tensions are a prerequisite in the creative process. The process serves as a tension-relieving agent.*

In the third grade where Terry wrote the haiku poem about strawberries, the teacher introduced the children to the haiku form of writing poetry one day. Then, on another day she brought in a box of strawberries. Each child studied his strawberry. Words which described the strawberry were written on the chalkboard. Then the children ate the strawberries. More words describing the taste of the strawberries were added. Then the children were allowed to choose a form of writing with which they could tell about the strawberries. Terry chose haiku.

From the opening of the lesson, Miss Mann, the teacher, built tensions within the children by introducing the box of straw-berries. She constantly asked the children to think by asking ques-tions which teased their imaginations. They saw, tasted, felt and smelled strawberries. The motivation to express themselves built positive tensions which were released successfully and with satis-faction in the written work of the children.

However, not every minute of every day in Miss Mann's room is keyed to the tension-building described in this lesson. Periods of relaxation, when the energies of the children are not high-pitched, are also important for creative production.

4. *In creative teaching, open-ended situations are utilized.* Miss Mann posed questions which were worded so that they stimulated more questions. Open-endedness in teaching means that children are presented with situations where they can put their knowledges, understandings, facts and skills to work. Miss Mann provided open-ended situations when she asked for *unique* words to de-scribe the fruit, and later when she suggested they use their emo-tions to describe the fruit, and later when she encouraged them to select a form from their own experience or make one of their own to express how they felt about the strawberries. The most important open-ended situation finally occurred when Miss Mann said, "Now you are on your own. Go ahead and write about the fruit—use any form you like, any ideas you like and write as many poems or phrases as you like."

5. *In creative teaching, there comes a time when the teacher withdraws and children face the unknown themselves.* Miss Mann told the children they were on their own and added, "What we want now is ideas—as many *different* ideas as possible. You may use the ideas on the chalkboard but only if you use them in a new way. Okay, let's go!" She made certain that she had built highly motivating tensions in the children and then she let them release these tensions in individual ways through writing their own pic-turesque speech.

6. *In creative teaching, the outcomes are unpredictable.* When Miss Mann withdrew as a guide and leader to the children she changed her role. Up to this moment she had been the organizer, the instigator, the leader, the *divergent* thinker and the children were the responders, the helpers, the *convergent* thinkers. From this moment on the children became the organizers, the instiga-tors, the leaders and the main source of *divergent* thinking pro-cesses. Miss Mann became the responder, the helper. She did not know what products would result from her motivations, she could only encourage the children and hope they would create. Her faith in them was obviously justified.

7. *In creative teaching, conditions are set which make possible*

preconscious thinking. Miss Mann encouraged the children to draw again and again from memory and from things they had heard or seen or felt. She accepted and used all their ideas. None was considered silly. In Chapter II a longer explanation of this principle is developed.

8. *Creative teaching means that students are encouraged to generate and develop their own ideas*. The other poems and picturesque speech which resulted from Miss Mann's lesson show that she is a master at this.

9. *In creative teaching, differences, uniqueness, individuality, originality are stressed and rewarded*. Notice how Miss Mann asked for *different* ideas. Her methods of inquiry and presentation, judged by the unique products she obtained, were successful.

10. *In creative teaching, the process is as important as the product*. The process of creative production has been defined by Marksberry[3] as follows: (a) a period of preparation when the creator becomes involved with and identifies with the problem at hand; (b) a period of incubation when the creator lives with, and is even tormented by the problem; (c) a period of insight when all parts of the problem seem to become clear; (d) a period of illumination or inspiration when the ideas or answers seem to come (this may also be classified as a moment of discovery) and (e) a period of verification, elaboration, perfection and evaluation when the product is tested for its worth and tension is relieved.

Because Miss Mann's lesson was one of minor problem-solving situations, all the steps of the creative process as defined by Marksberry are not as dramatically exposed as by some other illustrations which will come later. The period of incubation was short. It is a fact of creativity that it can be found in varying degrees. Lower degrees of creative problem-solving do not require as long a period of time to reach a solution as higher degrees of problem-solving, but in spite of this, each of Marksberry's suggested stages was present to some degree in the account of Miss Mann's lesson.

11. *In creative teaching, certain conditions must be set to permit creativity to appear*. Creativity cannot be taught. We can only set conditions for it to happen, and then by re-enforcing its appearance through reward, encourage it to appear often. Among the conditions which must be present are certain *physical conditions*. Miss Mann provided a comfortable classroom, a comfortable and suitable seating arrangement and all the necessary materials for her lesson.

Certain psychological conditions are also necessary. Miss Mann

---

3. Mary Lee Marksberry, *Foundation of Creativity* (New York: Harper and Row, 1963), pp. 17–20.

provided these through establishing good rapport with the students and by developing an "air of expectancy" for creativeness in her classroom. She also developed a permissive atmosphere and a feeling of acceptance. Psychological security was provided through putting ideas on the chalkboard, building a vocabulary to which all could contribute and from which all could draw and in accepting and praising all contributions. Her lesson was, therefore, success-oriented and all the children became involved. Divergent thinking processes developed as the teacher encouraged the children to use more and different ideas.

Intellectual conditions abound in the challenge of creative thinking, in teasing the imagination, in keeping all the children thinking, in drawing on former words and experiences for material and in putting this material into new patterns.

Sound social and emotional conditions were present in the rapport among the children, the acceptance of the teacher and the freedom allowed to explore ideas.

12. *Creative teaching is success oriented rather than failure oriented.* In Miss Mann's lesson, many children may have had a failure experience, but all were eventually resolved so they experienced success. There is a difference between failure experiences and failure. Failure experiences help children understand the true conditions of life and help build character, but repeated failure can only result in psychological damage.

13. *In creative teaching, provision is made to learn many knowledges and skills but provision is also made to apply these knowledges and skills in new problem-solving situations.* Miss Mann's lesson was a follow-up on other lessons in vocabulary building, word usage, punctuation usage, speech improvement and composition. Every creative lesson cannot develop *all* the principles of creative teaching any more than one lesson can teach all the uses of the comma. But Miss Mann developed most of them. The problems she posed were not of great magnitude, but they were important in that they gave the children the practice needed to deal with problems of magnitude which they encounter later on.

14. *In creative teaching, self-initiated learning is encouraged.* Miss Mann's questions helped children to draw on their own experiences, to perceive in new ways, to recognize new relationships and to produce new ideas.

15. *In creative teaching, skills of constructive criticism and evaluation skills are developed.* After the children wrote their picturesque speech, they read their ideas to each other. Helpful suggestions were given for a different word here or there. In some instances a whole new idea emerged. Miss Mann then helped

each child prepare his creation for a bulletin board by checking his punctuation and handwriting. A discussion was also held about the various patterns each child used in writing his idea on paper. Constructive criticism encourages creativity but evaluation is better deferred in the creative act, as we shall see later.

16. *In creative teaching, ideas and objects are manipulated and explored.* Miss Mann's lesson was a good example of this principle.

17. *Creative teaching employs democratic processes.* The exchanging of roles between pupils and teacher and the general tone of the classroom are good examples of the application of democratic principles.

18. *In creative teaching, methods are used which are unique to the development of creativity.* Among these special methods are those suggested by Alex Osborn[4] and Sidney Parnes[5] in their courses on creative problem-solving at the University of Buffalo:

a.   Deferred judgment—notice that no evaluation of ideas was offered until after all ideas were out, and all picturesque speech papers were read.

b.   Creative ideation—to stretch creative thinking Osborn and Parnes suggest the following with creative products: new uses, adaptiveness, modification, magnification, minification, substitution, rearrangement, reversing and combining. Dr. Parnes suggests attribute listing, forced relationships and structure analysis.

c.   Brainstorming—a method of creative ideation. In the account of the uses of the bathtub and paper cup above, we see a good example of brainstorming; see pages 10–11.

INDEPENDENT LEARNING THROUGH CREATIVE TEACHING: AN EXAMPLE

Creative teaching should develop the abilities of the children so they are able to learn and function with a minimum of guidance from the teacher. One of my student teachers was especially gifted in her ability to help children work independently. The coming of spring offered her an excellent opportunity for a project which integrated all the subject matter areas. I asked her to write a brief account of this project for me.

---

4. Alex F. Osborn, *Applied Imagination* (New York: Charles Scribner's Sons, 1963).

5. Sidney J. Parnes, *Instructor's Manual for Semester Courses in Creative Problem Solving* (rev. ed.; Buffalo, N.Y.: Creative Education Foundation, 1963), pp. 32–66.

"May Madness" was an original seven-scene program written and performed by fifth grade level students. Dona wrote this about it:

My students requested performing a program for their classmates and, after a two-day brainstorming effort, decided to write an original program for May, as opposed to performing a play or program commercially written for fifth grade students. These thirty-five students have shown many signs of creativity during their language arts and reading classes, as evidenced in their independence, unusual questions, unique poetry, and genuine interest in writing creative stories and doing independent reading. The class size is large, but all the students are reading and working at least one year above their grade level and, therefore, are easily motivated and work well independently. I felt they had the ability to write and perform a program with my guidance.

The program, performed May 6 for all fourth and fifth level students, included the following:

Scene 1: "Animals of Spring," a poem written and recited by four boys. These boys, each carrying a flower, decided on a take-off of Henry Gibson from the television program "Laugh-In." The presentation was very effective and the boys enumerated all those slimy, fluttery animals which seem to come to life only in the spring.

Scene 2: "Flowers," a poem written by three girls and three boys, depicting two flowers who bloom in the morning, play all day, during which time they are visited by busy birds and bees, and then their life is tragically nipped in the bud in the evening by an unknowing lawnmower. The children playing the characters do not speak, but wear signs denoting their part. They dramatically pantomimed the feeling of two flowers born and buried in one day.

Scene 3: "Mother's Day," a poem written by six girls and pantomimed by five girls and one boy, the father. It involved a narration of both the good and bad aspects of being a mother, i.e., housework, naughty children. But a bow of thanks is given to Mother on her special day, Mother's Day.

Scene 4: "Baseball," a poem in which the narrator describes this sport which begins in the spring and ends in the fall, "All you really need is a bat and a ball." Of course, every boy in the class wanted to take part, and they were very proud of their lines:

Baseball is a game
Which cannot be played with a dame!

Scene 5: "Sunny Days," a poem depicting all the beautiful things which happen and are seen when the sun shines in May. The students wear signs denoting their part: Maple tree, frog, polliwog, snake and bees.

Scene 6: "Rainy Days," a poem depicting those things which happen in the rain and those animals which visit the earth only when it rains: worms, snakes, toads and children who play in the rain—with galoshes and a broken umbrella.

Scene 7: "A Mad Day in May," a poem depicting a day in which all the elements in the weather come to life and perform. This particular scene was motivated by a recent Science Unit on, "Why Does the Weather Change?" Each student in the performance wears a sign denoting his part: The curtains part (shake hands), the sun rises (student rises from chair), wind blows, thunder claps, lightning strikes, rain falls, sun sets, curtains close, and the Mad Day in May is over—I wonder what June will bring!

The students seemed to thoroughly enjoy writing and performing this program. The applause by their peers made their efforts worthwhile. I feel it was a learning experience not only for these children, but also for myself. They were able to creatively express what they wanted to say to their classmates about May and what it meant to them.

SUMMARY

In American education the concept of "meeting" individual needs must be replaced by a broader one—that of "developing individual differences"—if the greatest resource of the nation is to be developed. The Davids, the Missies and the Jacks who come to the American schools carry with them the potential for solving their own problems: the job of the school is to release this potential. Creative teaching which makes learning interesting, dynamic and relevant to the children and which also develops their creative powers may well be one answer to this dilemma.

Recent research in the area of creativity has revealed some concepts which take a giant step toward reaching this goal. Studies of the creative child have caused educators to identify and accept new kinds of behavior. Creative teaching can be defined and planned around a set of basic principles.

In creative teaching the job of the teacher is three-fold: (1) she must be sure the children are taught certain knowledges and skills needed for the solution of any given problem, (2) she must be certain she has helped instill the attitudes essential for creative development and (3) she must set the necessary conditions so these skills can be combined with the experiences of the children into new patterns. In other words, by adhering to the principles outlined above she must utilize problems in the classroom in such a way that creative processes will be used to solve them.

This chapter clearly shows how all the principles may be employed to develop creative expression through the language arts.

TO THE COLLEGE STUDENT AND THE CLASSROOM TEACHER

1. The author listed his objectives for writing this chapter on page 4. Did he accomplish these objectives? To what degree did he do it creatively?

2. Take the cases of David, Missy and Jack. Even though there is little evidence presented for each child, do you see differences in them? Do you feel you know children like them? Make a set of plans to develop the creativity in each, and the ability to help each of these children handle his own problem.

3. An extremely creative book of open-ended situations is Remy Charlep's *Arm in Arm* (New York: Parents Magazine Press, 1969). Both you and your colleagues (and students, if you are a teacher) will enjoy reading this delightful departure from the commonplace.

4. Brainstorm this idea: What are all the uses of a paper plate in teaching *all* curriculum areas? Have children brainstorm it also.

5. Make a list of all the blocks set in your way to prevent creative production, both in your job and in everyday living.

6. Read Sylvia Ashton-Warner's books, *Spinster* and *Teacher*, and discuss the following topics:
a. Creative people often are forced to be antisocial in order to accomplish their creative drives.
b. To be creative in current times means to be courageous.
c. The practical aspects of a school curriculum must always be considered before the creative aspects.
d. Noncreative people seek security in rules and conformity.

7. Try some divergent thinking in class while discussing these problems:
a. What is an appropriate theme to use for our college spring dance? How can we decorate and have appropriate refreshments for $100 total expenses?
b. Assume your May Day Float Parade will have as its theme, "Storybooks for Children." Divide into groups and have each

group design a float appropriate to the theme. Try to limit your expenses by putting available materials to creative uses.

c. Plan a good field show for your band and cheerleaders for the half period of your next football game.

d. Plan an aquatic show to be given for fund-raising at your college swimming pool. Incorporate as many props as possible.

e. Plan an unusual spring picnic for your class using none of the ideas ordinarily used at a typical picnic.

8. Make a list of the principles of creative teaching stated in this chapter and check your own teaching against them. In how many areas are you proficient? In how many are you deficient? If you are a student, check your student teaching against this list.

9. Search your own opinions regarding intellectually gifted and creatively gifted children. Do you feel you can identify the creatively gifted in your classroom or among your peers? Try some of the following questions on your children and notice which ones have the greatest number of ideas, the greatest fluency of ideas, the most original ideas and the most unusual ideas.

a. How many ways can we use an apple?

b. To how many uses can we put a rock?

c. What two things in our classroom can we put together to make something new?

d. Using only a volley ball and a wastepaper basket, make up a new game.

e. How many different yet appropriate names can you make up for the story "Hansel and Gretel"?

10. Apply the principle of deferred judgment when using the above ideas.

11. Here are some other ideas to stretch children's imagination:

a. Ask them to design an invention which will show how fast the wind is blowing outside while they are inside.

b. Ask them to draw twenty circles on a page and then in five minutes see how many things they can make out of the circles. If ideas begin to run out, suggest that the children think of all the circular forms in their mother's kitchen, in their living room, etc. Note whether or not there is a flurry of greater production after each suggestion.

c. Ask them to think of all the ways they can make the bulky records in the school office take up less space.

12. Assume a group of manufacturers find themselves left with a million monster dolls when the craze suddenly dies down. Think of all the uses to which you can put a monster doll so the manufacturers will not lose their initial investment.

13. Take any lesson you taught today that developed convergent thinking skills and replan it so it becomes open-ended; that is, use the information in a problem-solving situation.

14. Think how the process was as important as the product in:
a. The invention of the ice box.
b. The discovery of the Salk vaccine.
c. The launching of the first rocket into outer space.
d. The invention of the safety pin.

15. Take any one of the poems written in this chapter by the children and reconstruct the creative lesson which brought about its conception.

16. Record a random set of incidents from your observations in two different classrooms. Then submit both sets of incidents to an interaction analysis, such as Flander's Matrix, and note the items he suggests, such as teacher participation, pupil participation, interaction between the two, kinds of mental functioning called into play and the like. Determine which of the two situations you felt was more creative and then try to formulate some hypotheses of creative teaching that are not stated in Chapter I of this text, which might become problems for research studies.

SELECTED BIBLIOGRAPHY

Anderson, Harold H. (ed.). *Creativity and Its Cultivation*. New York: Harper and Row, 1959.

Anderson, Harold H. (ed.). *Creativity in Childhood and Adolescence*. Palo Alto, Calif.: Science and Behavior Books, 1962.

Ashton-Warner, Sylvia. *Spinster*. New York: Simon and Schuster, 1959.

————. *Teacher*. New York: Simon and Schuster, 1963.

Baker, Samm. *Your Key to Creative Thinking*. New York: Bantam Books, 1968.

Barron, Frank. *Creativity and Personal Freedom*. Princeton, N.J.: Van Nostrand, 1968.

————. *Creativity and Psychological Health: Origins of Personal Vitality and Creative Freedom*. Princeton, N.J.: Van Nostrand, 1963.

Berman, Louise M. *Creativity in Education*. Madison: University of Wisconsin, School of Education, 1964.

Bernier, Norman. *The Affective Domain in Teaching*. Chicago: Association for Student Teaching, Speech-First Florence B. Stratemeyer Lecture, February 17, 1966.

Clark, C. H. *Brainstorming*. New York: Doubleday, 1958.

Clegg, A. "What Is a Humanizing Curriculum?" *National Elementary Principal* 49 (February 1970): 8–12.

Crary, Ryland W. *Humanizing the School: Curriculum Development and Theory*. New York: Alfred A. Knopf, 1969.

Eisner, Elliot. *Think with Me about Creativity: Ten Essays on Creativity.* Dansville, N.Y.: F. A. Owen, 1964.

Fabun, Don. *You and Creativity.* Beverly Hills, Calif.: Glencoe Press, 1968.

Gardner, John. *Self-Renewal: The Individual and the Innovative Society.* New York: Harper and Row, 1962.

Getzels, Jacob W. and Phillip W. Jackson. *Creativity and Intelligence.* New York: John Wiley, 1962.

Gowan, John Curtis, George D. Demos and E. Paul Torrance (eds.). *Creativity: Its Educational Implications.* New York: John Wiley, 1967.

Guilford, J. P. "Factors That Aid and Hinder Creativity." *Teachers College Record* 63 (February 1962): 386–92.

————. *Intelligence, Creativity and Their Educational Implications.* San Diego, Calif.: R. R. Knapp, 1968.

Halprin, Lawrence. *Creative Processes in the Human Environment.* New York: George Braziller, 1969.

Hopkins, Lee Bennett. *Let Them Be Themselves.* New York: Citation Press, 1969.

Hyman, H. *Some Experiments in Creativity.* New York: Random House, 1961.

Kagan, Jerome (ed.). *Creativity and Learning.* Boston: Houghton Mifflin, 1967.

Karagulla, Shafica. *Breakthrough to Creativity: Your Higher Sense Perception.* Los Angeles: DeVorss, 1967.

Kneller, George. *The Art and Science of Creativity.* New York: Holt, Rinehart and Winston, 1965.

Kornbluth, Frances S. *Creativity and the Teacher.* Chicago: American Federation of Teachers, 1966.

Marksberry, Mary Lee. *Foundation of Creativity.* New York: Harper and Row, 1963.

Mars, David. *Organizational Climate for Creativity.* Buffalo, N.Y.: Creative Education Foundation, 1969.

Massialas, B. G. and Jack Zevin. *Creative Encounters in the Classroom: Teaching and Learning through Discovery.* New York: John Wiley, 1967.

Michael, William. *Teaching for Creative Endeavor: Bold New Adventure.* Bloomington: Indiana University Press, 1968.

Miel, Alice. *Creativity in Teaching: Invitations and Instances.* Belmont, Calif.: Wadsworth, 1961.

Miller, James G. *The Human Mind.* New York: Golden Press, 1965.

Moustakas, Carl E. (ed.). *The Self: Explorations in Personal Growth.* New York: Harper and Row, 1964.

Muenzinger, Karl F. *Contemporary Approaches to Creative Thinking.* New York: Atherton Press, 1967.

Murphy, Gardner. *Human Potentialities.* New York: Basic Books, 1958.

Osborn, Alex F. *Applied Imagination.* New York: Charles Scribner's Sons, 1963.

Parnes, Sidney and H. F. Harding (eds.). *A Source Book for Creative Teaching.* New York: Charles Scribner's Sons, 1962.

Patrick, Catherine. *What Is Creative Thinking?* New York: Philosophical Library, 1955.

Reed, E. G. *Developing Creative Talent.* New York: Vantage Press, 1962.

Rowson, Joseph P. (ed.). *Impact '70.* Des Moines, Iowa: Polk County Board of Education, 1971.

Rugg, Harold. *Imagination: An Inquiry into the Sources and Conditions That Stimulate Creativity.* New York: Harper and Row, 1963.

Shumsky, Abraham. *Creative Teaching.* New York: Appleton-Century-Crofts, 1965.

Sigel, Irving and Frank H. Hooper (eds.). *Logical Thinking in Children.* New York: Holt, Rinehart and Winston, 1968.

Smith, James A. *Setting Conditions for Creative Teaching in the Elementary School.* Boston: Allyn and Bacon, 1966.

Taylor, Calvin W. *Creativity: Progress and Potential.* New York: McGraw-Hill, 1964.

―――. *Widening Horizons in Creativity.* New York: John Wiley, 1964.

Taylor, Calvin W. and Frank Barron. *Scientific Creativity: Its Recognition and Development.* New York: John Wiley, 1963.

Taylor, Calvin W. and Frank E. Williams. *Instructional Media and Creativity.* New York: John Wiley, 1966.

Torrance, E. Paul. *Creativity: What Research Says to the Teacher.* Washington, D.C.: National Education Association, 1963.

―――. *Encouraging Creativity in the Classroom.* Dubuque, Iowa: William C. Brown, 1970.

―――. *Guiding Creative Talent.* Englewood Cliffs, N.J.: Prentice-Hall, 1962.

―――. *Rewarding Creative Behavior.* Englewood Cliffs, N.J.: Prentice-Hall, 1965.

Torrance, E. Paul and R. E. Myers. *Creative Learning and Teaching.* New York: Dodd, Mead, 1970.

Williams, F. E. *Foundations of Creative Problem Solving.* Ann Arbor, Mich.: Edwards Bros., 1960.

Wilt, Marion. *Creativity in the Elementary School.* New York: Appleton-Century-Crofts, 1959.

CHAPTER II

The Nature of
Creative Communication

EFFECTIVE COMMUNICATION

"What do you hear?" Miss Brown asked while the children in the classroom closed their eyes.

"Someone is walking," said Tom.

"I hear steam in the pipes," said Kevin.

"Someone just opened and closed a door," added Andrea.

"The wind is blowing outside," said Sharon.

"There is a hose running outside, too," added Peter.

"Tell me what you hear in such a way that I can hear it, too, even if I can't actually," said Miss Brown. "In other words, use noise words to describe what you hear."

"I hear clomping, stomping walking," said Tom.

"Banging, pounding vapor in the pipes," said Kevin.

"A scraping, screeching door," added Andrea.

"I hear the soft, murmuring wind," added Sharon.

Peter said, "I hear the water splashing and gurgling."

"Good," said Miss Brown. "Peter, use some words to describe the leaves outside. "Crunchy, autumn leaves," said Peter. "I see," said Miss Brown, "use a word that tells us what the wind is doing to the crunchy, autumn leaves—an unusual but very effective word."

After a short pause, Peter said, "Tugging." "Oh, I like that!" said Miss Brown. "The wind is tugging at the crunchy, autumn leaves. That is a very effective sentence!"

TO THE READER

In spite of the fact that man has developed more hardware for the purpose of refining communication than ever before, the greatest problem he still faces is that of communication. It could very well be that too much emphasis is placed on "correct" communication rather than "effective" communication in our elementary schools.

As a result of reading this chapter the reader should gain some insights into the objectives for teaching the communication skills in the space age, and see where the new emphasis in methodology must be placed if these objectives are to be met and the desired outcomes realized. The reader will explore the nature of communication and the nature of language as it is learned by children, with some attention given to the work of the linguists and the effect of mass media on communication.

INTRODUCTION

To understand what is meant by "creative communication" an exploration of current research in communication is necessary. Interest in the area of creativity was stimulated by the launching of Sputnik, after which a realization swept the nation that creativity was a precious commodity. Research in this area has accumulated since 1957. Scholars in all disciplines have added to this growing body of knowledge which has contributed a great deal to an understanding of creativity and how it may be developed in elementary school children. This research affects the teaching of the language arts in terms of (1) objectives, (2) methodology and (3) outcomes.

OBJECTIVES

Basic objectives for teaching the language arts in the American public school have, in the past, centered largely around the teaching of the *correct* use of language. To this must now be added the teaching of the *effective* use of language—language which is clear, dynamic, forceful, imaginative, creative. In spite of the fact that man has now contrived more means of communication than any other time in history, communication is still one of his greatest problems. Devices for communication make it easier, but not necessarily more effective.

In this age of television, moving pictures, tape recorders, visual advertising, sound systems and hi-fidelity, the child is bombarded with visual and audio stimuli from the time he arises until he goes to sleep. He learns from all this experience with sight and sound; he reacts to it and learns to accept it. Today's child often learns through the dramatic and the highly dynamic means of communication which bombard him from the time that he awakes to the end of his day. Schools are forced to compete with the teaching media outside them; the means for communication within the school must be as dynamic and as dramatic as those outside in order to get through to the child.

We have at our disposal the one thing which the mass media does not have: the child! He is an active, participating, thinking, risk-taking, problem-solving machine all his own, and no one child machine is exactly like any other. This gives us an immediate advantage! In forming objectives for the language arts program in the elementary school for teaching and learning in the space age, it is essential that we make allowances for the changes in the times, for the needs and interests of modern children and for their individual differences.

Basic objectives to be kept in mind in building effective communication skills may be stated as follows:

Objective 1: Each child needs to experience language in dynamic and relevant ways all day, everyday, so he can communicate comfortably in every way open to him, and without unnecessary pressures.

The meeting of this objective implies that the skills learned in language arts and listed below in objective 2 should be obtained in such a manner that their use is normal and natural to the child. Language cannot be learned effectively under excessive, negative pressures. When tensions build up, speech is the first part of the human system to break down. The communication skills must be taught in a relaxed atmosphere of positive pressures and wholesome motivation. Language is part of the personality of the child and it grows with his personality. His attitude toward the use of these communication skills is as important as his ability to use them. Learning to read must be accompanied by success experiences or the child does not learn to read for any purpose of his own; he reads to please the teacher. To be a reader he must love to read; to write well he must enjoy writing; to speak effectively his speech must be satisfying and rewarding to him. A child's abilities in the language arts can be measured by tests for specific purposes, but in the long run these are meaningless measures of achievement. The factor which determines whether or not a school has a good reading program is not the grade level on which the children read but the attitude about books and the way they use them. Do they go home nightly with books tucked under their arms? Is the school library constantly filled with children? Do the children write profusely, leaving their creations on the teacher's desk as they leave the room each day? Can each child say what he wants to say in a class discussion without fear and embarrassment? If the answer to these questions is yes, the school has provided a facility and love of language that fulfills the purposes of a good language arts program.

Objective 2: Each child must acquire necessary communication skills so that he may express himself effectively in all mediums.

This objective implies there is a body of skills to be learned in order to use language effectively. Adventures in learning these skills are described in the following pages of this book.

Each child should learn:

a.   To listen effectively and for a variety of purposes (see Chapter IV).
b.   To speak effectively in many kinds of social situations (see Chapter V).
c.   To read effectively for many different purposes.
d.   To spell acceptably as a social courtesy (see Chapter IX).
e.   To write legibly and with ease (see Chapter VII).
f.   To learn common word usage as a social courtesy (see Chapter VIII).
g.   To use capitalization and punctuation as a social courtesy (see Chapter VIII).
h.   To use grammar as a social courtesy (see Chapter VIII).
i.   To use reference material effectively (see Chapter VIII).
j.   To use word forms correctly (see Chapter VIII).

Once these skills are acquired, adventures should be planned where they may be applied—adventures which are not unlike those children will have when they leave school. Such experiences should include adventures in story telling, dramatics, creative writing, radio broadcasting, television broadcasting, tape making, film making, dictating and transcribing and editing written materials.

Objective 3: Each child needs to come to appreciate the beauty of language itself, the effective use of words and the creative ways they may help him express his own original thoughts.

This is a study of language for language's sake. It is loving the rhythm of certain words; it is delighting in the way words are put together; it is using words and phrases to paint pictures. It includes the creative: the job of sorting, deciding and choosing the right word for the right spot. It means children evaluate according to what they can do to make language forceful and effective. It means children write their own literature and recognize beauty in the writing of others. It is the building of appreciation for authors, poets and composers. It is the knowledge of that which lifts language from the commonplace to the beautiful.

Objective 4: Each child needs to find such satisfaction in his communication experiences that he will develop a healthy attitude about communicating in all media and will develop his communication skills even without the assistance of the teacher.

In summarizing the objectives for the teaching of the language arts, we can see that effective communication does not necessarily take place when language is merely correct (in the sense that all the grammar, punctuation and sentence structure are perfectly written). Such perfection can, at times, impede communication. Effective communication means more than this; it means the ability to speak and write clearly, imaginatively, sensitively, beautifully and effectively whenever the occasion demands. To meet these objectives, relevant adventures must be encountered daily by children in our schools.

METHOD

The tendency to minimize the effect of *method* of teaching among today's critics of educational procedures must be neutralized by showing that, while the *content* of teaching gives children the knowledge necessary for living, it is the *method* of teaching which gives them the basic values, appreciations and skills which develop their creativeness. That some methods of teaching accomplish our purposes better than others has been proven by research.

That which appears on the surface to be logical in educational practice is often proven to be illogical when submitted to scientific investigation. Part of the job of the school principal and administrator is to keep his school patrons informed as to what are the emerging truths in pedagogical technique. Another of his jobs is to help his patrons and his teachers differentiate between fads and truths. Fads are unproven ideas often tried on a mass scale before they are proven to be worthy. Truths are those facts which remain constant when repeatedly subjected to research.

However, it must be observed that both have a place in the teaching process. In order for teaching to improve, the fads are necessary just as the search for truths is necessary, for the fads are the creative products and explorations of men's minds—a breaking from tradition, habit and outmoded custom. Often they are the first step toward posing creative solutions to new problems which can later be submitted to scientific investigation.

The methods used in Chapter I were geared to developing some objectives which were unheard of a decade ago. Creative teaching is a *method* of teaching which must differ from many current modes if the objectives for developing creativity *and* the objectives for developing language skills are to be accomplished. Many illustrations of these differences will be given in the succeeding chapters of this text.

OUTCOMES

Language teaching up to this point has been thought to be a process concerned largely with the memorization of rules and their application. A few creative teachers of past generations contributed to a change of concept in this respect. Language learning can be a creative process and can have creative outcomes. There is enough substance in the research instigated by this thinking to indicate that outcomes achieved through creative methods are vastly different and greatly superior to outcomes achieved through noncreative teaching.

The following pages consist of a review of some of the truths of our times culled from the vast amount of research in the area of creativity, linguistics, communication and language which apply specifically to the development of communication skills in children. Some of these are established truths and some are emerging truths which seem to be directives for the teaching of language arts in the elementary school in the immediate future.

THE NATURE OF COMMUNICATION

To be a creative teacher there is one other basic requirement— the teacher herself must have a knowledge of the basic established truths in every area of the curriculum for which she is responsible, in this case, the language arts. A command of this

FIGURE 2-1. *Levels of communication.*

knowledge is essential before effective and creative teaching can result. A review of the *nature* of communication follows. First we will deal with levels of communication.

Levels of Communication

Communication is possible basically on three levels: the *experience* level, the *verbal* level and the *conceptual* level. The figure above illustrates these three types of communication.

In Figure 2-1 (a), we see Mrs. Jones and Mrs. Fry making a cake. Verbal communication in this instance is possible with a minimum number of words spoken because these two women are experiencing the total process together. New words take on meaning because they are introduced in context. But words are not the only means of communication in this picture. The two women communicate in many ways: speech, actions, demonstrations, gestures, facial expression and movement. Once the cake is baked and eaten both women can refer to this experience and relive it with a minimum number of spoken words. Mrs. Jones may meet Mrs. Fry at the shopping center and say, "Remember that cake you showed me how to make? Well, I tried it out on my family and they just loved it!" Mrs. Fry answers, "I just knew they would!"

A bystander would know from this conversation that Mrs. Fry had shown Mrs. Jones how to make a cake which she had tried out on her family. But that is about all. Mrs. Jones and Mrs. Fry, however, have communicated more to each other than simply the words which they spoke; they know the kind of cake Mrs. Jones made, the circumstances under which the making of the cake was first learned, the ingredients of the cake and the number of people in the family who enjoyed the cake.

In Figure 2-1 (b), we see Mrs. Fry talking to Mrs. Ellis. Mrs. Fry is trying to explain to her new neighbor how to make the cake which her family enjoyed so much. Because the communication is taking place on the verbal level without the background of the *common* experience, Mrs. Fry must use more words and she must use more descriptive words to put across her ideas to Mrs. Ellis. What she really must do in order to be able to communicate here is to try to find word symbols from her own experience which match or nearly match those word symbols which identify similar experiences in Mrs. Ellis's background. She knows that Mrs. Ellis has experienced "one-half," she has experienced "cup," she has experienced "ripe" and she has experienced "strawberries." She is not so sure that Mrs. Ellis has experienced "avocado" so she embellishes the meaning for her by telling her what an avocado is, using words which are common labels to the past experiences of both women. These two women are able to communicate on this verbal level to the degree to which words (in the form of statements and questions, gestures, facial expression and voice inflection) make Mrs. Fry's experience meaningful to Mrs. Ellis.

In Figure 2-1 (c) we see communication taking place on a conceptual level. Here the cooking class teacher is assuming these mothers have already tried out (experienced) the avocado-strawberry dessert recipe and is talking on a level which requires a knowledge of a total experience and the ability to transfer or modify this experience to a new one. The teacher is dealing with concepts and in order to understand her, each member of the class must have experienced the acts on which the concepts are based. The class member who has not had these experiences is very confused because she has only a partial participation in the communication process which is underway. In every one of the three kinds of communication described here, common experience is necessary for full communication to take place.

Figures 2-1 (d), (e) and (f) show how the three kinds of communication function. In Figure 2-1 (d) the children of Miss Temple's first grade are visiting a farm. They see a tractor being operated and learn its name while watching it. They see the silo and the thresher and label these objects with a verbal symbol or a word. These new words are very meaningful to all of them because they are all experiencing them together.

In Figure 2-1 (e), we see the children back in the classroom. Now they are making a reading chart of their experience. Miss Temple is letting them see their new oral vocabulary in printed symbol form. Communication is easy because the symbolic experience rises out of a common experience. All the children know and understand the *meaning* of the words.

Figure 2-1 (f) shows these same children a few years later in the fourth grade. Since their original trip to the farm they have had many other contacts with the same printed symbols. They have added new experiences to their old ones and have generalized these experiences into concepts. Therefore, when Miss Temple says, "Modern farming equipment has helped the farmer produce more crops from the same land than our early ancestors," these children need no detailed explanation because they have developed common concepts and communication takes place.

Learning at the verbal and conceptual level is actually a rearranging of old verbal experiences into new meanings rather than living the experience oneself. When children have had a wealth of common experiences and have developed a reservoir of oral or verbal symbols to represent these experiences, the symbols *may* be rearranged into new understandings or new meanings in the child's mind so that new concepts are developed.

When teaching begins at the concept level without the base of the experience level, communication breaks down. It is when we cross over from one level of communication to another that we fail to communicate. The diagram below shows how this is likely to happen.

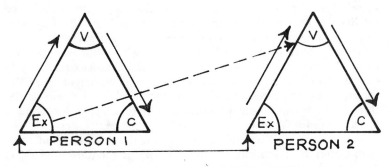

FIGURE 2-2. *Levels of Communication.*

In Figure 2-2 each triangle represents a person. The solid line illustrates Mrs. Jones and Mrs. Fry communicating on the experience level. Their understandings are clear and concise. The dotted line shows a teacher who is talking on a concept level to a student —the verbalization is present, but there is meaning only if the student has experience to interpret or translate the teacher's words.

Figure 2-3 shows that understanding between people is possible to the degree that their common fields of experience overlap.

Methods of Communication

In the above discussion we have dealt largely with oral and written communication. Sometimes other forms of communication replace the verbal phase or the conceptual phase. Gesture is one such form. Such substitution is possible because a culture has de-

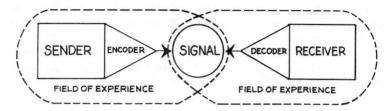

FIGURE 2-3. *The human communication system.*

veloped common experiences which can be represented by a symbol of some sort. Examples of this might be: a cross, a Bible, a green light, a red flag or a dove; all convey meaning as they appear in various places in everyday living.

Look at the problems listed below on a continuum. Try to do them.

1. Communicate some idea or thought by a pose; do not use movement or voice.
2. Communicate something by adding movement to your pose.
3. Communicate something through the use of movement and voice.
4. Tell about a trip you took recently. Allow the class to interrupt to ask questions.
5. Write about your trip.
6. Write about your trip in one paragraph.
7. Write about your trip in one sentence.
8. Write about your trip in one word.
9. Write about your trip in one letter.

In trying to communicate through the above techniques, which proved the easiest of all? Probably No. 4 enabled you to communicate more freely than any of the others. As you moved away from No. 4 both up and down the continuum, communication became more difficult. Let us see what might happen on each level of communication mentioned above.

No. 1: Communication here could take place by having someone assume a prayerful attitude by bowing his head and folding his hands. Persons entering a room and encountering someone in such a pose would probably drop their voices and even tiptoe to a seat. Because the pose has changed the behavior of a listener or observer, it has communicated something. Other poses might be assumed such as a salute, arms crossed on chest, the boxer's pose or the pose of a runner ready to sprint. Each would communicate *something* to the observer. That *something* might be different to each observer because the pose could only be interpreted in light of the experience.

No. 2: Ideas can be communicated more easily by movement than by a pose. Many movements have been developed in every society which have common meaning: the thumb of a hitchhiker moving across his body as it follows the passing car, the circle motion of the finger winding around the ear as one child tries to show another that his teacher is a little "touched in the head," the motion of the two index fingers making the pattern of a square as one teenager tries to describe the new boy in school to another or the thumbs down motion that indicates the rejection of a candidate from the club.

No. 3: Adding voice to movement makes communication easier for the speaker but not always for the listener.

No. 4: This probably proved to be the most satisfactory kind of communication to both listener and speaker. Free to use his hands, voice, and facial expression, the speaker can put his ideas across. The listener can interrupt to ask questions and put the speaker in a situation where he must use words within the understanding level of the listener.

FIGURE 2-4. *Motions communicate.*

No 5: Freedom to write as you choose makes communication easier than through simple gestures, but here is lost the tone quality of the voice, the facial expression, the right to question and to clarify statements. Here is a teenager's story about a trip:

My Trip

Last week I flew to Florida. When I left New York City the temperature was around zero. When I arrived in Florida the temperature was 78 degrees. Such a delightful change!

The flight down was perfect! We flew non-stop so it took only three hours. It was one of the most beautiful flights I have ever taken. The sky was a clear azure blue all the way. At times cloud banks cut off our view of the earth, but most of the way the panorama of the countryside stretched out clearly below us in the bright, sparkling sun. It was a fascinating experience to watch the clean, white ground give way to bleak, barren terrain, which in turn became green and lush. We stepped into the plane in a cold, winter world and stepped out of it three hours later into a warm, summer climate. It was sheer magic!

My stay in Florida was just wonderful. I had such a good time! Our plane was met at the airport by a limousine which whisked us off to a swank hotel. As soon as we arrived we were invited to a reception on the terrace.

No. 6: To write about this trip in one paragraph becomes difficult because much of the writer's excitement and feeling of the trip is lost. Of necessity, the writing becomes almost a summarized factual account of the experience.

My Trip

I flew to Florida for my vacation. The flight was delightful; the weather was perfect and the people were very friendly and gracious. From the moment I arrived at my hotel until the time I left to come home, I was busy with a variety of exciting activities. Needless to say, I had a wonderful time.

No. 7: Writing about this trip in one sentence handicaps the writer hopelessly. The result probably reads something like this:

My Trip

I went on a trip to Florida and had a wonderful time.

No. 8: What can one do here except to write "Florida"?
No. 9: This assignment becomes an impossibility.

We have taken a look at various types of verbal and conceptual communication skills, or substitutions for them. At some time in our own experience each type plays an important part. However, we feel most comfortable and communicate most readily when we operate in area No. 4, where we can communicate in a face to face manner using all our resources. Communication without voice is difficult but possible. This is exemplified by the tourist in the foreign country where gestures and actions must be used to communicate because of the language barrier. In like manner, written communication is more difficult than spoken communication because of the loss of gesture, facial expression and body movement.

The type of communication used depends on the situation. The tourist does the best he can in a limited way. So does the hitch-hiker who has to get across a message as quickly as he can. Short sentences generally are best suited to communicating one idea, not a whole series of ideas. Letters of the alphabet communicate almost nothing because they are less than ideas—they are fragments of ideas.

Much of the misunderstanding regarding report cards among parents arises from the fact that the reports do not communicate what the school intends them to. The use of a numerical grade, or a letter (whether it be an *A* or an *S* or a *U*) communicates almost nothing to the parent except as grades were used within his own experience on his own report card while he was a boy in school. To assume that the whole story of a child's academic, social, emotional and physical growth over a ten-week period can be told by the use of one letter is naive. The writer once asked a group of ten parents to write what an A meant to them when it was used on Junior's report card. There were six different interpretations of this letter grade from the ten parents although the school meant that there should be but one.

What "A" Means to Me

1. It means that my son is one of the brightest children in his class.
2. It means to me that my daughter is capable of doing excellent work and is living up to her capabilities.
3. It means that my child is doing what he is able to do although he may not be the brightest child in the class.
4. It means my child is in the top ten percent of his class.
5. It means my child was able to do what the teacher expected of him.
6. It means that my son is doing work somewhere between 90 percent and 100 percent.

Many school systems have realized the inadequacy of such reporting and have resorted to the individual parent-teacher conference which falls in the category of area No. 4. This is the only justifiable type of reporting to parents in terms of sound communication in this day and age when improved methods of communication and transportation make it possible to reach them so easily.

THE NATURE OF LANGUAGE

What has research told us in recent years about the acquisition of language by children and what of this material may be applied to the teaching of language? A child enters this world with a physical and mental potential for language. His language ability will be determined to a high degree by his intellectual capacity and his physical well-being. He comes into a culture where a structure of symbols is already in use. How does he acquire it so he too can become civilized?

According to Smith, Goodman and Meredith,[1] two human qualities explain the development of language. The first quality is the capacity of man's mind to imagine and use symbols; the second quality is man's need to communicate. So universal is this need for communication that man invented language not once but perhaps many times, wherever, in fact, man congregated. The ability of children to think symbolically and to produce sound symbols makes it *possible* for children to learn language. The need for children to communicate makes it *necessary* for children to learn language.

Following are some generalizations about language development which will help us in forming objectives and in planning activities for the development of communication ability in children.

GENERALIZATIONS ABOUT LANGUAGE DEVELOPMENT

Smith et al. make some generalizations from current studies which seem to give significance to the child's language development as it relates to his learning processes.

---

1. Brooks Smith, Kenneth Goodman and Robert Meredith, *Language and Thinking in the Language Arts in the Elementary School* (New York: Holt, Rinehart and Winston, 1970), pp. 11, 17–26.

1. The closer the language development of the child comes to the speech norms of the adult community, the more effective is his communication.

2. There is a continuous tendency, therefore, for the child's language to move toward adult norms.

3. The more opportunity the child has to communicate, the more skill he will develop in use of language and the more acceptable will be his language by adult standards. He needs to be spoken to, listened to, responded to.

4. Anticipation of his needs by a parent or a teacher before he communicates to them will tend to retard a child's language development.

5. In literate societies, a communicative need will place the same prime motivation role in the child's learning to read and write as it does in his learning to speak and listen with understanding.

6. Before change can be achieved in an individual's idiolect, the individual must strongly feel that the change will help him to communicate more effectively.

Other generalizations can be made from recent research studies.

1. Language learning is not a natural part of maturation. Children who have been isolated from humans while maturing have not developed a language.

2. Every normal child achieves near mastery of at least one language by the time he is five or six years of age. Studies reported in 1963 indicate that most children's speech by the time they are five or six years old is a close approximation of adult speech in their immediate environment.[2]

3. One of the most important ideas to become accepted over the past few years is that language is not learned in isolated fragments or "words." It is best learned in total situations. From the very beginning of life a baby finds himself bombarded and drenched by sounds and words around him. From this smorgasbord of sounds, he eventually selects those which best meet his needs. He sorts out a particular aspect of the total situation and forms firm associations to that aspect before he is able to reproduce the sound associated to it or to speak.

This process may be the method most suitable for language development in the school situation: not to teach language in isolated words but in situations such as described in this book,

---

2. Susan M. Ervin and Wick R. Miller, "Language Development," *Child Psychology*, 62nd Yearbook, Part I (Chicago: National Society for the Study of Education, University of Chicago Press, 1963), p. 20.

and to focus on particular *aspects* of a situation only when a child needs help in forming certain specific concepts or in speaking certain words.

4. Because of the recent interest in the work of Piaget, some of his views on language development in children are pertinent to an understanding of language as a part of the greater adventure called life. Piaget has this to say about language, "Words are probably not a shortcut to a better understanding . . . the love of understanding seems to modify the language that is used rather than vice versa . . . Mainly, language serves to translate what is already understood; or else language may even present a danger if it is used to introduce an idea which is not yet accessible."[3]

Piaget felt that language was an outside agent that serves the purpose of helping the child express his own symbols in a manner meaningful to society and that his use of speech and language does not effect the development of personal symbolic structures, they each develop independently from the other. He indicates that children show that they understand many ideas through action which they cannot express in words. Piaget points out that when children are presented with an idea to be learned in adult language, structures are being forced on their thinking, and he asks whether it is proper to teach the structure or to present the child with situations where he is active and creates the structure himself. He states that when we teach too fast, we keep the child from inventing and discovering himself. Piaget defines teaching as creating situations where structures can be discovered, not the transmission of structures which may be assimilated at the verbal level only. The material in this book has been presented with Piaget's concepts in mind: teaching in learning situations where structures can be discovered.

THE INTERRELATEDNESS OF LANGUAGE

Some of the most significant research in the studies of children's language of late have been carried out by Loban.[4] Loban shows certain interrelationships among the language arts. He forms the following conclusions:

---

3. Eleanor Duckworth, "Piaget Rediscovered," *ESS Newsletter*, (Watertown, Mass.: Elementary Science Study, Educational Services Incorporated, June 1964), p. 15.
4. Walter Loban, *The Language of Elementary School Children* (Champaign, Ill.: National Council of Teachers of English, 1963), p. 89.

1. Reading, writing, listening and speaking are all positively related. Children who are low in general oral language ability tend to be low in reading and writing achievements. Children high in language ability tend to do well in gaining literacy skills.

It is the major premise of this book that the language experience concept is the most practical and logical for the teaching of the language arts (see pp. 86–87). Studies in language development in the past twenty years have repeatedly called attention to the fact that an effective language program in the elementary school must begin with a carefully planned, goal-directed program in oral expression (see Chapter V). It would seem that Loban is re-enforcing the concept that a good reading or writing program is based on a sound program of speaking.

2. A positive correlation was found between health and language proficiency. The vitality necessary to speak fluently can only be generated by a healthy body. Physical fitness and continual checks on eyes, hand-eye coordination, sleeping and eating habits of children may be vital to a child's language development.

3. Reading and writing are related to sociometric position.

One wonders as he reads Loban's conclusions, whether or not the commercial material designed for use in teaching children from a certain socioeconomic background has much, if any, effect on language development in children from a different background. These studies seem to re-enforce the concept that the teacher must sometimes create the materials to be used with a child from a particular environment, or the child who deviates from the classroom norm.

4. All language ability and vocabulary correlates highly with success on I.Q. tests.

Here Loban reinforces a concept revealed by research studies of the past. There still seems to be a high correlation between intelligence and language usage.

5. Chronological age, effective use of language and sociometric status correlate positively with complexity of grammatical structure in the speech of children.

Once again, research shows that the use of language, especially at the spoken level, is one of the most successful ways of developing language ability. It is safe to assume however that in most schools the emphasis is not on the oral use of language: most of the time allocated to the language arts program is used in completing written exercises.

Loban[5] points out the very important fact that the major categories of language difficulties that elementary school children

---

5. Ibid., p. 89.

are likely to have come from the kind of teaching which presents language that is limited and inflexible and that does not serve the expanding needs of the child, particularly in school tasks, and language that is considered nonstandard or socially unacceptable for use by educated members of the society. This should say something to all teachers. If language that is different, new or unique is not used in school, children are being inhibited in their ability to develop and they are not assessing school learnings as relevant.

LIFE PATTERNS OF LANGUAGE DEVELOPMENT

What are the life patterns of language development? Many studies of children's natural development from preschool years to adulthood have been made. In the preschool years the home plays a vital part in launching the child successfully or unsuccessfully in his life pattern in language development. This life pattern of language development is highly individual for each child, and little is gained by comparing one child's language development to that of another except as a diagnostic procedure to locate areas where future instruction may be of benefit to the child.

Upon school arrival, the child reflects a mastery of the grammar of the home, which may mean the acquisition of a nonstandard system. Lewis[6] has said that a child, on school entrance, incorporates in his speaking all those forms of grammar about which he needs to know for life. His speech contains sentences that are declarative, exclamatory, questioning and demanding. Children have verbal control of the use of tenses. They may make mistakes in grammar forms because they speak the words in forms they hear and if their mistakes are common in the dialogue of the parents the child can only use what he has heard.

Lewis' studies[7] remind us that children the world over move through a succession and procession of experiments and experiences with sound: from babbling to first words to a phase of immature speech to speech which falls within accepted language norms. Even the sounds are made in pattern sequence showing the relationship between physical development and ability to reproduce the sounds. Studies of school beginners indicate that the speaking vocabulary of these children is at least 8,000 words and

---

6. M. M. Lewis, *How Children Learn To Speak* (New York: Basic Books, 1957).
7. Ibid.

that these children may know and understand over 20,000 words. Seashore[8] states that a child at the age of six is likely to know 17,000 words plus 7,000 derivatives and that he can reasonably expect to add approximately 5,000 words each year thereafter.

By the age of six the child's spoken language has reached 90 percent of its mature level when judged on the basis of sentence structure according to McCarthy.[9] The single child performs better in spoken language than twins.

Hearing acuity affects growth in all language abilities. The age of six marks the beginning of complicated speech, manual performance, and behavior restrictions required of the child in adjusting to the school situation. Stuttering often begins at this time. Boys develop more slowly than girls in their language, and there are more stutterers and more speech defects among boys than girls. Handedness is generally well established by the age of four. Yedinack's research indicates that there is a strong relationship between reading disability and articulation defects at the second grade level.[10]

Loban found that all children in his study of 11 classes used all basic patterns of English sentence structure, even in the kindergarten. He found that the differences between groups of children who were rated high or low in language ability was not in the patterns they used. Children who rated "poor" tended to use more partial utterances. Those who were rated as "better" in use of language used more complete utterances and more complex utterances. More subordinate causes were used by the "high" group. Loban arrived at some conclusions about the general direction of language growth which appear obvious, such as: As children become older they tend to use more language; they tend to use more communication units (similar to sentences) when they speak; the communication units tend to get longer; the units tend to be more complex grammatically and language becomes more coordinated, more articulate. Less obvious is the fact that their language tends to express more tentativeness, more supposition, more hypothesis, more conditionality.

Loban also stresses the fact that children literally grope for words in the middle of an utterance. Children whose language

8. Robert H. Seashore, "The Importance of Vocabulary in Learning Language Skills," *Elementary English* 25 (March 1948): 137–52.
9. Dorothea McCarthy, "Language Development in Children," in Leonard Carmichael (ed.), *Manual of Child Psychology* (2d ed., New York: John Wiley, 1954), pp. 492–630.
10. Jeanette G. Yedinack, "Study of the Linguistic Functioning of Children with Articulation and Reading Disabilities," *Pedagogical Seminary and Journal of Genetic Psychology* 74 (March 1949): 23–59.

was rated high tend to do less groping, but all children grope through "mazes" of words to some degree throughout the elementary school years.

Loban also found that boys are at the extremes in language ability. They tend to do very poorly or to excel.

Loban summarizes the key findings of his research as follows: during the first seven years of schooling, children speak more words in each succeeding year, produce more communication units, and increase the average number of words in those units. Children rated as skillful in language reduce both their incidence of mazes and the number of words per maze. At the kindergarten level, vocabulary and proficiency in language appeared to be related. Not pattern but what is done to achieve flexibility within the pattern proves to be a measure of consecutiveness and control of language at this level of language development. Children who are rated as most proficient in language are also those who manifest the most sensitivity to the conventions of language.

Of importance to the teacher of language arts are additional findings reported in Loban's summary:

1. Both the low and high groups of subjects used the same number of words from among the 12,000 most commonly used words of the English language; after that, the low group shows a higher incidence of words selected from the next 20,000 of the most commonly used words in the language (from 13,000 to 33,000). Thereafter the high group gains ascendency in the use of the least commonly used words of the English language.

2. For subject nominals, the low group depends almost exclusively on nouns and pronouns. The high group can use noun clauses, infinitives and verbals.

3. Boys in the low group are clearly more limited in their repertoire of syntax than girls in the low group. On the other hand boys in the high group tend to excel the girls in the high group.

4. Problems with use of verbs prove to be the most frequent kinds of deviation from conventional usage in the elementary school.

5. Lack of agreement between subject and predicate, particularly in the third person singular, proves to be a major difficulty in the use of verbs. Consistency of verb tense is another difficulty.

6. Adverb and noun clauses are used by the total group much more frequently than adjective clauses.

7. In this study, reading, writing, listening and speaking show a positive relation.

8. The subjects in the lowest and highest groups in writing are also lower and higher in reading achievement. Those who write well in grade three are also those who are above average in speak-

ing and reading. Those who rate in the highest group in proficiency in all language areas are also those who are completely above the median in reading (developed for the random and low groups).

An interesting concept is that of Smith, Goodman and Meredith[11] who have summarized some research and stated some interesting theories. These men say that throughout the process of language acquisition there are four continuing cycles: increasing experience, increasing conceptualization, increasing communication need and increasing effectiveness in communication. The last can be considered synonymous with increased control over language.

They state that child language development can be viewed as a series of stages through which the child passes. Each of the stages overlaps with the next; the child enters into higher stages well before he has completed earlier stages.

The authors then proceed to identify these stages and their characteristics. First is the *random stage* which is a prelinguistic stage where the infant babbles and experiments with sound. The second stage is designated by the authors as the *unitary stage*. In the unitary stage the child begins to produce sounds purposely to express a need or a desire. Often sounds are produced on cue but have no communication value, such as when a parent urges a child to say bye-bye and he does—he parrots the adult. The authors label the next stage as the *stage of expansion and delimiting*. Here language is still a collection of utterances but the utterances move in two directions at the same time. They are expanded from a one-syllable to a two-syllable utterance to approximate adult speech. It is not a process of combining words to make sentences but is an expansion of the nucleus so that minor features are included; a filling out of utterances rather than the building up. At the same time the child is delineating the use of his utterances; they come to be more and more precise in expressing more and more particular needs or wishes or feelings. The next stage is recognized as the *stage of structural awareness* and is characterized by the child's ability to generalize, to find pattern and order in the situations he experiences. He notices the common elements of similar utterances. He generalizes a pattern in which a series of things or people are inserted in the objects slot, such as "I want milk, I want apple, I want Mommy" and so

11. Brooks Smith et al., *Language and Thinking in the Language Arts* . . ., pp. 17–26.

forth. In generalizing, the child must reflect on the utterance he uses, generalize a pattern, induce a rule, generate an utterance consistent with the rule and evaluate the rule and modify it. The *automatic stage* is next. At this stage the child has internalized the grammar of his language. He can now generate utterances which he has, and has not, heard before but which are fully grammatical. The last stage, which is of particular interest to the readers of this book, is defined as the *creative stage*. Up to now the child has conformed to the language of a community because this language has been his model and he had to know it in order to be able to communicate. His language has become a vast collection of clichés, tried expressions, neat and trite ways. Children pass into a stage of creative manipulation of language which may be due to their increasing ability to conceptualize and think in metaphors and abstractions. New needs arise, outside the realm of the "model" adult needs, so children invent new language to meet these needs. An obvious example of this is the teenager's creation of new language. In teenagers, part of this can be attributed to the drive to be an entity—to be independent and to be identified with his peers rather than his family. Much of this creative language finds its way permanently into the language of the society.

Great storytellers and literary giants have retained this ability to create language. Smith et al. feel that all people create language to some degree but only the great language artists rival the young in creative use of language. The authors say, "In their (literary giants and great storytellers) hands, language does not so limit the human capacity for self-expression; it becomes the supple tool of thought and communication. So much a master of language is the great writer that he transcends all language conventions; he makes rules work for him."

Creative thoughts require creative language to express them. Emphasis on conformity in language in school or at home stifles not only expression but also thought. Fortunately, the tendency of children to be creative with language is almost universal. Parents and teachers can encourage this tendency. If they do so, there will eventually be more adults with the courage to use language creatively.

THE NATURE OF LINGUISTICS

Of great interest in recent years is the study of linguistics and the contributions made by the linguists to the study of language.

What is linguistics? The linguist narrows the definition of language: "the fundamental forms of language activity are the sequences of sounds made by human lips, tongues, and vocal chords."[12] To the linguist language is speech. Thus the linguist would put great emphasis on the oral program, as the author has done in this volume. All other language arts experiences are derivatives of speech. Often, school curriculum developers desecrate the difference in the linguists' concept of language by labeling speech as oral language and all other forms as written language.

The linguist identifies five basic characteristics of language: (1) language is symbolic; (2) language is systematic; (3) language is human; (4) language is a social instrument; (5) language is learned. All of these assumptions are used as the basis for much of the material presented in this book.[13]

The linguist is concerned not only with the sequences of sounds but also with how they are uttered; that is, the effect of pitch, inflection and rhythm on the communication process.

Linguistics, therefore, is the study of human speech and all its components; the nature of speech, the structure of speech, the modifications of language, the units of speech.

Lamb[14] defines it further as follows: "Such study may concentrate on the sounds of language (phonology), the origin and changing meaning of words (etymology and semantics) or the arrangement of words in a meaningful context in different languages (syntax—structural or transformational grammar)." Linguistics is also considered by many to be the *relation* between writing and speech.

Linguistics, as such, finds little place in the classroom today, but the knowledge which has come from the study of linguistics has made a definite impact on the understanding of communication and how it takes place.

In Robert's *Linguistics in the Elementary Classroom*[15] these insights are listed:

---

12. Archibald A. Hill, *Introduction to Linguistic Structures* (New York: Harcourt, Brace and World, 1958), p. 1.
13. Harry A. Green and Walter T. Petty, *Developing Language Skills in the Elementary Schools* (Boston: Allyn and Bacon, 1971), pp. 17–18.
14. Pose Lamb, *Linguistics in Proper Perspective* (Columbus, Ohio: Charles E. Merrill, 1967), p. 4.
15. Paul Roberts, *Linguistics in the Elementary School Classroom* (Los Angeles: Los Angeles County Superintendent of Schools Office, 1968), pp. 3–4.

1. Language is a creative activity of each person.
2. Language patterns are well learned by the time a child is five or six.
3. He usually knows and uses all basic structures.
4. Language habits, once learned, change slowly.
5. Speech is the language; writing reflects the speech.
6. The writing system or code of English is alphabetic and has certain inadequacies.
7. Language is continually changing; it has history.
8. Language varies with the age, socioeconomic group and geographical region of the speaker; this is his dialect.
9. The concept of "correctness" is replaced by a concept of alternatives in pronunciation, word choice, phrasing and construction.
10. Every language has its own grammar. English grammar is not Latin grammar.
11. Everyone speaks his native language, to a degree, in his unique way with his particular resources for language. This is his idiolect.

These concepts are embedded in the practices advocated in the creative teaching of the language arts on the pages which follow.

SUMMARY

Creative teaching relates to the process of communication in many ways: (1) the objectives of teaching of the language arts must be concerned as much with the effective use of language as with the correct use of language; (2) creativity can be developed through the teaching of the communication skills; (3) to accomplish this objective special *methods* of teaching must be employed; (4) outcomes will be different but more effective.

Creative teaching of the language arts must be founded on our known truths about the nature of creativity and the nature of communication. Some of the basic principles of creativity which apply to the teaching of the communication skills are: (1) all children are creative; (2) creativity is determined to some degree by intelligence; (3) creativity is a process and a product; (4) creativity means individualism, nonconformity and uniqueness; (5) creativity is a set of traits, characteristics and values; (6) creativity is a way of learning which differs from the ways of learning commonly experienced.

Basic truths concerning the nature of communication are: (1) there are three levels of communication: experience, verbal and conceptual; (2) communication is possible through many techniques; (3) all communication is rooted in common experience; (4) verbal communication and conceptual communication are effective when meaningful symbols are assigned to common or like experiences; (5) there are many ways to communicate but the most effective way is talking in face to face contact; (6) the selection, arrangement and fluency of words determines the degree of feeling and the accuracy of the information which is communicated.

All language arts teaching should begin with basic experiences. New vocabulary must develop from these basic (direct or vicarious) experiences and eventually concepts should be built by adding depth and meaning to this newly acquired vocabulary.

Ideas are the important factor in communication; the mechanics of communication are secondary. A creative teacher is concerned about the ideas she uses to communicate effectively to her students. She sets conditions for effective communication in her classroom by providing common experiences from which she can build a rich, imaginative language arts program. The creative teacher uses language with skill, aware of the sequential development of words and concepts. Language is her main tool for teaching and her teaching skill is totally dependent on her ability to use language skills.

Creative communication is communicating with a fluency of ideas, with original and ear-tickling thoughts and with the ability to relate words in unusual patterns and to select the right word for the right place. On the following pages the concept of creative teaching is further developed and examples are given to show how some teachers have brought about the creative teaching of language through placing children in provocative vocabulary-building, thought-centered, problem-solving situations.

TO THE COLLEGE STUDENT AND THE CLASSROOM TEACHER

1. Over a short period of time collect new words that are created to symbolize man's new experiences.

2. An excellent film you will want to see which will give you new insights into the language structure is *Alphabet Conspiracy*, produced by the Bell Telephone Company. It may be borrowed from the company.

3. Collect newspaper articles about language for a class bulletin board. You will be surprised at the numbers of people who write about language.

4. Current magazines often publish a page of picturesque speech. Collect some of these sayings and analyze them. Why do they appeal to the reader so strongly? Would you say picturesque speech is creative?

5. A film which will help you to understand the historical development of communication is *Development of Communications* (2nd ed.), 10 minutes, black and white, *Encyclopaedia Britannica.* After you see it, discuss this question: Is there a pure language? Is English a truly phonetic language?

6. Have someone in the class make a research report on the origin of the basis for the rules of grammar in the English language.

7. A regular source of creative ideas for teaching the language arts (as well as other things) is the *Sesame Street Magazine,* published in October, December, February and April of each year (North Road, Poughkeepsie, New York, 13601). Even if children cannot watch the television program, the magazine is worthy of study.

8. In the description of the segment of Miss Brown's lesson at the beginning of this chapter we see a teacher artfully developing effective oral communication with her students. How much time from your day do you spend doing this? If you are a classroom teacher, check on your program to see what percentage of your day is spent in this activity. Study one of your day's schedules and note where you can work more of it into the classroom program.

If you are a college student listen carefully to conversations in the student union or in class. Would you say that college students are skilled at communicating effectively? Might they be if they had had more Miss Browns in the elementary grades?

9. You may properly conclude, after reading this chapter, that we set conditions for the creative teaching of language by understanding the function of language in our society and teaching language skills to children. Children cannot communicate without these language skills. Once a skill is learned, a child is better equipped to create with it. Think of this and then discuss these questions:

a. Where do you draw the line on the use of slang in school?

b. Can the teaching of speaking and listening be creative?

c. The use of proper forms in grammar and word usage are largely social courtesies. Are social courtesies necessary conformities? Why?

d. What are some ways you would handle the problem of the child who comes from a home where speech is in dialect?

10. Make a collection of picturesque speech used by children. Also, collect some verbalisms.

11. Keep a collection of new words or slang words you hear children using which you do not understand. Try to trace origins.

12. Referring to the language sequence charted on page 87, think through the value of introducing new words for a reading lesson by printing them on the chalkboard. What would be a better way to do it?

13. Here are some films you and your children will enjoy which will give them a better understanding of communication and language:
a. *Do Words Ever Fool You?* 11 minutes, Intermediate and Junior High level, black and white, Coronet.
b. *History of Writing,* 28 minutes, Intermediate level, black and white, *Encyclopaedia Britannica.*

14. Problems for discussion:
a. Is creativity an attitude or a method?
b. How can a teacher remain objective in judging individual creativeness?
c. Is it possible to fall into patterns of teaching creativity so that the act eventually becomes uncreative even though it evokes creative response?
d. Can I teach creatively when I, myself, am not creative?
e. How is it possible to teach grammar and spelling creatively?

15. If you are excited about helping children develop their perception skills, use David Webster's little book "Crossword Puzzles." This is an exciting book of mystery photographs and science puzzles about sights seen around the nation's highways. You will enjoy it as much as the children.

SELECTED BIBLIOGRAPHY

Anderson, John E. "Principles of Growth and Maturity in Language." *Elementary English Review* 18 (November 1941): 250–54.

Anderson, Paul S. *Language Skills in Elementary Education.* New York: Macmillan, 1964.

Britton, Lowenfeld. *Creative and Mental Growth.* Rev. ed. Englewood Cliffs, N.J.: Prentice-Hall, 1971.

Burns, Paul C. "Linguistics: A Brief Guide for Principals." *The National Elementary Principal* 4 (September 1965):37–42.

Burns, Paul C. and Alberta L. Lowe. *The Language Arts in Childhood Education.* Chicago: Rand McNally, 1966.

Burns, Paul C. and Leo M. Schell. *Elementary Language Arts Readings.* Chicago: Rand McNally, 1969.

Byrne, Margaret. *The Child Speaks.* New York: Harper and Row, 1965.

Carroll, John B. "Words, Meanings and Concepts." *Harvard Educational Review* 34: 178: 202; 1964 (b).

Cober, Mary E. "Creativeness in the Language Arts." In James C. MacCampbell (ed.). *Readings in the Language Arts in the Elementary School.* Boston: D. C. Heath, 1964, pp. 114–17.

Corcoran, Gertrude B. *Language Arts in the Elementary School: A Modern Linguistic Approach.* New York: Ronald Press, 1970.

DeBoer, John J. "Some Sociological Factors in Language Development." In James C. MacCampbell (ed.). *Readings in the Language Arts in the Elementary School.* Boston: D. C. Heath, 1964, pp. 77–89.

Donoghue, Mildred R. *The Child and the English Language Arts.* Dubuque, Iowa: William C. Brown, 1971.

Educational Service, Inc. *Create.* Stevenville, Mich., 1969.

Emig, Janet A., James T. Fleming and Helen M. Popp. *Language and Learning.* New York: Harcourt, Brace and World, 1964.

Ervin, Susan M. and Wick R. Miller. "Language Development." *Child Psychology.* 62nd Yearbook, Part I. Chicago: National Society for the Study of Education, University of Chicago Press, 1963, pp. 108–43.

Fries, Charles C. *Linguistics and Reading.* New York: Holt, Rinehart and Winston, 1963.

Greene, Harry A. and Walter T. Petty. *Developing Language Skills in the Elementary Schools.* 4th ed. Boston: Allyn and Bacon, 1971.

Hughes, John P. *Linguistics and Language Teaching.* New York: Random House, 1968.

Labov, William. "Linguistic Research on the Non-Standard English of Negro Children." Paper presented at the New York Society for the Experimental Study of Education, 1965.

Lenneberg, Eric H. *The Biological Foundations of Language.* New York: John Wiley, 1967.

Letton, Mildred C. "How Do Children Communicate?" In James C. MacCampbell (ed.). *Readings in the Language Arts in the Elementary School.* Boston: D. C. Heath, 1964, pp. 48–51.

Lewis, M. M. *How Children Learn to Speak.* New York: Basic Books, 1957.

Loban, Walter. "The Language of Elementary School Children: A Study of the Use and Control of Language, Effectiveness in Communication, and the Relationships among Speaking, Reading, Writing and Listening." *Research Report No. 1.* Champaign, Ill.: National Council of Teachers of English, 1963.

Lodge, William J. "Developmental Characteristics of Childhood Related to the Language Arts Curriculum." In James C. MacCampbell (ed.). *Readings in the Language Arts in the Elementary School.* Boston: D. C. Heath, 1964, pp. 52–65.

MacCampbell, James C. "Child Growth and Development." In James C. MacCampbell (ed.). *Readings in the Language Arts in the Elementary School.* Boston: D. C. Heath, 1964, pp. 42–47.

MacGinitie, Walter. "Language Development." In Robert L. Ebel (ed.). *Encyclopedia of Educational Research,* rev. ed. New York: Macmillan, 1969.

McNeil, David. "Developmental Psycholinguistics." In Frank Smith and George A. Miller (eds.). *The Genesis of Language.* Cambridge, Mass.: M.I.T. Press, 1966, pp. 15–85.

Petty, Walter T. (ed.). *Research in Oral Language.* Champaign, Ill.: National Council of Teachers of English, 1967.

Reed, Carroll E. (ed.). *Learning of Language.* New York: Appleton-Century-Crofts, 1971.

Smith, Brooks, Kenneth Goodman and Robert Meredith. *Language and Thinking in the Language Arts in the Elementary School.* New York: Holt, Rinehart and Winston, 1970.

Stauffer, Russell G. *The Language-Experience Approach to the Teaching of Reading.* New York: Harper and Row, 1971.

Strickland, Ruth G. "The Language of Elementary School Children: Its Relation to Language of Reading Textbooks and the Quality of Reading of Selected Children." *Bulletin No. 38,* Bulletin of the School of Education. Bloomington: Indiana University Press, 1962.

Torrance, E. Paul and R. E. Meyers. *Creative Learning and Teaching.* New York: Dodd, Mead, 1970.

Wells, Charlotte. "The Child's Equipment for Language Growth." In James C. MacCampbell (ed.). *Readings in the Language Arts in the Elementary School.* Boston: D. C. Heath, 1964, pp. 66–75.

CHAPTER III

A Creative Approach to the Language Arts

> *Enemies*
>
> *Roses are Red*
> *Violets are blue*
> *If I had an egg*
> *I'd throw it at you!*
>
> CATHY
Grade 3

TO THE READER

A sense of humor! That's what the world needs. Most children have it; creative children have it in abundance as the poem above indicates. What happens to children that they loose it as they grow older?

In his work with children, the author has found there are at least two ways that creativity can be developed: through creative teaching and through developing the characteristics in all children that are predominant in creative children. We can begin with a sense of humor: teachers and their students should laugh together more.

In Chapter I many of the characteristics of creative children were mentioned with samples of their manifestation in children's writing. More are developed below. Also in this chapter the reader will see how the language arts are the tools of communication and will explore some of the misconceptions about language. Most important of all, the manner by which language develops will be studied.

If you are using this book as a text in class why not divide the class into four numbered groups and let each group dramatize one of the misconceptions about language for the rest of the class. In this way you will not all have to read all of the chapter.

THE PERSONALITY OF COMMUNICATION

Children have a rare gift of communicating creatively. It is natural for them to do it; it is only because we clutter their minds and their hearts with trivia like commas and complete sentences, which get in their way, that they grow impatient and abandon their own way. The process, to us, becomes more important than the product. But this should not be; the process should *aid* communication not hinder it.

A teacher friend of mine selected the following piece of writing because she thought it was good. She based her judgment on its correctness and proper structure, I am sure.

Spring

Spring has come. How do I know? Today a robin sang on my window sill. Today a dandelion bloomed on the lawn. Today the sun burst forth and remained the entire day. Gold in the sky and gold on the lawn and a red red robin came hopping along. Yes, it is spring!

JILL
Grade 4

Personally, I found it dull and overwhelmingly adult. I chose these instead:

A Spring Stream

The snow melts into little streams,
Trickling over rocks and stones.
Like a laughing child
It gurgles along the way.
It has no cares, this little stream,
But to trip over stones that are in its way.
This little stream,
This lovely stream that gurgles along the way.

MARGO
Grade 4

The Color of Trees

Some things are yellow, some are green but the ever-green is the greenest of all green.

Some things are purple, some are gray but the beech is the grayest of all gray.

If I had to name all the trees and their colors, I would be going on, on, on, for ever.

VICKY
Grade 3

They appear to me to be beautifully direct, honest and uncontaminated with adult values. So fresh and pleasant and childlike.

This quality can be retained even after children have learned standard forms and usage, providing of course, that the forms and usage are taught as *means to assist a child in expressing himself.*

See the evidence below:

Spring

Spring is in the air.
And the weather is pretty fair,
Although there is a bit of snow,
The sun will come and make it go.

JACQUELINE
Grade 5

Spring

From the spring rains,
    the rivers all gain,
And every one's scared of a flood,
But when its all through,
    everything's new.
But some of the things are all mud.

JOHN R.
Grade 4

Spring

Spring is a lovely season
As you all know
The warm weather comes
And the cold weather goes.

DAVID
Grade 5

67

God Made Birds To Fly

Oh! Little bird
Why do you sit?
Soar up to the sky!
You sit on that branch
Like a frightened cat.
But wings have you to fly!

Do not neglect
God's gift to you,
For wings were made for flying.
So use your wings
My little bird,
Till you are sick or dying.

So little bird
Go! Fly away!
Oh yes, some day you'll die.
But now isn't the time
To think about that
For God made birds to fly!

DANA
Grade 7

There is a certain personality that creeps into effective communication. What makes it effective is the personality of the child. Creativity and creative expression may be developed by valuing those characteristics held by creative children and seeking to develop them in all children. Also, there are some skills that creative children possess which are not emphasized in all classrooms but could be. Let's look at a few.

A Sense of Humor

One of the objectives of the language arts program should be to develop a good sense of humor in children, especially since this is one of the attributes of creative children. Communication of ideas through verbal fun is a much required skill in our culture.

Jimmy shows his love for his gluttonous kitten with a wry smile.

A Kitten

A kitten soft and fluffy
It loves to jump and play
It feels so fat and stuffy
Because it eats all day.

JIMMY R.
Grade 3

This "tongue in cheek" paragraph was submitted by Kay when she chose to write on the topic "What I Enjoy the Most."

What I Enjoy the Most

There are many things that I enjoy, but the favorite one at the moment is Junior Band. I enjoy all music, and rhythm. This is my first year in the band and I eagerly look forward to happy Friday! My handsome instructor won't believe this, because my obstinate, uncooperative saxophone blows sour, squeaky notes. Scowls, inquisitive eyebrows and other "no-no's" do not discourage my love for the band. So give me music, music, music.

KAY C.
Grade 6

The Ability to Emphathize

Can children be helped to project so that they can sense other people's feelings? Indeed they can. First, however, they must have experienced the many emotions common to all men. The sensations created by these emotions can be called into play in situations contrived to relive them. Role-playing and dramatics are techniques which help children enter into the frame of mind of someone else and develop sympathy and feeling (see page 184).

In the language arts, empathy can be developed through the writing of projection stories involving both people and things. The samples given below of children's ability to empathize are self-explanatory.

Shiloh

My name is Shiloh. I am a hill. A war was fought on me. Many men had to leave their families.

The war was the Yankees versus the Confederates. Grant and Johnston were the generals of the two armies.

The fort on top of me is Fort Donelson.

Today is April 7, 1862. Many men are down, bloody and scattered about. Men aren't the only dead or wounded. Many horses are dead. The sun is now setting. The war is still going. Cannons and gun shots ring out.

The night passes. Morning dawns. The Confederate General is surrendering. Many men and horses are dead.

On they march to the next terrible battle. What is it all for?

DOROTHY
Grade 6

A Civil War Rifle

I am in a man's hands who is fighting for his life. He shoots man after man. Bullets come from here, there, everywhere. Everywhere there is blood. There is much weeping, crying. Will this terrible bloody battle never stop?

I am part of the cause of all this. I am a cruel weapon. Wives, children are crying for the ones they love. Night after night, day after day, cannons ring out! All around horses are dead. Besides men and horses, homes that took sweat and hard work were burned to the ground. Crops dead, fields with blood, soldiers lie there.

I hate to think that I helped cause much of this suffering.

JOHN
Grade 5

Imagination can be stimulated when children are asked to become abstract concepts such as colors, wind, air, sky or elements of nature. Here is one very outstanding poem written by a sixth grader when the children were asked to select a color and write how it would feel to be that particular color.

How Does It Feel to Be Green?

I wouldn't like to be green
To me green means "mean"
It's slimy and icky and sticky and sick
If I had to be green I'd change mighty quick
To yellow or orange or blue or red
Because things turn green when they are dead.

No—
I wouldn't even like to be green
If I were green I'd never be seen
Unless I was grassy or leafy or flowery
Or woodsy or watery or meadowy or bowery
Green in these places is rather fine
If I had to be green—this kind would be mine.

But I am a people and who's ever seen
Attractive people who are green?

No—
I wouldn't like to be green!

Empathy or biography?

Tomboys

A tomboy is a girl
Who likes to play with boys.
And doesn't like
To play with dolls and toys.
She likes to wear slacks
And play in haystacks.

JUDY
Grade 2

On feelings:

Bright as a daisy
Fresh as the sea
That's how being clean
Feels to me.

PAT
Age 5

Use of Metaphor and Simile

Many artists believe that creativity is best determined by a person's ability to use metaphor, or simile. This could well be for some very creative children in one school I visited seemed to have an unusual ability to use metaphor and simile in their writing as you can see below:

God's Feathers

The dainty, feathery, snow flakes
float softly to the ground.
From high, white fleecy clouds
where heavenly angels float around.
They float so daintily and always
light on bush or flower
They are so pretty we just have
to watch them by the hour.

PAT
Grade 6

Even second graders are capable of using imagery in their writing:

The Green Grass

One spring morning when I woke up. The green grass was starting to grow. And then flowers were starting to pop up. I love it when it sprinkles. Because I like to hear the rain drops on the house. They go pitter patter on the roof top. I like it also when it stops sprinkling. Because I like to go out and see the rainbow. And I like to look in the puddles and see all different colors. Did you ever see a rainbow? Yes I have seen a rainbow. It looks very pretty all different colors are in it red, green, yellow, purple and blue. I hate it when it thunders out. I like especially when it's sunny out. So I can play out. I like to play with my friend Teri when it's nice out.

Originality in Thinking

Creative children are able to use words fluently to express their imagination. Notice the easy, comfortable manner in which Kevin and Walter (age 10) describe a falling star.

A Falling Star

I saw a star slide down the sky,
Blinding the North as it went by.

Too burning and too quick to hold,
Very lovely, heavenly, and bold.

Making streaks and trails so long,
Going fast and going strong.

Streaking down the sky so fast,
Hard to see as it went past.

Good only to make wishes on,
And forever to be gone.

KEVIN G. AND WALTER B.
Grade 5

A teacher friend writes to me in the following memo:

I have a girl in my reading group who is able to express herself poetically.

She gets an idea and puts it on paper. Often the form or grammar needs polishing but she has such marvelous ideas.

Often I have found poems left on my desk with no explanation or name—sometimes—"To a Friend."

Here are two that I enjoyed. I hope you do, too.

She is a fifth grader who loves to read more than anything else in the world.

She wrote:

> *I love to read; I love to write,*
> *For a book, I'd put up a fight.*
> *Maybe a book as big as the sea,*
> *Is something that would interest me.*

Another sample of Joanne's spontaneous writing follows. A measure of true creativity is a child's ability to take off on his own as this little girl is able to do.

It Will End

> *Oh how beautifully the sun*
> *Rises over the great mountain*
> *And we know*
> *Respectfully so*
> *That the dusk is done.*
> *While on the other side of the earth*
> *There's a tide*
> *Coming in on the evening surf.*
> *While hunger, hurt and sin*
> *Are overcoming us*
> *This we know*
> *We cannot mind*
> *And thus*
> *The world will end.*

JOANNE P.
Grade 5

Variety: The Spice of Life

Creativity is well demonstrated by the different ways children express themselves about one topic:

Winter Wonders

> *In winter snow falls on the ground,*
> *Flakes go spinning round and round.*
> *Some icicles hang low and high,*
> *In different formations that catch the eye.*
> *Some of them are long and thin.*
> *That hang from my window's brim.*

JOYCE MENTER
Grade 6

Snow

Snow quiet, soft and lovely, it dresses everything in a velvet coat.

When Mother Nature shakes out her feathery pillow, they land shimmering on the ground. Drifting down so fluffy and white.

Snow is squishy, slushy and melty. When you go out you sink in the snow. You put it in your mouth it melts. It's so good! When cars drive along the snow splats out from their tires, it makes such a funny sound.

Snow is fun, light and cold. It is fun to go out and make snowmen and forts. When it falls on your tongue it feels so light. When you go out in the snow it blows into your face, and you go in the house and get cocoa, its nice and warm.

Snow is everything.

CYNTHIA TALBOT
Grade 5

Snow

I love the snow
So soft and white,
It is so clean and quiet and light
Just like feathers falling from the sky.
I love the snow,
I wonder why
Maybe its because the snow's so pretty
Cold and icy and sparkly glittery
It looks like stars upon the ground
And during a blizzard the stars whirl around
I love the snow, I don't know why but I'll
love the snow until I die.

MAXINE
Grade 5

THE TOOLS OF COMMUNICATION

The language arts are the tools of communication. They are not subjects in themselves for they have no body of content. We do not read reading or write writing or spell spelling. We read because we want to obtain a message or an idea from a printed page; we write because we wish to convey a message or an idea by symbols; we spell correctly because we wish to make our communication clear by utilizing those arbitrary written symbols agreed upon by our society. The fundamental objective of the language arts program is to develop correct, clear, imaginative and effective communication. The full realization of this objective is possible only when the tools of language are used *as tools* and children practice the use of them continually.

MISCONCEPTIONS ABOUT LANGUAGE

There are many misconceptions about language which interfere with its use as a creative tool for the development of effective communication.

Misconception 1. Language and the rules of language are "set." Actually, there is little about language that is rigid. Because its purpose is to communicate effectively and efficiently, language is continually being changed. Verb forms which were frowned upon twenty years ago have now found their way into common usage.

There are really few pure forms of language and sentence structures used in common everyday speech. The drive for efficient communication within people resolves itself in a continual evolution in language usage: a virtual "trimming it down to size."

Which Sounds Natural?

I'll take the omnibus to the city.	*or*	I'll take the bus downtown.
Our high fidelity phonograph set has given us much pleasure.	*or*	We've had a great deal of enjoyment from our hi-fi.
Let's watch television.	*or*	Let's watch TV.
He took an airplane to New York City.	*or*	He took the plane to New York.

In many cases, the economical version communicates better than the more correct and proper version. By this criterion, the trimmed down form is as acceptable as, or more acceptable than, the more proper forms as a media for communication.

Great literature is written so that it communicates unusual moods, plots, ideas. On one page in a Nobel Prize book there are twelve instances where grammar rules are violated so that the author can create a mood. It makes for powerful reading. Yet, few teachers accept this type of writing in themes or stories. Regard-

IN USING TOOLS WE APPLY THEM DIRECTLY TO THEIR PURPOSE. JOHN IS ONLY PRACTICING STROKES...HE IS NOT REALLY RAKING THE LAWN WHILE HE USES THE RAKE ON THE DRIVEWAY. WE WOULD CONSIDER THIS A FOOLISH WAY TO TEACH JOHN TO USE A RAKE AND YET...

drill
quietly
distance

COUNTLESS NUMBERS OF "BLUEJAYS," "BLUEBIRDS" AND "ROBINS" MARCH UP TO THE TEACHER IN A GROUP, ARE INTRODUCED TO A GROUP OF WORDS GO THROUGH A SERIES OF "SOUND" EXERCISES AND RETURN TO THEIR SEATS WITHOUT THE OPPORTUNITY TO APPLY THE NEW SKILL OR TOOL THEY HAVE LEARNED...WONDERING WHAT IT IS ALL ABOUT.

FIGURE 3-1.   *Language is a tool.*

less of the child's intent, these papers are generally marked with red pencil and returned to be corrected. Correct writing, in many instances, is dull and ineffective.

Misconception 2. Language and rules of language are determined by experts. Language is determined by common usage. The words which are used in any given society are the ones which rise from the experiences of the people. After a short period of usage, these words appear in dictionaries.

Vocabularies within a language evolve, sometimes slowly and sometimes dramatically. A group of college juniors in teacher education compared two newspapers printed six months apart to show how dramatically language can change in a short period of time. One paper was printed in September 1957, previous to the launching of the Russian Sputnik. The other was printed in February 1958, six months after this historical event. The average newspaper is printed on the vocabulary level of the sixteen-year-old. Yet in the feature article of this newspaper over seventy-five new words and phrases had come into common usage in six months time—almost a whole new language had been invented in order to communicate new ideas. Among those words and phrases were the following: satellite, Jupiter-C Rocket, trackers, bullet-shaped space vehicles, radio transmission, tracking operations, launching pad, Smithsonian Astrophysical Observatory, zenith, space bullet, meteor sensing devices, international astronomical usage, space module, maiden circuit, cosmic rays, moon-watching teams, missile, blast-off, minitrack, astronaut, cosmonauts, International Geophysical Year.

Experts serve the purpose of setting common rules by which language may be used for standard communication but not always for most effective communication. They make their contribution to language in those instances when proper communication is needed, such as in business letter writing, formal textbook construction, reporting and the like. But the people of a society use the language to say what they have to say, according to the social setting in which they find themselves. In such instances correct language forms may be abandoned for a more efficient or picturesque communication.

Misconception 3. Language is static. We have seen how language is continually changing. It is not static, it is dynamic, vibrant and alive with change. Change replaces old phrases and words with new ones, gives us new spellings and more realistic language forms, new punctuation forms to coincide with our use of machines in communicating and even changes the meanings of words.

New words are being born every minute while many words fall into disuse:

Words Recently Born	*Words that Are Dying*
recycle	coal scuttle
feedback	blacksmith
synectics	trolley car
yippie	hook and eye
futuristics	buggy
biodegradable	bloomers
Vietnamization	carpetbag
megalopolis	bundling
phonovision	icebox
ballistic	
minitrack	

Words Almost Dead (Rarely Used)	*Words Whose Meaning Is Changing*
hobble skirt	*Decay:* once meant decomposition of organic matter—now also means the deterioration of metal in outer space.
button hook	
surrey	
waterglass	
horseless carriage	*Fallout:* once a command—now the radiation effect of nuclear blasts.
gas light	
carfare	*Pot:* once a kettle—now a drug.
mumblety-peg	*Program:* once an account of an entertainment—now a system to feed a computer.
tenpins	

The symbols of language are constantly undergoing change. Children and adults are continually experimenting with language. When children cannot express an experience with a certain word, they put together other words to express the idea. Timmy, age four, who does not have the word *boost* in his vocabulary, says, "Will you please give me a *reach-up?*" when he wants to climb a tree. Stephen, age five, describes the difference between a layer cake and a loaf cake by saying, "This is an *up* cake." Such experiments with language are called *verbalisms*. (See pp. 144–45 of this book.)

We hear words in one context, reproduce them in another context and absorb them into our own speech patterns if they are accepted by all listeners over a period of time.

Slang communicates too. Another common way we see language undergoing change is through slang. This use is often frowned upon in school, yet our language is peppered with slang which was once rejected. Such expressions as *O.K., right on, scram* and *keep your cool* communicate in a way which no other words do. Slang has a unique factor—it seems to express a multitude of ideas and feelings with a minimum of words.

Slang fulfills many functions. To the teenager it is a way of asserting his independence and individuality by breaking away from adult restrictions and standards. It becomes a language all his own with which he can communicate with other teenagers but not with the adults who dominate his life. Yet, in most English courses, the use of slang as a means of communication is denied to children. This denial is an example of how teachers limit creative development by driving the use of words into the subconscious rather than allowing it to remain accessible in the preconscious or in what Rugg describes as the transliminal chamber.

When we refuse to allow children to use slang in school we do not realize that what we are doing is refusing them the right to use their newly formed language (slang) while we are often using it ourselves (as we once knew it).

This conversation, taken from a third grade class discussion, illustrates this point.

The children had been planning a trip to the bakery. Their plans were printed neatly on a chart. The teacher was reviewing the chart with the children. "Now let's remember," she said, "that we are going to walk by two's along the sidewalk. Do you all *get that?*" The children nodded. "Let's also remember that each has some special problem he is to find out about, *O.K.?*" Again the children nodded. With a twinkle in her eye the teacher continued, "And—let's also remember we promised each other there would be no *horsing around O.K.?*" The children smiled and Billy said, "O.K., *I dig it*, Miss Ransom." Immediately Miss Ransom's face sobered as she said, "Now, Billy, you know we don't use slang in *this* classroom!"

Slang Gone	Slang Sometimes Heard	Current Slang
Savvy?	Get with it.	Can you dig it?
Drop dead!	Knock it off!	Cool it!
Let's chew the fat.	Let's shoot the bull.	Let's rap.
He's off his rocker.	He's a kook.	He's freaked out.
He flew off the handle.	He blew his cool.	He flipped out.
Swell!	Groovy!	Heavy!

The creative teacher realizes the need for change in language. She accepts the creative forms of language being invented through common usage or by the children she teaches. She encourages the coinage of new words, recognizing the fact that creating a new word is as exciting as creating a painting.

Donald, age 10, could not find the word he wanted to describe the sunny, golden day he was writing about in his poem so he called it brightful. Shelly said there was no word to tell about the evening sky she was describing in her poem so she invented pink-sky. Ronnie, a teenager, named his jalopie "Shasta" because, said Ronnie, "Shasta have oil, shasta have gas, shasta have water everytime I drive her."

Language is changing. The children aid the process when they find new ways of saying things in their speech and their writing. The school has little justification for shutting off any communication form. This inhibits the creation of new language. It should recognize all communication forms and help the child find the most effective ways of using them (slang included).

If we are to teach children to speak and write creatively, we must place all known resources at their disposal and not force language forms into the subconscious mind. The new patterns of speaking and writing are dynamic and changing; through it language becomes a creative tool.

Misconception 4. There is a single language in a culture. There may be many languages within one culture. Even though the same words are spoken, they may have different meanings among different sets of people. Lumberjacks, teachers, doctors, railroad workers and laboratory scientists all have unique languages of their own. These groups also use words commonly used by other sets of people, but often with completely different meanings.

There is a story told of a little girl who went with her mother to a parent-teacher planning meeting. Although she appeared to be happily playing at the rear of the room, she apparently heard more than her mother imagined. After a busy afternoon with the group, planning which consultants should be called in to help with P.T.A. problems, the mother took her little girl home. At dinner that evening the father said to the little girl, "Well, what did your mother and her friends talk about all afternoon?" The little girl replied promptly, "Farmers."

The mother was perplexed. She could recall no instance when farmers had been mentioned. After careful questioning, she finally realized the little girl had heard the consultants referred to as "men outstanding in their fields," and to a little rural girl a man outstanding in his field was, who else, but a farmer!

There are languages within a language. Sometimes this is called "jargon." Educators have a jargon as do most people involved in a vocation or profession. Spoken out of context, jargon is meaningless to some people. It actually represents communication at the conceptual level.

In Figure 3-2(a) a musician would recognize the invitation to bring his instrument to his friends to play.

In Figure 3-2(b), cooks in a short-order diner will recognize the order for two poached eggs on toast.

In Figure 3-2(c), the statistician will recognize the language which tells about the falling of the data into the pattern of the normal curve.

FIGURE 3-2. *What does it mean? Who says it?*

In Figure 3-2(d), television crews and stagehands will respond by clearing the stage.

The nurse interprets Figure 3-2(e) as asking whether an extra nurse is working on the floor.

These languages within the language need an interpreter almost as much as the foreign language does. Nonetheless, they give the language a beauty and a picturesqueness which makes it exciting and colorful. Children who hear these subcultural languages are afforded opportunities to see how words can be used creatively to express different ideas. If their writing is to ring true, they must understand that some words and sentences can convey many meanings.

Language often gives status. Knowledge of accepted speech forms and appropriate grammar gives us a wider choice of usage. We can apply the forms of speech which we know to the social situation in which we find ourselves. Speech is, above all, a social

FIGURE 3-3.   *Can this be the same person? Is it?*

process. One can be accepted or rejected in his social setting because of his speech. Many educated young men, in their drive to be accepted, abandoned their learned speech patterns while in military service and assumed the unique speech of the platoon in order to be able to communicate and hold status within that group.

Just as there are many languages within the language, so there are many levels of language.[1]

Levels of Usage

ILLITERATE	HOMELY	IN-FORMAL	FORMAL	LITERARY
We've done et.	We just had chow.	We've just finished eating.	Dinner has been served.	Ah, how hath the groaning board been lightened of its burden.
He's maddern a hornet.	He's all riled up.	Boy, is he sore at me.	He is extremely distraught.	The turmoil within him all but erupted in a volcanic outburst.
We're gonna shake a leg.	C'mon let's trip it.	May I have this one?	May I have the pleasure of this dance?	Let us bow and curtsey to the melodic strains of Strauss.

Effective communication may take place at one level as well as when levels are crossed. Often a child coming from a home background which is different from other children is confused by the phrasing of his teacher because the words are used in different patterns or contexts from those he is used to hearing. These children often experience spelling difficulties simply because they hear words as their parents say them and then spell them by sound. A farm boy in the sixth grade wrote "refrigeador," "stoopid" and "breffast" in a story. A visit to his home revealed this to be exactly the way his parents pronounced these words. Many years of listening had fixed these patterns so well in his mind, that they predominated over his teacher's pronunciations. This boy needed to

---

1. R. Pooley, *Teaching English Usage* (New York: Appleton-Century-Crofts, 1946), pp. 16–24.

hear and see these words. He had good phonetic sense, but he did not have the word sound or picture imprinted on his mind. This situation is a delicate one because under no circumstances should the teacher cause a breakdown in communication between the parents and the boy, nor should the teacher do anything to cause friction or loss of respect in the boy-parent relationship. Yet, the boy must see and hear the correct ways of saying and writing words.

Few people operate on any one level of language. Actually, most of us use all levels at one time or another, depending on the social situation in which we find ourselves. We fluctuate from the literary to the illiterate level frequently in the course of one conversation.

To help children cope with language and to better develop communication skills, it is important that they come to recognize levels of language, not as criteria for determining the social status of the speaker, but as a literary style or a means of communicating a specific idea within a certain context. Children are exposed to these levels of language all the time and they need help in understanding, interpreting and using them.

Figure 3-4 is a sample of the material a ten year·old girl read in a ten-minute period which shows four different levels of language.

Every person has many vocabularies. Often our grammar and reading books refer to the child's vocabulary. This becomes a confusing concept because all people have many vocabularies rather than one vocabulary. As children acquire words, they categorize them within the memory operation of the brain. Some words they use continually, while others are stored away for special usage. Because language is a social skill, we select from our reservoir of stored up words those which best suit each situation in which we find ourselves. Some words appear in all vocabularies, but many are unique to only one and are used only at one time. A child's comprehension vocabulary may differ from his speaking vocabulary; he can hear and understand words he never uses.

Although there are many different vocabularies, we can sort out three basic ones for the language arts: the speaking, the reading and the writing vocabularies. In a child, the largest of these is the speaking vocabulary. Second largest is the reading vocabulary. Smallest is the writing vocabulary. In adults the largest is the reading vocabulary, next is the speaking vocabulary and smallest is the writing vocabulary.

Adults read many words they never or rarely speak. The adult rarely talks on a literary level, but he can think or read on this

FIGURE 3-4. Levels of language of a ten-year-old.

level with ease. Somewhere between early childhood and later childhood or adulthood, the individual amasses enough words so that his reading vocabulary becomes greater than his spoken vocabulary. But young children rarely read words meaningfully if those words are not common to the oral vocabulary.

It is important to note that the smallest vocabulary of both adults and children is the writing vocabulary. This is probably true because children never, and adults rarely, write words they do not say. All this bears significance when we realize that we must place a great deal of stress on the oral vocabulary of children in order to build the necessary vocabulary for effective reading and creative writing.

HOW LANGUAGE DEVELOPS

Language develops through a logical sequence. First in the sequence comes *listening*. Children learn the names of things by hearing them identified. Listening and experience go hand in hand. A child can only understand the abstract verbal symbols we call words when they represent a direct or a vicarious experience which he has had.

After the child has experienced and listened he can *speak*. *Oral communication* is nothing more than the substitution of oral sounds for a vivid direct or vicarious experience. When the oral symbols or sounds become a fluent part of the child's vocabulary, he is ready to recognize them in print. This is *reading*. After his reading ability has developed sufficiently to afford him a true visual impression of these words, he is ready to imitate or reproduce these words in *writing*.

Spelling, handwriting, word usage, capitalization, punctuation and *grammar usage* are refinements to the writing act. They make communication clearer but not necessarily richer. Actually, they are social courtesies learned in order that all people may communicate through writing. They are the examples of some of the necessary conformities of a society.

Figure 3-5 helps explain the sequence of language development. This sequence of development is longitudinal as well as lateral. It is longitudinal in that it is the way language develops over a period of years. The baby listens for a period of time, varying from a few months to two years, to the people around him using verbal symbols in meaningful context. He listens and experiences. He hears mother say table in a host of ways during this period of time. She says: "Helen, help Mother set the table"; "See the pretty flowers Daddy bought, in on the coffee table"; "Answer the telephone on the table in the hall"; "Here's a lovely picnic table under these trees"; "I left my book on the dining room table"; "Pull your chairs up to the table"; and so on until one day, when he is physically able and psychologically ready, he thumps his hand on the object in mind and says, "tabbul." He re-enforces his learning when Mother gleefully shouts, "Did you hear what he said. Say it again, Honey—tell sister. What is this?" Then he tells Daddy and all his relatives and so fixes the word in his mind. Here is an example of the word appearing in the child's vocabulary at the concept level, for he has generalized his experiences with many tables.

This sequence of development is also lateral in that the same process is used over a short period to introduce new words to children. For instance, a teacher calls a reading group to the front of the room. They are to construct a reading chart from an experience they had at the farm the previous day such as the one constructed by Miss Temple in the last chapter. They learn some new words such as silo, tractor, thresher, milking machine, milkcooler, furrow and acre by labeling their experiences. The teacher re-enforces their learning by showing pictures of these words and

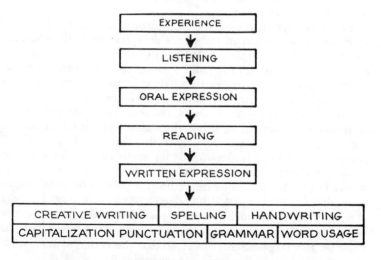

FIGURE 3-5. *The normal sequence of language development.*

the children recall the oral symbols. The teacher then introduces the printed symbol by use of the experience chart, and the children learn to read the chart. Some children, if they are advanced enough, may even copy the words in a story of their own later at their seats. In this situation, the child has widened his vocabulary and has developed language skills in one period, where he progressed from experiencing to listening, to oral expression, to reading and on to writing.

Intelligence enters into the picture here. It has been pointed out that intelligence is highly related to vocabulary development. Therefore, as the child progresses down through the above chart, his intelligence becomes more and more important in terms of his ability to use language. Slow learning children do not read as well as normal or bright children, and we can never expect them to be able to punctuate, capitalize and spell as effectively.

For effective teaching, the sequential development of language must always be followed; whenever it is violated, problems result. A primary teacher, about to give a reading lesson, often introduces a list of words on the board. If these words are not within the range of the children's experiences, they do not communicate effectively. The children can only resort to memory or name-calling of the printed symbol. Unless the word takes on meaning during the subsequent lesson, it does not become a part of the child's usable vocabulary. It is only a meaningless arrangement of letters looking like many other meaningless arrangements, and he will forget it out of lack of use.

Teachers once introduced spelling words for the week's lesson from a textbook. Many of the words were foreign to the child and unrelated to his experiences. When this was so the teacher's first job was to see to it that the child experienced the word, then used it orally, then saw it in print and then learned to spell it, so he could use it to help him communicate in his written work.

Unless these steps are followed, the motivation for learning the word becomes something other than communication. It may be fear of failure or desire to please the teacher. The child will memorize the word under this latter motivation, pass a test on Friday, and often not know the word on a succeeding test two weeks later. The word has never been a part of his total experience, and his memory of it has deteriorated. In a good language arts program then, much emphasis must be placed at the top level of this chart: *experience*. In the primary grades this experience must be, to a large extent, direct, so that the verbal symbol which represents it may be accurate and meaningful.

This sequence is vitally important in developing the creative aspects of the language arts. *It is only when children receive the opportunity to talk frequently and freely that they develop an extensive oral vocabulary. It is only when conscientious efforts are made on the part of the teachers to use normal experiences to build new vocabulary that children develop a rich written vocabulary. It is only when teachers contrive experiences to keep children using these vocabularies in new and creative ways that creative writing can take place. It is important to remember that children rarely write words they do not speak.*

SUMMARY

The language arts are the tools of communication and because communication is a complicated process, learning to use the tools is also a complicated process. There are many misconceptions about language which interfere with its creative use in developing effective communication.

Language develops in a logical sequence, and when this sequence is violated the teacher may cause communication disability among the children. The importance of experience as the base of language development cannot be overstressed.

TO THE COLLEGE STUDENT AND THE CLASSROOM TEACHER

1. Take any one of the characteristics or unique skills of the creative child which are mentioned in this chapter and design a lesson which will develop it, such as a sense of humor, empathy or the ability to use metaphor and simile.

2. Take one basic idea such as pollution or drugs, identify the major problems about it. Divide the class into five or six groups and have each group communicate the idea in a different manner. One group might do it through dance, one through dramatics, one through speaking, one through poetry and another through pantomime. What other ways can you think of?

3. Think of a public figure (or some classmate) who has the talent of communicating well. List as many of the components of good communication as you can. How would you define creative communication? Where does it fit into your list?

4. Think of how difficult it is to understand children when they tell about having seen a television show which you have not seen.

This is a good example of the points made in this chapter. How many ways can you think of to use a television program to develop creative oral expression?

5. Examine some teaching manuals. If meaningful communication between children and teacher develops from fields of common experience, are not some of the lessons in the manuals planned backwards?

6. Apply what you have read in this chapter to the reading lessons you are teaching or have seen taught. Did the teacher provide an experience for every word symbol before introducing it into the communicative process? Discuss this question: Is there ever a time when vicarious experiences are superior to direct experiences in learning?

7. *Mrs. and Mr. Peacock* is a film written and made by a child with the help of her father and some technicians who were interested in her work. View the film and discuss this child's ability to communicate. (*Mrs. and Mr. Peacock*, 12 minutes, color, distributed by Syracuse University.)

8. When you were in high school, you probably learned to speak a foreign language. Foreign languages are now taught in the elementary school by what is often called the "conversation" method. In light of what you have just read, can you see why the conversation method is a logical way of teaching a language?

9. *Creative* communication means something different from *correct* communication. These two concepts well illustrate the problem of conformity and individuality. Correct communication means teaching children to conform to predetermined patterns of writing and speaking. Creative communication means helping children to use language to suit their own needs. Find examples of each type of communication among children.

10. Ask your colleagues to search for writing among children or among the works of famous authors which show the "personality" writing mentioned in this chapter. Did you ever try to write a poem? Try it and then read it as an objective observer and analyze it for signs of your own personality.

11. Put a word or phrase on the chalkboard and have each member of the class write a metaphor or simile about it. Fold the papers, put them in a hat box, have everyone then draw one and share it with the rest of the class. How many *different* ideas were created? Group creativity is generally a more productive kind of creativity than individual creativity in terms of quantity.

12. Discuss this statement: "Because verbal communication springs from common experiences, creative communication is more likely to result from creative experiences."

13. Creative communication means helping children to express themselves in oral and written forms which are primarily their

own. Consider what you read in this chapter and list as many ways as you can to set conditions for teaching standard communication forms to children. Then list ways you can set conditions to teach creative communication to children. Can the teaching of standard communication forms be creative?

14. Your author generally has difficulty in telling the age level of a child who writes a particular poem. It seems to him that children in the middle school who are beginning to write creatively write quite similarly to primary children who have been writing creatively over a period of time. Following are two poems written by children. At what age level were the children, would you say?

May Flowers

Beautiful, beautiful May flowers,
Look so bright and graceful,
Look so gay and fresh,
Shocking pink and bright colors
Look so pretty with different colors
Gorgeous petals
Bright happy roses
A little cheery
That's what makes May graceful and gay.

The Mouse and the Motorcar

A mouse all whiskery, in his motorcar speedy,
Zoomed all day along a shady road,
In among the flowers tall and bold.

This tiny brown creature, short and small,
Was not much more than two inches tall.
His rattly car carried him far.
With a boom and a bang and a big loud clang.

He drove around in all kinds of climate,
While in his motorcar he sat.
One day he caught a cold and coughed,
And his back tire went rolling off.

This light little mouse, had a red brick house,
With a red car shed, for his motorcar's bed.
And he lived happily in his house all red.

15. Problems for discussion:

a. The degree to which a child uses metaphor is an indication of his creativity.
b. Grammar rules should be memorized by children.
c. Parts of speech should be taught in the fifth grade.
d. Diagramming sentences is a necessary skill to acquire in order to be a truly good writer.

e.   The poems and stories by primary children which appear thus far in this book are indications that children have and use all forms of language by the time they are school age.

SELECTED BIBLIOGRAPHY

Anderson, Verna D., Paul S. Anderson, Francis Ballantine and Virginia M. Howes. *Readings in Language Arts.* 2d ed. New York: Macmillan, 1968.

Burns, Paul, Betty Broman and Alberta Lowe. *The Language Arts in Childhood Education.* 2d ed. Chicago: Rand McNally, 1971.

Commission on the English Curriculum of the National Council of Teachers of English. *The English Language Arts.* Chapter XIV. New York: Appleton, 1952.

————. *Language for Today's Children.* Chapter IV. New York: Appleton, 1954.

Dallmann, Martha. *Teaching the Language Arts in the Elementary School.* 2d ed. Dubuque, Iowa: William C. Brown, 1971.

Goldstein, Miriam B. *The Teaching of Language in Our Schools.* New York: Macmillan, 1966.

Greene, Harry A. and Walter T. Petty. *Developing Language Skills in the Elementary Schools.* 4th ed. Boston: Allyn and Bacon, 1971.

Kornbluth, Frances S. and Bernard Bard. *Creativity and the Teacher.* Chicago: American Federation of Teachers, 1966.

Lamb, Pose. *Guiding Children's Language Learning.* 2d ed. Dubuque, Iowa: William C. Brown, 1971.

Loban, Walter. *The Language of Elementary School Children.* Champaign, Ill.: National Council of Teachers of English, 1963.

Lundsteen, Sara W. "Language Arts in the Elementary School." In W. B. Michael (ed.). *Teaching for Creative Endeavor.* Bloomington: Indiana University Press, 1968.

McCampbell, James C. (ed.). *Readings in the Language Arts in the Elementary School.* Boston: D. C. Heath, 1964.

Petty, Walter T. *Issues and Problems in the Elementary Language Arts.* Boston: Allyn and Bacon, 1968.

Platts, Mary E., Sr. Rose Marguerite and Esther Shumaker. *Spice: Suggested Activities to Motivate the Teaching of the Language Arts.* Benton Harbor, Mich.: Educational Service, 1960.

Pooley, Robert C. *Teaching English Usage.* New York: Appleton-Century-Crofts, 1946.

Shane, Harold G. and Jane G. Mulny. *Improving Language Arts Instruction through Research.* Washington, D.C.: Association for Supervision and Curriculum Development, 1964.

Shane, Harold G., Mary E. Reddin and Margaret C. Gillespie. *Beginning Language Arts Instruction with Children.* Chapters VIII and XII. Columbus, Ohio: Charles E. Merrill, 1961.

Smith, James A. *Creative Teaching of the Language Arts in the Elementary School.* Boston: Allyn and Bacon, 1967.

————. *Setting Conditions for Creative Teaching in the Elementary School.* Boston: Allyn and Bacon, 1966.

Trauger, Wilmer. *Language Arts in Elementary School.* 2d ed. New York: McGraw-Hill, 1963.

Vygotsky, L. S. *Thought and Language.* Cambridge, Mass.: M.I.T. Press, 1962.

The Nurture of Creative Communication

CHAPTER IV

Creative Teaching of Listening

No Sounds At All

We blew milkweed seeds up in the air.
Down they came real, real soft.
We could not catch them;
We could not hear them.
They were so very still.
Little soft white feathers
Floating in the air.

This is a poem written by a kindergarten teacher. Each line was contributed by a child after the children had taken a walk around the school and had blown milkweed into the air.

TO THE READER

Now is your chance to see how creative you can be! In this chapter I have made no attempt to organize the material according to grade levels because I feel each suggestion can be adapted to any grade level. One way to begin to be creative is to break away from set ideas and patterns. As you read this chapter think of how you can add, substitute or adapt these ideas to a primary grade and an intermediate grade. Then try to adapt them to varying socioeconomic levels and subcultures. You will want to try some of the ideas presented in this chapter, but your greatest satisfactions will come from trying your own.

As a result of reading this chapter, you should better understand how conditions can be set for the creative teaching of listening and what the various types of listening are. It is the hope of the author that the reader will be convinced that the teaching of listening can be creative.

INTRODUCTION

Listening is the newest skill to be added to the language arts program. Not long ago the teaching of listening was not considered important. Children were to be seen and not heard, and it was expected that they would also listen. Indeed, there were few distractions to keep them from listening. Much of the time in the classroom was spent listening to the drone of the teacher's voice. Much of the time outside the classroom was spent listening to relatively few people and to familiar sounds day after day.

But times have changed. Today's child snaps on his radio or TV set as soon as he awakens, and many sounds fill his room. In a neighboring room his sister has tuned in another station. In the kitchen, mother has tuned in on the weather report in order to know how to dress the children for school. From the bathroom comes the sound of Dad's electric razor and the water running in his shower. Little sister has tuned in on "Captain Kangaroo" in the living room.

Soon he climbs onto the school bus where he sees and hears many children from families all chattering and telling about their home experiences. The bus unloads him at a large central school where he meets many people in small and large groups in the classroom, the gymnasium, the cafeteria, the library and the auditorium. In the afternoon, he again rides the school bus, then drives to the shopping center with mother where he meets and hears more strange people in an hour than his great-grandfather heard in a year! Today's children are bombarded with sounds from the moment they arise until they retire.

The constant flow of words around them engulfs them to the degree that they quickly learn to shut off all those words and sounds which they do not wish to hear. This is perhaps necessary if they are to remain sane.

Because children are subjected to endless numbers of sounds, they do not always know *what* to listen to or *how* to listen. Even in the listening-for-listening's-sake situation there are distractions present which make training in the listening skills necessary. For this reason, continued emphasis is being placed on the teaching of listening as a necessary language skill to be developed in the classroom.

While speaking is the most common form of communication, it is ineffective without a listener. Listening constitutes half of the communication process.

In a study conducted by Wilt[1] it was estimated that children listened 77.6 minutes of the school day, according to the teacher. In her follow-up observations, however, Wilt estimated that children actually were supposed to listen more than half the time they were in school. The highest percentage of time children were supposed to listen was when they were listening to the teacher. The listening activity with the second highest percentage of "supposed to listen" time was when children answered questions asked by the teacher and answered by one child. In the same study the author concluded that the highest percentage of supposed listening time came in the first, third and sixth grades. The lowest occurred in the second grade; the second lowest was the fourth grade. Children are expected to spend more time listening than in any other activity, yet the writer concluded that teachers considered listening less important than reading and speaking. The writer felt she gained substantial evidence to conclude that teachers do not teach *listening*.

The importance of teaching listening is well illustrated through a study conducted by the Central New York School Study Council, in which the following conclusions were drawn.

1. *Test Result:* Children in the elementary grades get information through listening.
   a. *Conclusions and Suggestions:* If we did more direct teaching of listening we could improve the quality of learning.
2. *Test Result:* Children through the sixth grade level get directions better from listening than reading.
   a. *Interpretation:* Children at lower grade levels have not mastered enough reading skills to rely upon reading for information.
   b. *Conclusions and Suggestions:* Teachers should be conscious of teaching listening as a language arts skill.
3. *Test Results:* Listening results do not necessarily parallel reading achievement.
   a. *Interpretation:* Slow learners are not necessarily poor listeners.

---

1. Marion Wilt, "A Study of Teacher Awareness of Listening as a Factor in Elementary Education," *Journal of Educational Research* 42 (April 1950), 626–36.

b.   *Conclusions and Suggestions:* Listening is a good technique for teaching slow learners.
4.   *Test Results:* While sixth graders were both better readers and listeners than fourth graders, there seemed to be greater improvement in listening than in reading at the sixth grade level.
5.   *Test Results:* There is a limit to the number of things a child can listen to and recall.
   a.   *Interpretation:* The tests did not show how many items children can remember from listening, because some children had perfect scores. Children seem to remember the first direction better than the last.
   b.   *Conclusions and Suggestions:* Teacher should be aware of the limitations of the group and should give directions accordingly.
6.   *Test Results:* There appeared to be no significant difference in listening abilities of the sexes from kindergarten through the sixth grade.[2]

In another study conducted in 1953, Pratt found that even a short training period of five weeks can be instrumental in raising the general level of listening ability, thus re-enforcing the idea that listening can be taught.[3]

SETTING CONDITIONS FOR TEACHING LISTENING

Can listening be taught creatively? This author believes it can. He has seen countless numbers of teachers wasting precious minutes standing before classes of children, waiting until everyone was ready or because "John isn't quiet." He has also seen teachers who receive immediate response for each listening experience the children are to have, and the children come to the experience eager and excited.

The teaching of listening involves the setting of proper conditions so listening can take place. These conditions may be *natural* ones. Natural experiences are those where the conditions present themselves, where the teacher makes almost no preparation, because the motivation is so high that the children all listen immediately. Conditions, on the other hand, may be *contrived* ones

---

2. Central New York Study Council. *Some Helps for Building Guides for Skill Development in the Language Arts: Listening,* Report No. 7 (Syracuse, N.Y.: Syracuse University Press, 1957).
3. L. E. Pratt, "The Experimental Evaluation of a Program for the Improvement of listening in the Elementary School" (unpublished Ph.D. dissertation, State University of Iowa, 1963.)

where the teacher plans, constructs or utilizes materials, situations or gimmicks to motivate children for the purpose of teaching listening skills.

One excellent example of such a contrived situation follows. A particular first grade teacher found herself with an especially noisy and vigorous group of six-year-olds. Try as she might, she wasted many precious minutes getting these children orderly and quiet in order that they might listen to everything she said—even to the reading of a favorite story. Finally she had an idea. She had often said to the children, "Let's put on our listening ears." Now, she thought she would make it literal. During the next art period she and the art teacher had the children make "listening ears." On a headband, each child pasted ears cut from construction paper. These he decorated with any kind of material he wished, making each as different as possible. "Because," said the teacher, "we will want to recognize whose ears they are even when they are not being worn." The results were fantastic. Some ears were decorated with seashells, some with beads, others with sequins and glitter and some with pipe cleaners and crepe paper. The ears could only be worn when teacher said, "All right, let's put on our listening ears," and while they were being worn, it was the rule that all mouths had to close until the children heard what teacher had to say. What fun these children were having, and once they saw reasons for listening, they learned to listen more readily!

This contrived experience is a creative way to help children to approach the beginning steps of attentive listening—simply paying attention! On the pages that follow are many successful ways which teachers have set conditions for effective listening. Some of these are skills, others are gimmicks. It is hoped the reader will begin to see the possibilities of developing creative listening situations by reading these ideas and adding ideas of her own. The ideas have been categorized so the teacher may better understand the specific situations in which they were used.

In the teaching of listening, there are some important, general conditions which should be considered before each teaching situation. They include the following:

1. Be sure the physical conditions are properly set up. Remove all the distractions that you possibly can—both noise and movement. Make sure that chairs face the right direction so that eye strain and uncomfortable sitting positions are erased. Place materials in a prominent place and remove materials which are not to be used. Make sure each child is comfortable and that he can see well.

2. Speak in an animated and interesting manner, as though you

yourself could hardly wait to tell the children what you have to say.

3. Make sure your speaking speed does not exceed the children's listening speed.

4. Help children make up rules for good listening.

5. Help the children to understand what they have heard, much the same way as you would check comprehension in a good reading lesson. Ask such questions as, "What did Bill tell us about?" (selecting main idea); "What was the first thing that happened to Bill?" (sequence of ideas); etc.

6. Praise the children often for good listening. When you give directions and they are carried out well, motivation for listening is enhanced when the teacher says, "Good. I am proud that you did such a good job! It shows that you all listened well!"

7. Be a good listener yourself. Teachers so often only half-listen to a child as their eyes roam around the room taking in all the other children at work. Develop the habit of looking directly at a child when he talks and responding specifically to him.

8. Avoid needless repetition, especially in giving directions. It is better to say, "Do all of you understand that?" than "Listen once more and I'll say it all over again." The child who thinks he has it correct (and most of them will), will not listen the second time. This discourages good listening.

9. Avoid needless demands of pupil attention. Instead, try using interesting gimmicks and devices to gain immediate attention. (See page 109.)

10. Allow the children to talk. Remember that most teachers talk too much!

11. Adams[4] and Murphy[5] both emphasized four aspects to listening. These authors state that listening must be (a) purposeful, (b) accurate, (c) critical and (d) responsive or appreciative. They neglected, however, the creative aspects of listening.

12. Help children eliminate bad listening habits. Make a list of the poor listening habits you notice in your children. One teacher's list looked like this.

a. Children are distracted by playthings on or in the desk.
b. Children "fake" attention—they are really daydreaming.
c. Children interrupt each other with unrelated thoughts.

---

4. H. M. Adams, "Learning to Be Discriminating Listeners," *English* 36 (January 1947).

5. G. Murphy, "We Also Learn by Listening," *Elementary English* 26 (March 1944): 127–28.

FIGURE 4-1. *Miss Peach.*

Bring these habits to the attention of the children. Let the children help to take care of them. Here is how the children in the fifth grade class mentioned above went about their problem: They made a list of ideas which included the following:

a. Put everything on our desks away during listening time.
b. Listen carefully to the speaker.
c. Raise hands to ask questions about what the speaker is saying.
d. Face the speaker directly.
e. Get comfortable to listen.
f. Think about what the speaker has said.
g. When the speaker finishes, try to think over what he has said.

13. Do not place too much emphasis on regurgitative material. A basic goal in education today is creativity. To foster creative listening, seek to develop an attitude of mental alertness in children. Attitude or "set" toward listening is important. Much of the time that children are required to listen is for the purpose of reproducing what they hear. More emphasis should be placed on encouraging them to *think about* what they hear. Avoid overuse of these reproductive sets, and plan conditions for creative thinking sets.

14. In the teaching of listening, teachers should be sure that the children realize that there are varying degrees of attention required for different kinds of listening. Children can be helped to listen properly if they are told at the onset of each lesson just how important the listening for that particular lesson is, how they can best listen to get from the lesson what they should and the guides or directions for the particular kind of listening needed for the lesson.

Part of the task of the teacher is to set the mental and physical conditions necessary for listening in each new lesson throughout the school day.

SETTING CONDITIONS FOR THE CREATIVE TEACHING OF LISTENING

The generalizations stated above apply to the teaching of *all* listening experiences. However, there are some basic differences between the teaching of listening and the *creative* teaching of listening. The creative teaching of listening must include the above stated principles, but must go a step beyond to include the following principles as well.

1. In the creative teaching of listening, a unique or original idea is used by teacher or children which obtains the required response, so that creative teaching may follow.

2. The creative teaching of listening not only develops the skill of and need for listening among children, but it also results in an unusual response from the children, or a unique product as a result of the listening.

3. The creative teaching of listening accents highly motivational tensions; the listening experience is planned in such a manner that tensions are built immediately in children which make them want to listen. Little or no time is spent in waiting until John is ready or until all are quiet.

4. In creative listening experiences, the motivational experiences are planned so that divergent thinking processes begin to take place at once. Emphasis is not placed on the attainment of any *one* answer.

5. Consequently, the creative teaching of listening involves *all* children almost immediately.

6. The creative teaching of listening utilizes many open-ended techniques.

7. The creative teaching of listening may require that some unique conditions be set.

8. Creative listening experiences are the motivational forces which build proper tensions so that creative teaching may follow. As such, they encompass or lead into the basic principles for creative teaching listed in Chapter I.

The following description of a lesson on the teaching of listening will illustrate the use of the above principles.

The teacher's objectives were listed as follows:

1. To check children's ability to listen (a) on the appreciative level, (b) on the attentive level, (c) on the analytical level and (d) on the marginal level.
2. To provide some new, creative experiences in listening.
3. To help children become more aware of the importance of listening.

4. To help children establish good listening habits.
5. To help children evaluate good listening habits.
6. To help children realize that there are different kinds of listening.

The teacher motivated the children by putting before the group a gaily decorated box on which she had printed the words Sound Box.

"What is that?" the children immediately asked, "What is it for?"

"It is a sound box," answered the teacher, "and everything in it is something to listen to. I have it here today to see how well you can listen and if you know what makes a good listener. Let's get ready to listen. All eyes up here, desks clear, lips closed. Good. Now what is in the box? Max, put in your hand and draw out the first thing you feel!"

Max pulled out a yellow card on which was printed "The magic word is *story*."

"This," said the teacher, "is a word everyone will listen for this afternoon. Everytime I use this word today the first one who raises his hand gets a point! Now, I will take something out of the box."

The teacher then took from the box a small tray covered with a cloth.

"Well," said the teacher, "we are going to see how attentive you can be. I am going to take the cloth off this tray and you will see many things on the tray which make a noise. I will walk among you with the tray and you will have to look hard and try to remember all the things you see."

She took the cloth off the tray to disclose an eggbeater, a Halloween noisemaker, a clamp, a small bottle of water, a piece of paper, a music box, two sticks, a pair of scissors, a baby's rattle and a rubber band.

After all the children had looked at the tray, she asked them to number a paper from one to ten and then she put a folded cardboard upright on her desk behind which she made the noise of the object; she whirled the eggbeater, snapped the rubber band, tore the paper, sloshed the water, etc. After all ten noises had been made, she removed the cardboard and made the sounds in the same order so the children could check their papers.

"Here is a book in the sound box," she said next. "Now I am going to read you the story to see how well you listen for fun—only you will have to listen and watch at the same time because you are going to help me read this story." She then read "Gerald McBoing-Boing" and every time a noise was mentioned the teacher stopped reading, placed a card on the chalkboard and the children filled in the noise. After the story was over and they had discussed it, the teacher said, "Well, let's see what else we have in the box. I have a game to play which will show how well you can listen. Each one of you may draw one of these cards from the pack. Look at it but do not allow anyone else to see it." The teacher had a pack of cards with pictures pasted on one side. All the pictures were of noise-making objects. Each child then came to the front of the room and made the sound of the object pictured on his card while the rest of the class guessed what the picture was.

Alvin got up and said, in a deep voice, "Ho-ho-ho!" His picture was a Santa Claus.

Marie got up and clicked her tongue once. No one could guess her picture.

"Can you give us a clue by dramatizing your sound?" asked the teacher.

Marie closed one eye, held her finger up near the other, moved the finger down and up and clicked her tongue again. Her picture was a camera.

"There are two more things in the sound box," said the teacher, and she took out a recording and some drawing paper. "Oh, it is a record. I am going to play it and while I do, you draw or write about something that the music means to you."

In about ten minutes the children shared their creative products. Some had written poems, some had drawn pictures and some had written stories.

To summarize the afternoon's activities, the teacher said, "Well, the sound box is empty. How well do you think we listened today?" The children agreed they had listened well. John had ten points because he had heard the word "story" mentioned ten times. They had made good scores on their games, had good ideas from the records and only Marie had stumped them on the pictures.

"Well, I agree—you did listen well and we did have a good time. Did we have to listen the *same*, that is did we listen as *hard* or in the same manner to all the things we did? How would you say we listened to the different experiences we had?"

A lively discussion followed from which came the following chart:

Kinds of Listening

WE LISTEN HARD—	WE LISTEN EASY—	WE LISTEN FOR FUN—
to hear small sounds.	to stories.	to games.
to put sounds and objects together.	to records. for enjoyment.	to draw or write. to two things at one time.
to find one sound among many.		
to fit words in correct places.		
for special ideas.		
to directions.		

In this lesson the teacher applied the principles of creative listening, and although the children had not, at the third grade level, used the different labels of appreciative, attentive, analytical and marginal levels, their summary chart shows a consciousness of these four levels of listening.

The illustrations of creative teaching which constitute the remainder of this chapter were selected because they meet the criteria outlined above. Many fine examples of the teaching of listening have been omitted due to lack of space. The author has concentrated on those instances when *either* the teacher *or* the pupils applied the above criteria to obtain a creative product.

THE NATURE OF LISTENING

There are basically four types of listening:

1. Attentive listening.
2. Appreciative listening.
3. Analytical listening.
4. Marginal listening.

Each type will be discussed below. Skills must be developed for each of these types of listening.

Berry[6] suggests six ways we can improve the listening of children: (1) by sensing relationships of listening to other phases of communication; (2) by understanding the psychological process of listening; (3) by providing general conditions conducive to listening; (4) by utilizing opportunities for children to listen; (5) by understanding the development levels of listening and (6) by keeping alert to new inventions and equipment which will aid the program.

ATTENTIVE LISTENING

This is the type of listening where most distractions are eliminated and the attention of the listener is focused on one person or one form of communication, such as a radio broadcast, a play, a television show, a recording, a lecture or a telephone conversation. Attentive listening is used in the following "natural" ways in the classroom:

1. Gaining attention of children to take roll, prepare for a lesson, etc.
2. In giving directions for assignments.
3. For daily planning and organizing of the class into groups.
4. For audience-type situation reading.
5. In making announcements and reports.
6. For dramatic presentations and puppet shows.
7. For lectures or presentations by the teachers.
8. For announcements and programs over the school's sound system.
9. For directions on the playground and gymnasium.
10. For taking examinations.
11. For taking notes.
12. In searching for answers to questions in reading assignments.
13. For listening to tape recorders.
14. For teaching rote poems and songs.
15. For teaching music and for playing instruments.
16. For ordinary conversation.
17. For the show and tell period.

Attentive listening may or may not involve two-way conversation. In some cases it is a one-way communication process.

---

6. A. Berry, "Listening Activities in the Elementary School," *Elementary English Review* 23 (February 1946): 69–79.

Contrived Ways to Get Attention

Formal teaching cannot take place until there is order in the room and children are listening attentively. In any large group of children, however, children have much to say to each other and they shut out sounds that do not pertain to their immediate interests. Teachers can use several devices to bring children back to order quickly and pleasantly.

Create a signal or signals at the very beginning of the school year which tell the children they should stop what they are doing to listen at once. Here as some signals:

1. Flick the lights.
2. Tap a pleasant sounding bell.
3. Play a few chords on the piano.
4. Put on a favorite record.
5. Play chimes.
6. Hold hands up high and children stop what they are doing and mimic teacher as soon as they see her.
7. Carry a chair to the front of the room asking each child you pass to follow with his chair.
8. Play a music box.
9. Agree that the children will stop what they are doing when they see you put your head on your desk; each will do likewise.
10. Tap a rhythm with a stick or with your knuckles on a nearby desk. The children within hearing distance stop what they are doing and repeat the rhythm until all children are doing it. To vary this procedure, change the pattern of the rhythm.

These are commonplace attention getters. Following are some which are more creative, because they not only get attention at once, but they provide a strong motivation for developing the principles of creative teaching mentioned above.

a. "Let's all listen and see if we can hear the grass grow."
b. "Let's listen to the snowfall." (the clock tick, the rain fall, the wind blow, etc.)
c. "I'd like to see the color of everyone's eyes."
d. "I'd like to see how wide everyone can smile."

1. A game: The teacher touches a child and says "Shh" by putting her finger to her mouth. That child, in turn, touches another and does the same thing. Every child who has been touched may touch others so everyone is quiet as quickly as possible. The object of the game is to catch on quickly and be quiet, and *not* to be

the last one talking. The last one talking pays a penalty; he has to do some little job such as putting the books away.

2. Make an irrelevant statement and begin a discussion with the children around you—or write the statement on the board. Soon all will come to see what is going on. Some statements to use:

a.   "I wonder how long it takes to go by rocket to Mercury?"
b.   "I wonder what Christopher Columbus really looked like?"
c.   "I wonder who invented cheese?"
d.   "I wonder what it would be like with no sunshine?"

3. Lower your voice to almost a whisper and say something humorous or tell a funny story. When the children around you laugh, the rest will come to see what they are laughing about.

4. Use words of praise as much as you can. Children always respond to words of praise. "My what a bright happy group of faces I am looking at today," generally creates bright happy faces.

5. Instead of speaking all the time, turn and write or print simple directions on the board.

6. Sing commands or directions for a change. This is especially effective in the lower grades.

7. Also effective in the lower grades is singing the child's name for taking roll. The child sings back his name to the same tune or to a tune that completes the tune. For example, the teacher sings to the tune of "Frère Jacques":

> *"Are you here*
> *Are you here*
> *Mary Brown?"*

And Mary sings:

> *"Yes, I am."*

8. Stop in the middle of a sentence for just a moment and wait.

9. Call children by name by singing the name such as "Yoo-hoo, Henry Adams. Are you here?" and have the child respond in a singing sentence such as "Miss Wilson. Yes, here I am." The response should be a blending tune to Miss Wilson's question. Different tunes can be sung to each child. Tape this. Sometimes results are delightfully creative.

Creative Teaching of Attentive Listening

Attention getters serve the purpose of getting children ready for any lesson, but they should not be confused with actual lessons planned to develop attentive listening skills. Suggestions for the creative teaching of attentive listening follow.

1. Read stories that draw attention to the value of listening to sounds, words, letters or sentences. Examples: "The Sound That Turned Around" (*The Listening Book* by Dan Safier, pp. 13–19); "The Sound That Was Lost and Found" (*The Listening Book*, pp. 62–67); "The Changeable Clock" (*The Listening Book*, pp. 71–85); *Ounce, Dice, Trice* by Alastair Reid; "The Sound That Kept On" (*The Listening Book*, pp. 103–20); "Mr. Menton" (*The Listening Book*, pp. 103–20); "The Fish Who Said" (*The Listening Book*, pp. 125–45); *The Listening Walk* by Paul Showers; *Word Bending with Aunt Sarah* by Al Westcott.

2. Use of puppets. In the primary grades the children may have a friend who comes to talk to them once a day. In one room it was Jo-Jo, the puppet. The teacher had made a laundry bag from some colorful material. The laundry bag had a slit in the back through which she put her hand. Inside the bag lived Jo-Jo. Every once in a while Jo-Jo came out. He was shy so he only whispered to the teacher, and she had to relate to the boys and girls what he said.

Jo-Jo always had a surprise in his bag. Some days it was a letter or an invitation from another class. Some days he had a new book or a new game or a new story. One day he had a packet of seeds to plant. On another day he had a note from the principal telling of the Halloween party plans. All the teacher had to do was to stand by Jo-Jo's bag and there was immediate silence.

3. Choose ten "sound" makers. Fold a piece of cardboard to make a screen on a table concealing the ten items. Suggest to the children that they number a paper from one to ten. Call a number and make the sound. Let the children write down what they think it is. Younger children may raise their hands when they know instead of writing it down.

Some good ideas for sound makers are:

a. Pouring water from one glass to another.
b. Bouncing a rubber ball.
c. Turning an eggbeater.
d. Rubbing together two sand blocks.
e. Hitting together two rhythm sticks.
f. Crinkling cellophane.
g. Hitting a triangle.
h. Snapping an elastic.
i. Letting the air out of a balloon.
j. Playing a music box.

After this game has been played a few times, the teacher may ask the children to work by twos and think up sounds they can use on the rest of the class. When a group is ready, a few minutes may be used each day to develop listening skills.

4. Another variation of this game is to have the children categorize sounds under such topics as "Sounds Heard on the Playground" (the thud of a ball being thrown into a mitt, the sound of a medicine ball bouncing, the smacking of a ball and bat, the thud of the football on the floor, the sound of the beanbag landing on the floor, etc.). Other categories might be gym noises, cafeteria noises, hall noises, classroom noises, party noises, etc.

5. Teachers may carry this idea further by taking home a tape recorder over the weekend and making a recording of kitchen noises (water dripping, water running in the sink, refrigerator door closing, dishes being washed, setting the table, scraping vegetables, turning on the electric mixer or the pop-up toaster, starting the washing machine, bringing in the milk bottles); living-room noises (the vacuum cleaner, the fire crackling on the hearth, turning on the television set, popping corn, snapping on the lights, moving furniture, slamming closet doors); outdoor noises (the lawnmower, the sprinkler, shaking or beating rugs, bird calls, the bus going by, the ice-cream man, cars honking). Many variations can be taped and used in various ways with the children.

6. Children, too, can tape noises and bring them to school.

7. Children can make up stories, but instead of telling them with words, they tell them with sounds. Here is one made up by a third grade boy.

a.   He sat in a chair pretending to do his school work.
b.   He made the sound of a bee in the distance coming closer and closer.
c.   He slapped his hands a few times in the air but the droning of the bee went on.
d.   Finally, he hollered, "Ouch!"

Children may make up sound stories at home and bring them to school to tell the other children. Adding pantomime is fun!

8. Begin the period by playing records or playing a variety of musical sketches on the piano. Have children listen for music that is alike or different. Use some of these ideas for comparisons.

a.   Alike in rhythms.
b.   Alike in tone.
c.   Use the same musical instruments to get an effect.
d.   Fast—slow.
e.   High notes—low notes.

f. Clapping—tapping.
g. Rhythm patterns.
h. Spanish rhythms—Japanese rhythms.
i. Folk music—classical.
j. Jazz—popular.

9. Read stories to the children which have plots constructed around a breakdown in communication due to faulty listening. Discussions of these stories will help bring out the need for careful listening. Some such stories are:

a. "Espaminandos."
b. "The Hot Weather Mix-up" (*Jack and Jill,* July 1957).
c. "The Story of Slow Joe" (Safier, *The Listening Book*).
d. "The Tar Baby" by Joel Chandler Harris.
e. "Keeping Still in the Woods" by Charles G. D. Roberts.
f. "Henny Penny," fairy tale.
g. "Lazy Jack," English folktale.
h. "Rumpelstiltskin," Grimm fairy tale.
i. "Bambi" by Felix Saeten.
j. "The Midnight Ride of Paul Revere" by Henry Wadsworth Longfellow.
k. "The Forty Thieves" (from the Arabian Nights) by Andrew Lang.
l. "You Can't Please Everybody," an Aesop's fable.
m. "Ask Mr. Bear" by Marjorie Flack.
n. "The Funny Noise" by Romny Gay.
o. "The Emperor's New Clothes" by Hans Christian Anderson.
p. "Alice in Wonderland" by Lewis Carroll.
q. "Gerald McBoing-Boing."
r. "The Nightingale" by Hans Christian Anderson.
s. "The Tale of Peter Rabbit" by Beatrix Potter.

10. Group discussion provides rich opportunities to develop listening skills. A variation of the group discussion is the panel discussion. Some good samples of good group discussion are described in W. Pronovost,[7] *The Teaching of Speaking and Listening in the Elementary School.*

11. A good "audience-type" situation can be provided for listening by inviting a consultant to speak to the children and preparing them to listen for specific things. Some people to invite might include: a parent who has an unusual occupation or hobby, the librarian, the school physician, a forest ranger, a town person

---

7. W. Pronovost, *The Teaching of Speaking and Listening in the Elementary School* (New York: Longmans, Green, 1959), pp. 74–110.

who has just returned from a trip, the school nurse, the principal, the custodian, a state trooper, a fireman, a policeman, a visitor from a foreign country, etc.

12. Children spend large blocks of time listening to television. A television guide can be of invaluable use to teachers in planning structured listening experiences for their children. This listening can be put to good use by assigning children homework such as the following:

a. Watch "Film Festival" tonight to see if they tell the story as it is written in this book I am about to read to you.
b. Listen and watch the President's Press Conference and jot down the points he makes which tell how he feels about the education bills now in Congress.
c. The television awards will be given tonight. Here is a sheet which tells in what categories the awards will be made. See how many of the blanks on this sheet you can fill in.
d. It is difficult to produce mob scenes on TV due to the small screen area. See how "Treasure Island" is produced tonight to give the illusion of a mob during the mutiny.

13. To sharpen children's sensitivity to listening, it is sometimes fun to make a list such as "What Interfered with Our Listening Today?"

a. The lawnmower outside.
b. People interrupted.
c. An airplane flew over.
d. The fire bell rang for fire drill.
e. We were worried about getting our work done on time.

14. Listening signs placed around the room can help to develop listening habits. Examples:

What did you hear today?
The magic word today is *time*. How many times will your teacher say it during planning period?
Listen: What is the new sound in our room?

15. Some machines help promote the teaching of listening. Through the use of the tape recorder, the teacher may dictate special assignments on tapes and one group may listen in, even though many other activities are going on in the classroom.

16. Children can reproduce sound effects from the stories in their basic readers while other children guess the stories.

17. Obvious endings: The teacher makes up poems or stories with obvious words missing and accepts any logical rhyming words such as:

> *Once there was a little mouse*
> *He lived in a little* _____.
> *Every day he said, "Oh please,*
> *May I have a piece of* _____?"
> *"Cheese," his mother then would cry.*
> *"You will get some bye and* _____.
> *Right now with me you'd better scat*
> *For down the street comes Tommy* _____."

Encourage the children to create some for each other.

18. Have the children clap for various reasons when they are being read to. For instance:

a. Clap at every word that rhymes with *hat*. (Use Dr. Suess' books, "The Cat in the Hat" and "The Cat in the Hat Comes Back.")
b. Clap for every word that is a noun.
c. Clap for every word that describes something.
d. Clap for every word that begins with a certain sound.

19. Have children play at television broadcasting. A good audience type listening situation may be created by cutting a hole in a large box, painting the box like a television set and having one child appear in the opening as Uncle Don or the Space Boy to tell stories or reread the textbook story to his audience.

20. Several games to teach listening are listed on pp. 169–72 of *Beginning Language Arts Instruction with Children* by Shane, Reddin and Gillespie.[8]

21. Creating sound: In the early grades children enjoy the opportunity to translate real sounds into word sounds. Allow the children to listen to sounds and then substitute a word sound to take its place. For example:

a. For pounding clay a child said, "Bim, bam."
b. For pounding with a hammer a child said, "Bang, bang."

---

8. Harold G. Shane, Mary G. Reddin and Margaret C. Gillespie, *Beginning Language Arts Instruction with Children* (Columbus, Ohio: Charles E. Merrill, 1961), pp. 169–72.

c.   For a ringing bell, a child said, "Bong, bong."

d.   For a pound-a-peg board, one child said, "Boom, boom, boom."

e.   Squeezing clay, one child said, "Squashy, squashy."

22. Some good games to develop attentive listening:

a.   *Whisper:* Teacher (or a child) whispers ten sentences, words or sayings, each is in a softer voice and children try to see how many they can hear.

b.   *Gossip 1:* One child starts a sentence down his aisle or around his table by whispering a sentence *once* to the child next to him, who, in turn, passes it on until the sentence reaches the last child. This child tells what he thinks he heard. The first child tells what he said and children can compare to see how well they whisper and listen.

c.   *Gossip 2:* One child whispers a word to the next. This child in turn repeats to the next child and so on until the whole class has heard the word. The last child says aloud what he heard. Variations in the upper grades may be that children use sayings, proverbs, book titles, etc.

d.   *Fruit Basket Turn Over:* Give each child the name of a fruit. One child becomes "It." He calls the names of two or more fruits. The fruits called exchange seats. "It" tries to get into one of the vacated seats. The person remaining without a seat is "It." Every once in a while "It" shouts "Fruit Basket" at which time everyone exchanges seats.

Variations of this game may be played on many occasions, such as the beginning of the year when everyone is learning the names of classmates. They may call names directly, and call "Register" instead of "Fruit Basket." On Halloween, each child may be assigned a Halloween name (witch, cat, ghost, spook, pumpkin, broomstick, etc.) and exchange seats. "Witch's Ride" may be the signal for all to exchange seats.

e.   *Keep Talking:* This is an excellent game for older children. It originates from a popular television show of a few seasons past. Some children are each given a phrase. At the signal from the teacher, Child 1 begins a story. He tries to include his phrase in his story without giving it away to the rest of the group. The teacher taps a bell every thirty seconds and the next child must keep talking, picking up where the first child left off, and trying to include *his* phrase in the story and so on until all the group has had a chance, whereon they start at the beginning again. If, at any one time, one child guesses another child's phrase, the child who loses his phrase loses his chance.

23. Give the class three titles and ask them which one best fits the story or poem to be read to them.

24. Begin a rhyme and let children make up a new ending.

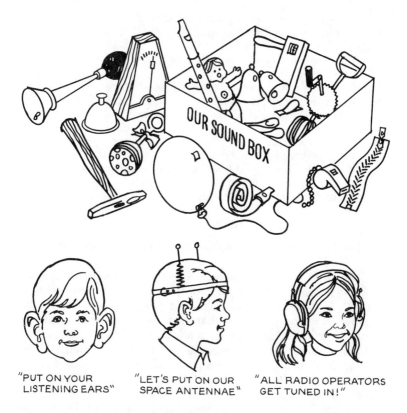

"PUT ON YOUR
LISTENING EARS"

"LET'S PUT ON OUR
SPACE ANTENNAE"

"ALL RADIO OPERATORS
GET TUNED IN!"

FIGURE 4-2.   *Contrived experiences that promote attentive listening.*

APPRECIATIVE LISTENING

Appreciative listening is the type used when one listens for enjoyment. Appreciative listening is not as concentrated as attentive listening. It is more relaxed, and the listener is in a less tense state. Appreciative listening was demonstrated above when the children listened to "Gerald McBoing-Boing." They react to this type of listening in pleasant or emotional ways. Suggestions for the use of appreciative listening in the classroom follow:

1.   Listening to musical or art recordings.
2.   Listening to radio and television programs for enjoyment.
3.   Listening to a play or puppet show.
4.   Listening to a concert.

5. Listening to stories or poetry being read.
6. Listening to a speech—particularly if it is about another country or a new idea.
7. Listening to recitations, shadow plays and other forms of dramatizations.
8. Listening to roll movies, filmstrips and slides.
9. Listening to enjoy lovely sounds: the song of the bird, the chirp of the cricket, the babbling of the brook or the tramp of elephants.
10. Choral speaking.
11. Responding to a mood or setting.
12. A child brings a good book to school and the children are immediately interested.
13. A child brings an interesting recording to school.

Creative Contrived Situations That Develop Appreciative Listening

1. *Reading stories and poems.* Some stories lend themselves to *listening* exercises. Noises are repeated which children can reproduce. Every time the teacher comes to a certain word the children are told to make the sound that goes with it. For example, the word *dog* evokes a "grr," the word *telephone* evokes a "ding-a-ling."

2. Play some beautiful records and have the children paint, draw or fingerpaint while the music is playing. Suggestions: *Nutcracker* Suite by Tchaikovsky; *Slavonic Dances* by Dvořak; *Peer Gynt* Suite by Grieg; *William Tell* Overture by Rossini; *Sleeping Beauty* by Tchaikovsky; "A Summer Place"; "Tara's Theme"; *Rhapsody in Blue* by Gershwin and "Blue Star." A variation is to play the music, listen carefully, and then have the children draw, paint or write what it means to them.

3. Choral speaking provides endless opportunities for careful listening so children may work out patterns of their own. Much of choral speaking should be with the children's own creative work and with familiar selections.

4. Use a round-robin listening drill: one child will say a word, the second child repeats it and adds another, a third child repeats both and adds a word and so on until a story results.

5. Have the children create a round-robin story. One child tells the first sentence, the second child the next, etc., until the last child (or the teacher) ends it. This is special fun at Halloween or Christmas or when used to commemorate other holidays.

6. Listen to recordings and dramatize the ideas suggested by the music—or the stories.

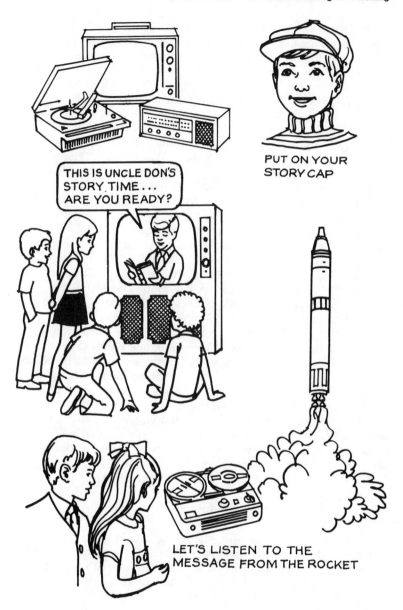

FIGURE 4-3. *Contrived experiences that develop appreciative listening.*

7. Often a poem such as "The Sugar Plum Tree" by Eugene Field can be read. Then the teacher asks the children to draw a picture showing everything they can remember about the poem.

Other poems which are adaptable to this sort of activity are: "Wynken, Blynken and Nod" by Eugene Field; "My Shadow" by Robert Louis Stevenson; "Song for a Little House" by Christopher Morley; "Animal Crackers" by Christopher Morley; "I Like House-keeping" by Dorothy Brown Thompson; "Stopping by Woods on a Snowy Evening" by Robert Frost; "White Fields" by James Stephens; "Written in March" by William Wordsworth; "Halloween" by Harry Behn; "Thanksgiving Day" by Lydia Maria Child; "A Visit from St. Nicholas" by Clement Clark Moore; "Block City" by Robert Louis Stevenson; "Roller Skates" by John Farras; "The Kite" by Harry Behn; "The Fishing Pole" by Mary Carolyn Davies; "A Sledding Song" by Norman C. Schlichter; "Caterpillar" by Christina Rossetti; "The Little Turtle" by Vachel Lindsay; "My Dog" by Marchette Chute; "Holding Hands" by Lenore M. Link; "Stop-Go" by Dorothy Baruch; "Song for a Blue Roadster" by Rachel Field and "The Locomotive" by Emily Dickinson.

8. Finger plays are excellent devices to foster good listening habits, especially when the children write their own.

9. *Game:* The Tiger Hunt: Almost every teacher knows the story of the tiger hunt where children use their hands to dramatize the story as the teacher tells it. Try other stories which include the children's experiences working out the accompanying sounds. Samples: The Haunted House, The Playground Accident, The Wild Ride for the Doctor, A Day in a Lumber Camp.

10. *Television Commercials:* Ask the children to listen to and reproduce as closely as possible their favorite television commercials or the opening phrases of their favorite television shows and then to change them to suit themselves.

11. Listen in order to learn to do folk dances or ballroom dances to popular music.

12. Listen to interpret the music with simple rhythm instruments.

13. Courtesies in listening should be taught—but courtesy is practiced also through listening. Have the children dramatize social courtesies such as: introducing a man to a man, introducing a man to a woman, introducing a child to an adult, conducting a club meeting, answering the telephone properly, asking a girl to dance, etc.

14. A picture book of sounds may be made with several ideas being used in it. One page might be devoted to sounds at home, with pictures for the lower grades or words for the upper grades.

Children might also use this in connection with reading by finding pictures or using words beginning with various sounds, blends, etc.

ANALYTICAL LISTENING

Analytical listening is attentive listening for the purpose of responding in one way or another. Analytical listening means one thinks carefully about what he hears. Instances where analytical listening are used naturally in the classroom are as follows:

1. Listening to solve arithmetic problems.
2. Reading-discussion assignments where children are:
    a. Reading and discussing to find specific points.
    b. Reading and discussing to outline.
    c. Reading and discussing to select main ideas.
    d. Reading and discussing to determine the true meaning of a word as it is used in a new context.
3. Discussing social problems, i.e., seeking a solution to a playground fight or solving problems through a school senate.
4. Any discussion involving a decision, such as, "What day shall we go on our trip?" or "Which textbook is correct?" when the texts do not agree on certain facts.
5. Analyzing a selection of poetry, literature or music.
6. Analyzing a speech, television program, tape recording or radio presentation.
7. Discussions on deciding what should fill restricted space in a school newspaper, etc.
8. Listening in an oral reading situation to:
    a. Find a sequence of events.
    b. Find supporting details.
    c. Find emotional persuasion.
    d. Draw comparisons.
    e. Make judgments.
    f. Find relationships.
    g. Make inferences.
    h. Follow directions and instructions.

Creative Contrived Experiences That Promote
Good Analytical Listening

1. *Analysis records.* Both children and teachers do this. How aware are we of the sounds in the world around us? Each can keep a diary over a given period of time wherein each lists all the

sounds he can remember having experienced during the day, from the ringing of the alarm clock early in the morning to the playing of the "Star-Spangled Banner" on television late at night.

2. Science experiments and demonstrations provide excellent situations for developing analytical listening.

3. Children may number a half-sheet of paper as for spelling words. Teacher asks, "Where do you hear the "t" sound?" The teacher then pronounces words such as report, tinkle, tank, part, etc. If the child hears the sound he is listening for, he marks it on the left side of the paper if it is found in the first part of the word, on the right side of the paper if it is found in the last part of the word. He then adds all the words he can think of to fill in both sides of his page.

4. Using a flannel board, build listening skills for details, for main ideas, etc. For instance, the teacher places a cutout of a girl in a blue dress holding a doll, and a girl holding a doll in a blue dress. The teacher says, "The girl in the blue dress is holding the doll" or "The girl is holding the doll in the blue dress." She asks which picture goes with the sentence just read. Children take over by compiling imaginative combinations of words.

5. Quiz games provoke good listening.

6. Use motion picture films with creative listening assignments. For example:

a.   How does the musical score help to tell the story?
b.   Look and listen for these three important facts; list them.
c.   How does the opening line set the theme for the rest of the film?
d.   Toward the end of the film there is a line which tells the main theme of the whole film. Can you find it? It comes during the prison scene. What other ways might this theme be developed?

7. *Scramble.* Oral sentences are scrambled and children arrange them in correct order. They make up scrambled sentences for each other.

8. Read a short paragraph containing several words that have the same or similar meanings. Children are to pick out the words that mean the same. Older children may write them down. Example:

Soon the little man came to a small dining room. He peered through the tiny door and saw a lovely, petite room all set up with miniature furniture. There were even minute dishes on the dining-room table.

122

Encourage children to write paragraphs of this nature for each other.

9. Ask children to listen on the way to school to special sounds which they reproduce (when possible) in the classroom where lists are constructed. Categorize them on charts into such headings as:

a. Building noises (ditch-diggers, hammers, saws, pounding, buzz saws, etc.)
b. Play noises (shouting, balls bouncing, skipping rope, playing hopscotch, running hotrods, etc.)
c. Beautiful noises (birds chirping, bees buzzing, wind sighing, ice cream man ringing, church bells ringing, children laughing, etc.)
d. Other categories might be: unpleasant sounds, funny sounds, happy noises, school noises, unusual noises, common noises, machine noises, circus noises.

10. Have the children close their eyes and see how many sounds they may hear in a two-minute period. Make a list. It might look something like this:

feet scraping
dishes scraping
radiator knocking
chalk squeaking
people talking outside
cars going by
trucks or school buses going by
steam pipes rattling
clock ticking
teacher walking
fans in air-vents
children in corridors
movement in the next room

11. A good way to begin a unit with sounds is to say something like like this: "Everyone put his head on his desk and close his eyes. I am going to open the window for two minutes. Listen to hear all the sounds that were not here when Columbus discovered America." The class tries to see how long a list it can get. *Variations:* "Since the Wright brothers flew their first airplane," "Since the covered wagons went west," etc.

12. Read poems to children which require responses. Examples:

a.   "The Children's Calendar" (*The Listening Book*, pp. 87–98).
b.   "The Humming Song" (*The Listening Book*, pp. 99–102).
c.   "Soon, Soon, Soon" (*The Listening Book*, p. 155).

13.   Have a toy telephone in the room. Encourage a child to talk into the telephone as though she were calling her mother, her father or a friend. The children try to guess what the person on the other end of the line is saying by listening to the one-sided conversation.

Middle grade students are especially clever at this. One sixth grade boy used only the word, "Yes," but he said it in fifteen different ways. The children had to listen carefully to that conversation. The next day one of the girls carried on a similar conversation using the word "Oh" with twelve expressions.

14.   Have the children tell stories or read into a tape recorder and listen to their own presentation in the play-back.

15.   Use a series of pictures which describe an event or a process such as frosting a cake, making a valentine, carving a jack-o-lantern, etc. Tell about the picture but omit one of the steps and have the children find the step omitted.

In the upper grades, the same procedure can be followed using words without the pictures.

16.   Riddles are fun. Children can create their own.
Here is one:

> *I am tall.*
> *I grow in a garden.*
> *I wear a green dress.*
> *I have on a bright hat.*
> *I am very beautiful.*
> *What am I?*

17.   A visit to a museum or an exhibit requires careful listening in the planning as well as in taking the trip, and also in the follow-up discussion.

18.   Use the records, *Sounds Around Us* by Scott Foresman and Company for Developing Listening Skills, and *Listening Activities* by RCA Victor Record Library for Elementary School (Volumes I–II).

Other records suitable for this use in the primary grades are: *Come to the Fair*, Young Peoples Records; *Muffin in the City*, YPR; *A Walk in the Forest*, YPR; *Little Cowboy*, YPR; *Listen and Do Series*, Vols. 1, 2, 3, 4, American Book Company; *Rainy Day*, YPR; *Let's Play Zoo*, YPR; *Little Indian Drum*, YPR; *Hot Cross Buns*, Children's Record Guild; *Songs, Games and Fun* (Dorothy

Olson), RCA; *The Merry Toy Shop*, CRG; *Little White Duck* (Burl Ives), Columbia; *Little Engine That Could*, RCA; *Muffin in the Country*, YPR; *Train Sounds*, RCA; *Children's Concert Series*, CRG; *Fun with Instruments* (Little Nipper Junior Series), RCA; *Let's Dance*, CRG; *Train to the Zoo*, CRG; *Peter, It's Pancakes*, CRG; *Who Wants a Ride?*, CRG; *Let's Play* (Children's Musical Action Stories by Kay Ortman. Set I—Farm Lands, Set II—Adventures in the Forest), Kay Ortman's Productions; *Sounds We Hear* (Illa Polendorf), Grosset & Dunlap.

For the intermediate grades: *The Shearing Piano* (George Shearing), Capitol; *Peter and the Wolf*, Columbia Long Playing; *Hansel and Gretel* (Basil Rathbone), Columbia; *Caught in the Act* (Victor Borge), Columbia; *Rusty in Orchestraville*, Capitol; *Big News Series*, Columbia; *Alice in Wonderland* (Jane Powell), Columbia.

Some Good Games for Teaching Creative Analytical Listening

Verbal tennis: This is a good game to teach listening as well as rhyming sounds. Children face each other in rows or across tables. Teacher gives a word like "head." The first child rhymes it with "dead." The child across from him tries to think of another word that rhymes and so on down the line until they can think of no more. Then the teacher supplies another word. Points may be used to show which side thought of the greatest number of words.

I'm packing a bag: Use variations such as taking all words with long or short *a* sounds or group together all things ending with same sound, e.g., I am packing a bag and will take a cake. Next player repeats previous player's word and adds one such as "a rake."

Go to the store: One child begins by saying "I went to the store to buy something that begins with _____," (he names a sound). When someone guesses, he becomes "It" and makes up the next sound.

Shopping at the supermarket: Prepare word cards using the names or pictures (collected from women's magazine advertisements) of items that may be obtained at a supermarket, e.g., bag, book, bottle, cake, can, corn, etc. (Duplicates are all right.) Choose a leader who can then distribute several cards to each player.

The leader says, "Who has bought something that begins with the same sound as banana?" etc. The players whose cards answer the question will read them aloud and then give their cards to the leader. To make the game more realistic, the leader may hold a grocery bag into which the children can deposit their "purchases."

Sound effects: Let the children try to produce sound effects as if they were the sound man on a radio program. Some good examples are:

1. crinkling cellophane to imitate fire.
2. patting half a coconut shell over the legs and chest to imitate a horse galloping.
3. clopping blocks on a table top to imitate soldiers marching in unison.
4. gently tumbling dried peas in a round cardboard hat box to imitate rain.

What is it?: Attention may de directed to the timbre of sounds by having children try to identify the instrument or agent that produces the various sounds. Use descriptive words wherever possible, such as *whir, swish, rattle, crash, bang, click, buzz, squeak, murmur, rumble, snort, hiss, gurgle.*

MARGINAL LISTENING

Marginal listening is that kind of listening where there are two or more distractions present. Children listen to the radio while doing their homework, apparently with no ill effects. An example of marginal listening was when the children wrote and drew in the lesson above while the record was playing. Instances where marginal listening might be used naturally in the classroom are as follows:

1. Teacher provides music for the children as a background for creative writing.
2. Teacher plays music for rhythms.
3. Children paint to music.
4. Teacher counts while children learn a folk dance or popular dance.
5. Children are planning together and writing plans on a chart or the blackboard.
6. Children read parts of a play.
7. Children work at one job, while other groups of children work at other jobs.

Creative Contrived Experiences to Develop
Effective Marginal Listening

1. Take the children on a field trip around the school to listen to all the sounds around them.

2. Run a short cartoon film, then shut off the sound and have the children tell the story or reproduce the speaking parts while the film is rerun.

3. "Musical Chairs" is a good marginal listening game.

4. Dramatize action poems that require careful listening. Examples: "The Piggyback Merry-Go-Round" (*The Listening Book*, pp. 57–59); "Bell Horses," nursery rhyme; "A Cat Came Fiddling," Mother Goose; "Feet" by Irene Thompson; "Trains" by James S. Tippett; "Soft Steps" by Georgette Agrew; "Pop Goes the Weasel," nursery rhyme; "Peas Pudding Hot," nursery rhyme; "To Market," nursery rhyme; "Ride a Cock Horse," nursery rhyme; "The Horsemen" by Walter de la Mare; "A Stick for a Horse" by Sybil Fountain; "Mrs. Hen" by M. A. Campbell; "The Elf and the Doormouse" by Oliver Herford; "Three Little Mice," Mother Goose; "Conversation" by Anne Robinson; "Mix a Pancake" by Christina Rossetti; "I Had a Little Pony," Mother Goose.

For intermediate grades: "Casey at the Bat" by Ernest Lawrence Thayer; "Stopping by Woods on a Snowy Evening" by Robert Frost; "Fog" by Carl Sandburg; "A Visit From St. Nicholas" by Clement Clark Moore; "The Duel" by Eugene Field; "The Landing of the Pilgrim Fathers" by Felicia Dorothea Hemans; "Barbara Frietchie" by John Greenleaf Whittier; "The Flag Goes By" by Henry Holcomb Bennett; "The Pied Piper of Hamelin" by Robert Browning; and "The Leak in the Dike" by Phoebe Cary.

5. Listen to records which can be dramatized or interpreted that require special listening skills. Example: *Peter and the Wolf*, Prokofiev; "I Went for a Walk in the Forest," Young Peoples Records; *Hansel and Gretel*, narrated by Basil Rathbone; *Pictures at an Exhibition*, Ravel-Mussorgsky; *Prelude a l'Apres-Midi d'un Faune*, Debussy; *Sorcerer's Apprentice*, Dukas; *Fantastic Symphony*, Berlioz; *Swan Lake*, Tchaikovsky; *Danse Macabre*, Saint Saëns; *Jeux d'Enfants*, Bizet; *La Mer*, Debussy; *Mother Goose Suite*, Ravel; *Night on Bald Mountain*, Mussorgsky; *Norwegian Dances*, Grieg; *Carnival of the Animals*, Saint Saëns; and *Children's Corner Suite*, Debussy; *The Children's Suite*, Copeland; *Going West, Christopher Columbus*, Young Peoples Records; The Bailey-Film Associates Records; *Rudolph the Red Nosed Reindeer*, Educational Record Sales; *The Story Teller*, Record Library.

6. Children who play instruments can listen to accompaniment recordings by famous artists such as Joan Baez, *Joan Baez Sings Folk Songs* (Vanguard); Harry Belafonte and Belafonte Singers, *My Lord, What a Mornin'* (R C A Victor); Logan English, *American Folk Ballads* (Monitor); Burl Ives, *Songs of the Colonies, Songs of the Revolution, Songs of the North and South, Songs of the Sea*, and *Songs of the Frontier* (Columbia); John Lomax Jr., *John Lomax Jr. Sings American Folk Songs* (Folkway Records); Alan Mills, *Oh Canada: A History of Canada in Folk Songs* (Folkway Records).

7. Children can develop skills by listening to recordings which teach them to play simple classroom instruments such as the following: Ginmund Spaeth, *Golden Autoharp Melodies* (National Autoharp Sales Co.); Evelyn Waldrap, *Autoharp Song Folio* (William J. Smith Music Co.); Sally Golding and Lucille Landers, *Melody Makers* (Carl Van Roy Co.); Pete Seeger, *The Folksingers Guitar Guide* (Folkway Records); Frederick Beckman, *Classroom Method for Melody Flute* (Melody Flute Co.); Margaret Bradford and Elizabeth Barker, *How To Play the Recorder*, Books I and II (E. C. Schirmer Music Co.); Lorena Johnson Keen, *Sing and Play the Ukelele* (Peripole Inc.).

SUMMARY

There are basically four kinds of listening; attentive listening, appreciative listening, analytical listening and marginal listening. Each type can be developed creatively and with creative results in the elementary school classroom. The creative teaching of listening requires different skills and produces different outcomes from regular listening experiences.

In a democratic society where we must learn to respect each other's viewpoints and contributions, children must be taught the skills and courtesies of listening so that effective communication can take place. We have seen how these skills may be developed in interesting, meaningful and creative ways when the proper conditions are established. These conditions are affected by the following factors:

1. The child's maturity level.
2. The child's general ability.
3. The child's interest in the topic at hand.
4. The child's previous experience with the material being presented.

5. The type of material being presented.
6. The listening "climate" created by the teacher.
7. The children's rapport with the teacher or the speaker.
8. The quality of the teaching.
9. The attitude and ability of the teacher (or speaker) to relate to the child.
10. The demands made on the child during the listening period.
11. The child's listening readiness.
12. The child's established listening habits.
13. The child's ability to adjust to any abnormal or unpredicted situation.
14. The physical-emotional tone of the room.
15. The child's acquired listening skills.
16. The adjustment of speed of reception with the speed of delivery.
17. The creative set to listen.

TO THE COLLEGE STUDENT AND THE CLASSROOM TEACHER

1. Blindfold a member of your class and have him identify a sound made by every member of the class. Try using some of the recordings of various sounds in class and guess what the sounds are.

2. Ask each member of the class to demonstrate one of the experiences or materials described in this chapter. Discuss how you feel children would react to it. If possible, try some of the ideas on children. Better yet, try some of your own ideas on children.

3. Have a class committee make a report on the effect of mass media (television, radio, etc.) on communication.

4. What part does listening play in your study habits? When is it helpful, when is it a distraction, when is it unimportant?

5. Keep a record, on any chosen day, of the time you use waiting for your children or your colleagues to listen. Is it exorbitant, average, below average? Might you cut down on some of this time if you use a more creative attitude toward listening and set more creative conditions for listening? Try it and see if you can save some time.

6. Note particularly the times your students or colleagues tune you out. Keep a record over a week's time and see if any pattern evolves: for instance, do they listen less at the beginning or the end of the day, are they better listeners during one subject than another, do they listen to each other better than they do to you, do they listen to some people better than others? Whatever the answers, seek to discover causes. Are they, perhaps, sitting too long, is the lesson dull, do they have concentration problems? When you know the cause, you can do something about it.

7. Find out what your students or colleagues think about listening by allowing them to hold a debate or discussion on its importance.

8. Think through a list of the things which cause you to listen readily. How can you apply these techniques to children?

9. Teenagers often do their homework with a television set or a radio blasting. This is marginal listening. Does this have any effect on grades? Some research has been done on this. Have some class members do some reading and make a report on it.

10. Think of all the ways *you* use the four types of listening.

11. Many articles are being written on listening. Collect as many as you can and share them on a bulletin board. Start a file of listening resources.

12. Prepare a television show (a listening-viewing media) on listening. Present it over your local station if possible.

13. How well were you able to adapt the material in this chapter to different age levels as suggested by the author at the beginning of the chapter?

14. Some of the books in the bibliography below contain some very interesting suggestions for teaching listening creatively. Have various class members demonstrate some of these.

15. Some interesting recordings have been made to help children learn grammar and word usage. Below some from Educational Record Sales are listed. Play them and evaluate their effectiveness.
a. *Saying the Right Word* (an audio approach to learning correct grammar at an early age).
b. *Billy the Lonely Word* (an introduction to the eight parts of speech).
c. *Building Language Power* (a set of albums of language development exercises).
d. *Building Verbal Power* (a set of albums on word usage).

SELECTED BIBLIOGRAPHY

Anderson, Rhea, Lucille Minshall and Iris Tracy Comfort. "How to Teach Better Listening." *National Education Association Elementary Instructional Service Leaflet.* Washington, D.C.: National Education Association, 1962.

Brown, Charles T. "Teaching Listening Comprehension." *Journal of Communication* 3 (November 1953): 127–30.

Brown, James I. "How Teachable Is Listening?" In James C. Mac-Campbell (ed.). *Readings in the Language Arts in the Elementary School.* Boston: D. C. Heath, 1964, pp. 132–40.

Canfield, Robert. "How Useful Are Lessons for Listening?" *The Elementary School Journal* (December 1961):147–51.

Central New York School Study Council. *Some Helps for Building Guides for Skill Development in the Language Arts: Listening,* Report No. 7. Syracuse, N.Y.: Syracuse University Press, 1957.

———. *Some Helps for Teaching in the Language Arts: Reading,* Report No. 4. Syracuse, N.Y.: Syracuse University Press, 1957.

Chambers, Dewey W. *Story Telling and Creative Drama.* Dubuque, Iowa: William C. Brown, 1970.

Denby, R. V. "NCTE/ERIC Report on Research in Listening and Listening Skills." *Elementary English* 46 (April 1969): 511–17.

Devine, Thomas G. "Reading and Listening: New Research Findings." *Elementary English* 38 (March 1961), 170–74.

Ernest, Carole H. "Listening Comprehension as a Function of Type of Material and Rate of Presentation." *Speech Monographs* 35 (June 1968).

Greene, Harry A. and Walter T. Petty. *Developing Language Skills in the Elementary Schools.* 4th ed. Boston: Allyn and Bacon, 1971, pp. 152–84.

Hall, Edward. "Listening Behavior: Some Cultural Differences." *Phi Delta Kappan* 50 (March 1969).

Keller, Paul W. "Major Findings in Listening in the Past Ten Years." *Journal of Communication* 10 (March 1960): 29–38.

Monaghan, R. R. and J. G. Martin. "Symbolic Interaction: Analysis of Listening." *Journal of Communication* 18 (June 1968): 127–30.

Petty, Walter T. "Listening: Directions for Research." *Elementary English* 39 (October 1962): 574–77.

Pronovost, Wilbert. *The Teaching of Speaking and Listening in the Elementary School.* New York: Longmans, Green, 1959.

Reddin, Estoy. "Characteristics of Good Listeners and Poor Listeners." *Journal of the Reading Specialist* 7 (March 1968): 109–13.

Ross, Ramon. "A Look at Listeners." *Elementary School Journal* 46 (April 1964): 369–72.

Russell, David H. and Elizabeth F. Russell. *Listening Aids Through the Grades.* New York Teachers College Press, 1963.

Safier, Dan. *The Listening Book.* Rev. ed. Caldwell, Ohio: Caxton Printers, 1954.

Smith, James A. *Creative Teaching of the Language Arts in the Elementary School.* Boston: Allyn and Bacon, 1967.

Taylor, Sanford. *What Research Says to the Teacher: Teaching Listening*. Washington, D.C.: National Education Association, 1964.

————. *Listening*. Washington, D.C.: National Education Association, 1964.

Wachner, Clarence. "Listening in an Integrated Language Arts Program." In James C. MacCampbell (ed.). *Readings in the Language Arts in the Elementary School*. Boston: D. C. Heath, 1964, pp. 141–47.

Wilt, Marion. "Children's Experiences in Listening." In Virgil Herrick and Leland Jacobs (eds.). *Children and the Language Arts*. Chapter VII. Englewood Cliffs, N.J.: Prentice-Hall, 1959.

————. "A Study of Teacher Awareness of Listening as a Factor in Elementary Education." *Journal of Educational Research* 42 (April 1950): 626–36.

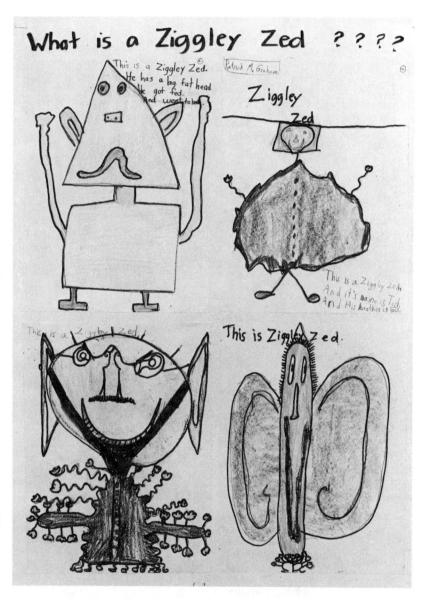

FIGURE 4-4.   *Developing creative oral expression and creative writing: "The Ziggley Zed."*

FIGURE 4-5. *Freddie had a bowl of popcorn. His teacher said, "You may not eat the last few kernels until you write about it." Freddie wrote:*

I ate a bowl of popcorn
Buttery with salt just right,
Golden and white and fluffy
Each kernel curled and light.
I thought I was full of popcorn.
All the kernels were gone but three.
But, I can't wait to eat them
To smell them is torturing me!

FIGURE 4-6. "John J. Plenty and Fiddler Dan" was read to nine-year-olds. The events of the story were listed in sequence and each child drew pictures of his own selection. Arranged on shelf paper in proper sequence the pictures made an exciting roll movie. The project was enhanced when the children made a "sound track" by reading parts of the poem into a tape recorder against a musical background.

FIGURE 4-7a. *The children build an oral vocabulary of descriptive words by writing some on cards. Each child draws a card and acts out the descriptive word with his feet. Here we see* hopping feet.

FIGURE 4-7b. *"I know! I know! They are* tired feet!*"*

FIGURE 4-7c. *". . . and* happy *feet!"*

FIGURE 4-7d. *". . . and* dancing *feet!"*

FIGURE 4-7e. *The game can also be played with hands, and these are angry hands.*

FIGURE 4-7f. *While this is a* strong hand.

FIGURE 4-8. *Developing creative writing: Miss Crown said, "Several monster dolls were left over in a warehouse when the sales dropped. So, they got together and told each other the sad story of their lives. Be a monster doll, draw your picture and then tell or write your own story." Later the children made huge papier-mâché monster dolls.*

FIGURE 4-9. *Nine-year-olds enjoy making puppet shows of their own stories. Here children are planning to present Tommy's creation called "The Clown and the Hippie."*

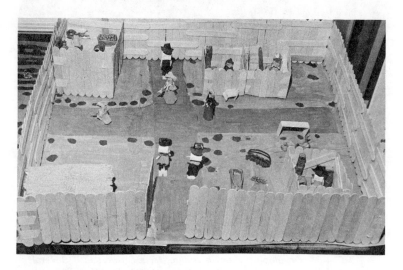

FIGURE. 4-10.   *A stockade constructed as a social studies project provides motivation for endless imaginative stories.*

FIGURE 4-11. *In a dramatization about the senses, this huge face was painted to have no eyes, ears, nose, mouth or hands. It had no reaction to a passing parade because it could not see, smell, taste or feel. When the eyes were added it* saw *the gay costumes; when the nose was added it* smelled *the popcorn and cotton candy; when the ears were added it* heard *the music; when the mouth was added it* tasted *the ice cream; and when the hands were added it* felt *the softness of the animals, the texture of cloth.*

CHAPTER V

Creative Teaching of Oral Expression

Very Oral!
Whenever I go to take a walk
No one has to beg me to talk
I'm a woman.

ANGIE
Age 8

Angie exercises the prerogative of her sex in this straightforward, amusing poem. She has amply shown the need for a strong program in oral expression. We need to discover how that program can be made creative.

"What is happiness?" I asked.
And Larry said, "Happiness is everything!"
"Happiness," said Johnny, "is a kitten rubbing against my legs."
"It's a birthday party," said Eric.
"I think," said Deborah, "that happiness is looking up and seeing clouds and birds sailing across a blue sky."

Here we see that utterance by children can be creative in content.

TO THE READER

Have you often felt emotionally moved by a beautiful sunset and felt the urge to express these emotions to a companion, only to feel embarrassed at trying? Why do you suppose you felt this way?

What happens between the period of childhood and adulthood that often makes us timid about expressing ourselves emotionally or in beautiful language?

Read the first part of this chapter with the purpose in mind of noting how freely and beautifully children often express themselves. When you are with children listen carefully to some of the clever ways they express their ideas and feelings. Collect some of these sayings and share them with your colleagues.

Try some of the ideas in the last part of this chapter with children. If you are using this book in a college class, each of you devise a poster which would be a motivation device for creative oral expression with a group of children. Try them out with one person leading the discussion while another person takes notes on what the children say. Share your notes with each other.

As a result of reading this chapter, the author hopes the reader will gain insights into what a good program in oral expression is, why it is necessary and how it might be implemented creatively.

INTRODUCTION

Children who listen well stand a better chance of developing an extensive oral vocabulary than those who do not. Consequently, good listeners often speak more exactly and more creatively than poor listeners; they have more words at their command.

Lloyd, age 7, says on a foggy day, "If the church steeple didn't hold the fog up like a tent pole, it would all fall down and smother us."

Marcia, age 8, says, "Love is kinda like heart trouble."

Mark, age 9, returning from a cub scout overnight hike says, "The moon is a flashlight in the sky."

Kevin, age 5, says on a blustery day, "Gosh, the wind is grouchy today."

Marion, age 12, says, "Loneliness is being all by yourself even when there are people around."

Noel, age 3, pointed to the pansies in the garden and said, "Why are you growing all the faces?"

Children experiment with speech just as they experiment with art materials. They manipulate words and try them out to see if they understand their true meanings. These trials are called verbalisms. Adults use verbalisms also, as they manipulate and experiment with speech.

Timmy, age 6, who has not quite heard correctly puts meaning to his listening even though it is incorrect, when he says, "There's lots of sand in the *O'Hara* desert." Needless to say, Timmy is of Irish origin.

Verbalisms may be considered a part of the experimental stages of speech development. It is hoped that children will progress from this stage on to the aesthetic stage, where they find enjoyment in arranging words just for the beauty of the words themselves and for the word pictures they can paint with them.

From an early age, youngsters go around the house chanting words which fall pleasantly off the tongue. Teenagers pick up new words and make their discovery obvious by using the word six or seven times during the course of one conversation.

The first step in developing creative expression is to capitalize on the things children say. In the situation where Lloyd spoke of the church steeple serving as a tent pole to hold up the fog, Mr. Smith, his teacher, said, "I like what you just said, Lloyd. I'm going to put it on a chart so that we may use it later."

Later when the class had assembled, Mr. Smith said, "I'd like to talk about the fog which you have all enjoyed on your way to school this morning. Lloyd already had a way of telling me about it. Let's read it."

After the chart was read, Mr. Smith asked, "Can each of you think of a different way to tell me about the fog and how it makes *you* feel?"

Here were some of the things the children said:

> "The fog has drawn white curtains over our school windows and we cannot see out."
> "The fog is wet on my face like my dog's tongue."
> "The fog is like frost on my glasses and I cannot see."
> "The fog is like a white night."

"Can we think of some words which might describe the fog?" asked Mr. Smith. "You may want to use them later in your own poems and stories."

The list which followed included these words:

mysterious	gentle
creepy	misty
sly	opaque
soft	

Mr. Smith did not let the experience die at this point. "I know of a famous poet who wrote about the fog," he said. "I think I can remember how he told about it. There is only one word I will have to explain to you and then I think you will understand this poem."

Mr. Smith proceeded to explain to his "inland" group the meaning of the word "harbor" and then recited Carl Sandburg's poem, "Fog."

Imagine his delight when, upon finishing the poem, Lloyd, the innovator, commented, "Gee, that's pretty good, too!"

Later the children wrote about the fog.

Such experiences as this can be developed if a teacher is sensitive to the child's creative speech. A teacher must know her children well if she hopes to nurture creative expression among them. She needs to know the types of homes from which they come, the experiences they have had outside of school and the kind of atmosphere in which they live out of school.

Some children will have more experiences upon which to draw than others. These are experiences which the teacher can use. The teacher must remember, however, that it is not the quality or quantity of experience that matters. All children have experiences of a sort. Sometimes those who come from unwholesome or unpleasant environments find most striking ways of telling about their feelings. The experience supplies the content for the verbalization, but it is the teacher who helps the child put it in powerful and imaginative language.

A teacher working in a poor railroad community in a school servicing families of a low socioeconomic level, helped her children discover the beauty of language by talking each day about words. One day she said, "Miss Mack is always telling you to be quiet. Let's talk about that word, *quiet*. What does it mean? Tell me; what is quiet?"

Here are some of the answers she received from her six-year-olds.

> "Quiet is my kitty-cat walking over the piano keys."
> "Dead is quiet."
> "Quiet is when my mother rocks my baby sister to sleep."
> "Night is quiet."
> "Milk turning sour is quiet."
> "Flies walking on the ceiling are quiet."
> "A knife slicing bread is quiet."

Later one group of children made up this poem about quiet things.

What Is Quiet?

What is quiet?
Peace is quiet

No noise at all
Snails moving are quiet
When they are small
Butterflies flutter
And snowflakes fall
Clouds float on air
And babies sleep
. . . . That's quiet!

A common, natural technique often used by teachers to develop good oral expression is the "show and tell" period, or as it is often called in the upper grades, the "contribution" period. Show and tell can be a vital part of building creative oral expression, or it can be a farce.

The writer has observed teachers who start the day with show and tell by appointing a class chairman and allowing this youngster to call on each child who has something to say. Teacher sits in the back of the room and fills out her attendance report or attends to other menial tasks. While there is some value in training children to assume responsibility for their own work, the show and tell period in this instance is a waste of time. At this period, children introduce many new words, often in context, as they bring new objects to be explored or share TV shows they have seen the evening previous. This excellent opportunity for building an oral vocabulary is lost unless the teacher is sensitive to it and cashes in on the situation.

Take Miss Crane, for instance. One day in October, little Julie came running into the second grade room clutching a branch of brightly colored maple leaves and a branch of yellowed elm leaves. At show and tell time Miss Crane said, "Julie has something very lovely to show us. Would you like to get them from my desk, Julie?"

Julie proudly displayed her leaves. The children exclaimed over them and commented on them. But Miss Crane capitalized on them further.

"Let's talk about each leaf," she said, placing her hand under one of the brightest maple leaves. "Look closely, and say how you could tell me about it."

"Well, it's pretty," said John.

Miss Crane nodded.

"It's colorful," said Agnes.

"That's a good word," said Miss Crane, "We have two good words—colorful and pretty."

"It's speckly," said Peter.

"Good," encouraged Miss Crane.

"And it's smooth," said Betty.

"Pretty, colorful, speckly and smooth," repeated Miss Crane. "Notice the edges—what are they like?"

"Well, they're uneven," said Harry.

"Rough," added Gwen.

"And pointed," John added.

"Uneven, rough and pointed edges," repeated Miss Crane. "Now let's look at the other leaf—how can we tell about it?"

"It's yellow and brown," said Beulah.

"It looks kinda rusty," said Jimmy.

"I like that word," said Miss Crane. " 'Rusty.' You know, I'd like to tell you another word that poets often use to describe that rusty look in leaves. The word is 'russet.' Would you like to try saying it?"

Miss Crane went on, "Look how the edge of this leaf is—is it like the other?"

"Notice how the leaves hang on the stems—how could we describe that?"

"They dangle," said Joe.

"They are limp," said Molly.

"Anyone else?" asked Miss Crane.

"They tremble," said Brenda.

"They do all of those," repeated Miss Crane. "They hang limp, they dangle, and they tremble. Let me put some of the new words you have learned on our vocabulary chart so you may see them up there and use them in your stories and poems today."

Show and tell in this instance is a creative situation. Miss Crane utilizes a normal occurrence to help children explore their past experiences and to find new and creative ways to express a new experience. Later in the day, Joan placed this poem on Miss Crane's desk.

> *The leaves:*
> *So pretty*
> *So colorful*
> *So speckly*
> *Tremble, tremble, tremble*
> *And then they fall*
> *And the children come*
> *And gather them up*
> *So pretty*
> *So colorful*
> *So speckly*
> *To take to school.*

Miss Crane set conditions for creative oral and written expression by asking questions that led the children to think. She was not sure what would come. Sometimes nothing does, but soon the children build a sensitivity to words and the ideas begin to flow.

In the same manner that children share words and arrive at meanings, they arrive at definitions. Following is an example of good vocabulary building in a contrived situation, where an excellent definition also came into existence.

In a combined fourth, fifth and sixth grade in a rural school, a teacher had provided his children with many rich, vocabulary building experiences. One day Pat, a girl in the sixth grade, asked what adjectives were. The teacher asked where she had heard the word and Pat replied, "I have a sister in junior high school who is studying adjectives and she spends all her time at home underlining words." Soon the whole class was interested in the word "adjective." What were they? The problem of helping these children draw from their experiences the meaning to go with the verbal symbol confronted the teacher. The fourth graders did not have the background the sixth graders had so the task was not an easy one.

However, he worked out a plan. He gave each of the children a sheet of drawing paper and some crayons. Then he wrote on the board, "The house stood on the hill under a tree," and asked the children to interpret this sentence through a drawing. When the drawings were finished, they were placed before the class and discussed. As might be expected, there was a great deal of variety in the interpretations. There were steep hills and squatty ones, tall houses and rambling ones, high trees and low ones. The teacher then led a discussion on how an author would paint a picture with words instead of brushes—especially if he wanted his readers to get a definite picture in mind because of its importance to his story. The suggestions for adding more words from the children soon resulted in rewriting the sentence this way: "The low, rambling, ramshackle house stood on the gently sloping hill under a tall elm tree."

This time, when the children drew their pictures, there was more of a similarity among them. Next the teacher led the group to verbal expression by having them put their heads on the tables while he read the sentence: "The brook ran through the meadow past the mill."

The children described what they had seen and again it was decided there were not enough words to paint a clear visual picture. So again the teacher asked that they close their eyes and attempt to see this picture: "The winding, bubbling brook ran through the daisy-dotted meadow to the old deserted grist mill."

Pat, at this point, raised her head and excitedly said: "Hold it, Mr. Jones! I've got 'technicolor!'"

And adjectives, to that group of children, became technicolor words. This is a definition that far surpassed any in the books and was never forgotten by that group, for to them it was rich in meaning and experience.

Vocabulary building should "pepper" the school day. Teachers should seize every possible opportunity to awaken children to the joy of hearing, repeating and understanding new words, and teachers should provide opportunity for children to discover and invent new words themselves as Miss Crane's children invented the word "speckly."

Vocabulary building is essential if the teacher is to help equip the child for creative expression. Too often the concept of vocabulary building is linked solely to the reading program, and little is done to help children learn new words outside the reading or spelling class. This is unfortunate, for the speaking vocabulary of children is many times greater than the reading vocabulary; learning new words for everyday speaking must come first.

Developing a feeling for words is not difficult if the teacher bases her teaching at the early childhood level on the resources the child already has. The wonderful sense of rhythm inherent in children expresses itself through words as well as through bodily movement. From the time the child can speak, he repeats sounds and nursery rhymes, not because they bear a particular meaning, but because of the natural rhythm of the words or the line. Repeated consonant sounds or well-mouthed vowel sounds fascinate the child. Thus he sings and hums nonsense rhymes from an early age, and entering the gang stage in his intermediate grade experience, he works out gang-calls that are full of rich sound expression:

> *Hip-Ka-Ninny*
> *Ka-Ninny-Ka-sock*
> *Ka-boob-a-ley-ock,*
> *Ka-Yoo-Hoo.*

This may be meaningless to an adult but music to a child.

There are several ways to build vocabulary. One way used by many modern teachers is to have a vocabulary chart at the front of the room as Miss Crane did. All during the day when new words arise in classroom use, they are added to the chart by the children. Such a chart serves a three-fold purpose: it acts as a place to record new words, it makes a good reference chart for children who wish to use the words in their work, and it provides the spelling words for the following week. An accumulation of such charts over a period of time will show a wealth of new words rising from childhood experiences that do not appear in the books.

The flow of words that comes from children should never be checked—controlled and utilized perhaps, but never checked. The children bring new words to school to share just as they bring in new toys to share. Teachers can make use of these natural experiences.

And if at times the river of verbal symbols tends to dry up, then the teacher should have up her sleeve many clever and contrived situations to give children the opportunity to develop a rich oral vocabulary and to have fun using words. Every single second spent in the development of a good oral vocabulary is time well spent, because a good oral vocabulary is necessary before reading, handwriting or creative writing can be taught.

Many highly creative children "tune out" what is going on in a classroom simply because the sounds around them are not worth listening to. A purposeful oral expression program keeps the sounds around children in the classroom more interesting than those being heard in the corridor or out the window and keeps the children challenged, because they must think and pass judgment to be certain that the right word goes in the right place.

The materials on the following pages illustrate ways teachers may make the sounds of speaking interesting to children. They are drawn from the files and experiences of the author collected over a period of years.

I am aware that some illustrations are far less creative than others. Their inclusion is deliberate. They may help teachers who feel they are not creative to see that some of the things they do can lead to creative teaching. A challenging program in oral expression leaves a situation open-ended, so children must think through to the conclusion of the situation. This has been the basic principle behind the selection of the materials included in the remainder of this chapter.

I have not graded the material presented because it is adaptable to all grades. In many instances I have given an illustration of the same stimuli being adapted to both primary and intermediate grade levels. Creativity, like learning, is based in the child's past experiences. It is necessary, then, not to begin with a grade but with a child. Because of an impoverished background in some areas, the beginning of creative work may well begin on a very simple level with many children.

PLACE OBJECTS IN A BAG. CHILDREN MAY TAKE ANY BAG — THEN DESCRIBE OBJECT. HOW DOES IT LOOK? HOW DOES IT MAKE YOU FEEL?

PLACE FIVE OBJECTS IN A BAG. PASS THE BAGS OUT TO GROUPS. EACH GROUP WILL DRAMATIZE A PLAY USING ALL FIVE OBJECTS.

FEAR
MAKE FINGERPAINTINGS OR DRAWINGS ABOUT WORDS SUCH AS FEAR, LOVE, ANGER ETC.

YELLOW YELLOW
WHAT IS YELLOW?
GREAT GREAT
WHAT IS GREAT?
MAKE RHYMES BY BOUNCING A BALL. SOMEONE BOUNCES AND ANYONE WHO CAN FILLS IN THE BLANK_____THE MISSING WORD

Wow! look at my new teacher!
COLLECT BABY PICTURES AND WRITE CAPTIONS UNDER THEM ABOUT YOUR CLASSMATES

ROLE PLAYING
CHILDREN TAKE EACH OTHERS' PART IN CLASS DISAGREEMENTS SO THEY CAN BETTER UNDERSTAND THE OTHER FELLOW'S VIEWPOINT...

POINT

4.3

I GET THE POINT!

DRAW OR TELL AS MANY MEANINGS AS POSSIBLE FOR: POINT
HAT
SAIL
FAIR
FACE
ROLL
SET ETC.

TAKE THREE UNRELATED WORDS AND MAKE A STORY FROM THEM
• HORSE • ROCKET
• PERFUME

MAKE UP NEW GAMES AND EXPLAIN DIRECTIONS

O.K. COACH

...OR DO THE SAME WITH ANIMAL PICTURES

MAKE A RECORD OR TAPE ABOUT *YOU*

AND GIVE IT TO YOUR MOTHER AND FATHER FOR CHRISTMAS.

FIGURE 5-1. *Creative activities for oral expression. The first step in the creative process is to create close identification with a problem, and a strong motivation to it. Here are many open-ended motivators which help in developing a creative oral expression program.*

ELEPHANT WORDS

PLOD
CLOMP
WEIGHTY
LUMBER
HUGE
MASSIVE
IMMENSE
UNDIGNIFIED
DUMBO
HEAVY
TWO-TON

FUNNY WORDS

LAUGH
TITTER
GIGGLE
JOY
DELIGHT
FOOLISH
SILLY
JOKE
HAPPY
GUFFAW
CLOWN
HILARIOUS
JOVIAL

HEAVY WORDS

TON
FAT
OBESE
DEEP
STEEP
FULL
SODDEN
LEAD
SOLID
STRONG
SERIOUS
GRAVE
CUMBERSOME

2000LBS.

SOFT WORDS

CUDDLY
FUZZY
FURRY
SNOW
AIRY
LIGHT
MILD
WEAK
GENTLE
KIND
PEACEFUL
FOGGY
TENDER
SOOTHING
PLEASANT
BLURRED

WORDS FOR HOUSES

DEW-DROP INN
TARA
THE PILLARS   RAMBLING
DON ROVIN   HAUNTED
DAD'S DREAM   DESERTED
THE MAPLES   RANCH

FIGURE 5-2. *Creative activities for oral expression. Children should be given freedom to use and manipulate words. Start collecting words by classifying them on charts of this nature. Later they can be bound in a reference book. Other charts might be built around words that explain themselves (like evergreen) or words that are new (like Telstar).*

NATURAL, EVERYDAY SITUATIONS THAT DEVELOP GOOD SPEAKING VOCABULARY

1. The show and tell period.
2. Discussions: TV shows, movies.
3. Reading together—audience type situation.
4. Dramatizations.
5. Shadow plays.
6. Puppet shows.
7. TV shows.
8. Radio shows.
9. Programs over the loud speaker system.
10. Assembly programs.
11. Tape recordings of stories, poems.
12. Choral speaking.
13. Reports by groups or individuals.
14. Panel discussions.
15. Planning periods.

CONTRIVED EXPERIENCES THAT BUILD GOOD ORAL VOCABULARY

Playing with Words

One way to develop expressive oral speech is to dwell on the describing words in the language which add tone, humor and color to ordinary speech. This can be demonstrated to children in many ways.

The teacher can describe these words (largely adjectives and adverbs) as words that paint pictures. A discussion of the importance of the describing words can lead to a comparison between them and the strokes of color an artist puts on a canvas to paint his "paint picture" as we sometimes paint "word pictures."

Demonstrations of the effectiveness of word pictures may be developed in various ways.

Mr. Elkins asked all the children to sit quietly and without using their mouths, but only by using their fingers, to show him how the describing words changed an idea. On a pocket chart in front of the room he put a card on which was printed the word *water*. "Now I am going to put other words in front of the one," he said. "Show me with your fingers how they change the idea each time." In front of the word *water* he placed a card bearing the word *running*.

Immediately fingers began to wriggle up and down, to move along, to dance gently. "Look," said Mr. Elkins, "our fingers are moving in a somewhat similar way yet they are all different, too. Now watch while I add another word." This time he put the word *dancing* before the word *water*. At once fingers made fountains or danced in a variety of patterns across the desk, each different from the other. "Very good," Mr. Elkins went on. "Now, let's try this," and he added the word *quiet*. Other words added were *angry, tumbling, cool, deep*. In each instance he evoked many interpretations from the children.

Almost any noun can be used in this manner if the teacher is sensitive to the many forms of describing words which create visual images in the youngsters' minds. The word *cat*, for instance, brings to mind one's own cat. Add words such as *pussy, tiger, black, soft,* and *pretty* and the vision changes. Add other sets of words such as *frightened, angry, nasty,* and *foolish* and a whole new set of images appears. Words like *minister's, teacher's, educated,* and *captain's* placed before the word brings forth another whole set of pictures.

Another way to sensitize children to describing words is to have them collect words and categorize them. These words can later be used in the poems and stories they do for creative writing. A simple little sketch or a picture pasted at the top of a piece of colored construction paper is often enough motivation for children to compile lists of their own "describing" words.

Describing words can be accented when attention is focused on them solely. Write a story about the children and omit all the describing words. Draw a line in the place of each omitted word. Tell the children that you were asked to write a story about them for the newspaper and that you want them to help. Ask each child to think of a describing word. Tell them you are going around the class and will incorporate their word into the story in the order in which it is given (whether or not it fits). After this is done, an hilarious time can be had by the children in reading back the story.

One such story is reproduced here. The capitalized words designate the adjectives given to the teacher by the group.

A Silly Story

One FUNNY, SILLY day in the NUTTY month of May, some BRIGHT sixth grade boys and girls met at the FABULOUS Mayville Elementary School to write some SLOPPY stories and CRAZY poems with their BEAUTIFUL, ICY teacher.

> *The MISERABLE class and their TERRIBLE teacher had a*
> *SOUR time. They wrote some CORNY stories, some STUPID*
> *poems and drew some MARVELOUS pictures.*
>   *When the afternoon was over, the FAT teacher got into*
> *her FRUITY car and drove home. Each of the GORGEOUS*
> *boys and girls took the BUMPY school bus back to their FAN-*
> *TASTIC homes and their SICK parents. It was a REPULSIVE*
> *experience to all.*

Once children have had this experience they will want to write news accounts at home leaving out the describing words so that they may use them in class. This is a great deal of fun with Halloween stories and stories about individuals in the class, providing, of course, the children realize it is done for fun.

A variation to this idea is to find a story where words can be left out easily. Have the children make out cards with words on them which they have just discovered. Place the cards face down on the table. Every time the teacher reaches a blank in the story a child picks up a card and reads a word. The story is never the same.

Rhymes and songs are good for helping children build a sensitivity to rhyming words.

The teacher says, "Afraid, afraid, who's afraid?" and any child who can think of a rhyming word says it, as when Mary said in response to the above, "The maid!" The answers can be sensible or nonsensical, whichever the class agrees they should be. Almost any sentence can be made into a rhyming one such as:

> Great, great, what is great?
> High, high, what is high?

Use of Pictures

At no time in the history of the world have beautiful pictures been accessible to teachers as they are today. Almost every scene imaginable has been depicted by pictures—cartoons, photographs, paintings, drawings and reproductions. All of these are free for the asking from calendar companies, educational supply houses, poster agencies, travel agencies, current magazines and newspapers.

Teachers have always used pictures in their teaching, but not always have they attempted to exhaust the possibilities pictures have for developing oral vocabulary. The most common use of pictures is to tell a story or to decorate a bulletin board. While these are two excellent ways to excite discussion, they are only a beginning.

Here are other ways of setting up thought-provoking conditions for the creative use of words through the use of pictures.

Pictures which appeal to the senses help evoke a group of expressive words.

FIGURE 5-3.   *How does it taste?*

In a second grade, where Figure 5-3 was shown these words came from the group:

yummy	thick
warm	wet
good	hot
comfortable	

The teacher suggested a few more such as:

tasty	rich
delicious	creamy

From Figure 5-4 came this list of words:

cool	refreshing
soft	delightful
wet	wonderful
grand	

FIGURE 5-4.   *How does it feel?*

When a picture of a child watching an airplane was put on the bulleting board and the sounds were discussed, children in a third grade made these analogies. They said, "It sounds . . .

like bees
like flies buzzing
like airplanes far away
like Daddy's razor
like mosquitos
like burrs in my head
like millions of telephones far away."

When children draw analogies such as this, poetic expression is beginning to emerge. Poetry results as a combination of mind and heart, and these children have begun to put the feeling into their work which gives it a poetic quality.

Sometimes two or more questions can be asked about a "situation" picture to help children see that new words are required to describe different points of view. Figure 5-5 also helped develop empathy in the children when the teacher asked them to make a face like the baby and then said, "What would you be looking at to make a face like the baby?"

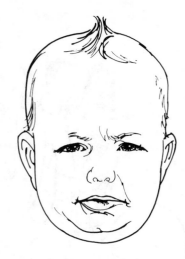

FIGURE 5-5.   *How does the baby feel? What does the baby see?*

The response to the first question in a second grade brought this list of words from the children:

afraid	like a crybaby
scared	frightened
hurt	like "oh my gosh"

The second question brought out these suggestions:

a dog	a car wreck
a bear	his rattle on the floor
a lion	his milk spilled over
someone hurt	

Pictures have always been good starters for telling a story. The picture with the unusual twist is a strong motivater for the unusual story. Instead of the phrase "Tell me about this picture," children are often stimulated to explore feelings more deeply and to search for expressive words when asked the question, "What happened?" or "How could this have been avoided?" or "Who was responsible for this?"

In Figure 5-6 some creative suggestions were made by fourth graders when asked, "What happened?" which were completely different from another group of fourth graders who were asked to tell the story of the picture:

The group that told the story labeled the items in the picture.

FIGURE 5-6.   *What happened? Tell a story.*

Little imagination was displayed as to what happened before or after the picture was taken. The other group had many unusual ideas, however, going into long build-ups to the situation depicted in the picture and offering solutions or logical endings to their stories.

Here is one example (as the teacher wrote it down).

> *Once there was a family, a mother, a father and a baby. It was a little baby and always had to have a baby sitter. One day the mother and father wanted to go to see the President. He was coming to town. There was going to be a big parade and the President was going to lead the parade. So, the mother called the baby sitter and the baby sitter said she would come.*

The father and the mother got all ready. But the baby sitter didn't come. They waited and waited, but the baby sitter didn't come. Finally the mother called her up, but she still couldn't come. She was sick.

The mother and the father were very disappointed. But the father said, "Let's go anyway. I'll wrap the baby inside my warm coat and he will be all right."

So they went. And soon the parade started. Finally the President came riding by. All the people cheered. This noise woke the baby. He wondered what the noise was all about. So, he stuck his head out of his father's coat. He wanted to see the President too. He might want to be a president some day.

Some pictures show a situation which has become unmanageable, such as Figure 5-7.

A whole flood of ideas will come forth if a teacher asks: "What happened *before* the picture was taken?"

There are pictures which are especially good to use in asking the question, "What happened *after* the picture was taken?" Certain magazine covers often show children and adults in various predicaments which supply excellent material for discussions built around this question.

Magazines and advertising material are filled with pictures of beautiful desserts, salads and other enticing foods. Some of these pictures, mounted attractively on a bulletin board, can bring out some imaginative prose or poetry when the label, "How does it feel to be your favorite dessert?" is attached.

Find pictures of people using one-way communication systems such as a picture of a person telephoning, a man or woman talking on TV or using a public address system. Put captions such as these over the pictures:

"What is she saying to you? Answer her."

"What is he saying? Tell us." Encourage children to take turns being the person in the picture and adding the sound to it. The label, "Make a sound picture out of me" is a good one to use on the bulletin board with many pictures.

Find unusual pictures, pictures that are misty, or show a scene taken through a window down which the rain is pouring. Ask the question, "What words describe this picture?" Unusual words are needed to describe unusual pictures. Find pictures that tend, in themselves, to depict some quality such as strength, or beauty, or joy. Use it to develop a specific vocabulary about specific parts of the picture.

FIGURE 5-7.   *What happened before this picture was drawn?*

FIGURE 5-8. *Using parts of pictures.*

These questions were asked of Figure 5-8:

1. Notice the man's arm in the picture. How could we describe it to others who could not see the picture? (Some of the words offered by a fifth grade class were: strong, tense, taut, tight, muscular and manly.)
2. Look at the rope. How could we describe it? (Words which were used included: strong, tight, taut, strained, stretched, heavy.)
3. Now let's look at the fish and tell about it. (Words such as these were offered: powerful, slick, slippery, wet, shiny, fluid, beautiful, graceful, strong, resistant.)

Often magazines publish pictures of beautiful designs. The caption at the top of the page asks, "What is it?" Close scrutiny proves the lovely circles to be onion rings, the beautiful flowing rivers turn out to be the cross section of a cabbage, the gorgeous sunbursts are crystals of sugar, all enlarged by the magic of the microscope. These pictures are excellent for classroom discussion, especially when their use results in making children closer observers of the beauty in the common things around them.

A variation of this use of pictures is to cut out an attractive picture for a bulletin board. Over it hang a piece of oaktag which has a small hole in it revealing only a part of the picture. The caption, "What is it?" creates the motivation for a discussion. Often a plate of spaghetti may look like a chocolate-chip cookie when only a part of it is exposed through a round hole. After children have tried to imagine what is under the oaktag, it is lifted for all to see.

This can be a springboard for other discussions on how things often are not what they seem. Often this can lead into the telling of mystery stories.

There are many pictures which can be partly covered and by so doing the whole idea of the picture is changed. Watch for pictures like this. Mount them on a bulletin board with a piece of tagboard over part of the picture. If it covers the bottom part, put this caption over the picture: "What do you think the bottom of this picture is about?" On the tagboard write, "Talk about it, then lift me up and see."

Children's imaginations can run rampant in a situation such as this, and the words will flow. The surprise of finding out what is really under the oaktag is fun too.

Pictures of inanimate objects are excellent to stimulate imagination. A caption such as, "If They Came Alive, What Would They Say?" can lead to a discussion or a dramatization, where different children assume the roles of the objects in the picture. Projection of feeling into inanimate and animate objects helps to develop a good "feeling" vocabulary.

FIGURE 5-9.   *How does the horse feel?*

Instead of asking children to tell about Figure 5-9, they were asked, "How does the horse feel—what does he think?" This brought out a flow of interesting "feeling" words: angry, frustrated, violent, unhappy, enraged, wild, vicious, furious, destructive, etc.

The use of pictures to develop vocabulary is unlimited. In the introductory chapter to this section, the point was made that oral vocabulary develops meaningfully when it grows out of the children's experiences. These experiences may be direct or vicarious. Pictures provide vicarious experiences for children. From these experiences comes a sharing of the vocabularies of all the group. Then new words, words developed this way, have meaning to the child and equip him with the tools he later needs to do creative writing. Children rarely, if ever, write words they do not say. The core of a good creative writing program and a good reading program lies in building a good oral vocabulary. Children ought to enjoy building their oral vocabularies—learning new skills should always be satisfying and fun.

Painting Word Pictures

The more children know about words and their meanings, the better they use them. Miss Gentry planned many lessons where the children played with words to develop an understanding of them. One day I observed her in an unusually creative lesson. Her objectives were as follows:

General

1. To study the word as a unit of meaning.
2. To understand that meanings of words are ascribed according to their use in context.

Specific—As a result of this lesson, each child will:

1. Realize that many words have multiple meanings.
2. Be acquainted with the multiple meanings of the following words: *fair, fast, sharp, plain, right.*
3. Understand that the meaning of a word is determined by the way it is used in the sentence.
4. Become familiar with a piece of literature, *The Blindmen and the Elephant.*

Miss Gentry read the folktale, *The Blindmen and the Elephant.* From a box she took cutout pictures of a wall, a spear, a snake, two tree trunks, a fan and a rope.

"Now," she said: "This is what each blindman thought he saw when he felt the elephant. Do you suppose we can make an elephant from these things?"

Figure 5-10 was the result of the arrangement of the articles on the flannel board.

"They still don't really look too much like an elephant—but they certainly look more like an elephant than any one of them—right?" The children agreed.

"Sometimes words are like pictures," said Miss Gentry. "You take them out of the story and you can't tell for one minute what they mean. Let's look at some."

She then held up cards that had these sentences on them:

1. We went to the state *fair*.
2. I want to be *fair* about the contest.
3. She was blonde and *fair*.
4. I went to see the movie, "My *Fair* Lady."
5. It was a *fair* day.

The children discussed the various meanings and concluded, that used out of context, the meaning of the word was as vague as the blindmen's impression of the elephant. Other words such as *fast*,

FIGURE 5-10. *How the blindmen saw the elephant.*

USING SOUNDS

PLAY BEAUTIFUL MUSIC
SUCH AS THE MEDIC THEME,
TARAS THEME ETC. AND
HAVE THE CHILDREN TELL
WHAT COMES TO MIND.

BUILD CHARTS OF
WORDS HAVING ONE
COMMON SOUND

LAW
LAWYER
LAWSUIT
LAW ABIDING
LAWLESS

PUT SOUNDS ON CARDS.
HAVE CHILDREN BUILD
A STORY AROUND THEM.
TRY:

SHHHH!
GRRRR
OUCH!
UGH!

MAKE NAME CHARTS
• NAMES FOR BABIES
• NAMES FOR WALES
• NAMES FOR AUTOS
• NAMES FOR DOLLS
• NAMES FOR DOGS

FIGURE 5-11. *After children acquire a reservoir of expressive and descriptive words, they need practice in the selection of the proper word for the proper situation. Many interesting conditions can be set where children must choose words precisely for a given situation. This can be very creative and, at the same time, a means of great enjoyment.*

sharp, plain and *right* were explored for meanings and the children soon volunteered a list of their own. Some words, they concluded, always meant the same thing and they produced a list of such words including *ouch, happiness, friend, enemy, help, true, love.*

Choral Speaking

A few years ago choral speaking fell into disrepute because of the way it was used. The purpose of using choral speaking becomes negated when teachers begin to rely on books which give selections to be spoken and the parts are all assigned to various rows, groups and individuals. When tense and strict drill develops, which is supposed to result in a highly polished choral masterpiece, little value to the children results. When used properly, choral speaking *can* be a very creative way to set conditions for good vocabulary development.

Choral speaking becomes creative when the children identify closely with a passage, decide to use it for choral speaking purposes and then proceed to work out an effective pattern by which to recite it. Even more creative is the group which makes up its own passages and poems to be set to choral speaking rhythms.

Choral speaking is especially effective because *all* children become involved. *All* children need to say words in order to acquire them, so they may be used later in their creative writing, reading and spelling. The shy child, who rarely volunteers in a class discussion, can enter into a choral speaking exercise with all the poise and security of the confident child. All children learn new words, because the words are spoken in meaningful context. Choral speaking must be conducted in a relaxed, happy atmosphere, where the product becomes secondary to the process. The learning comes in the doing and not in the end result. Often, the children will be so pleased with a passage they have created, they will want to perform for someone else. In this case time should be spent in "polishing it up." Most choral speaking should be carried on for the joy of using words in rhythmical patterns, much the way singing is.

Many teachers begin choral speaking by using material the children already know. Then they branch out by introducing unfamiliar material. Next they help the children write their own material.

Here are some ways teachers have begun choral work.

1. Select a poem with precise rhythm, allow the children to tap the rhythm and then say the poem to the rhythm.

2. Choose poems that *must* be walked or dramatized to be effective such as "The Merry-Go-Round" by Dorothy Baruch. Part of the class chants the poem while a group in the front of the room becomes the horses, working out various ways of going up and down like a merry-go-round.

3. Nursery rhymes are always good for establishing the idea of using words to rhythms. They can be used on any age level. The teacher will want to branch out soon, however, or children will consider the material tiresome or babyish.

Mr. Howard used a technique in his classroom which the children enjoyed very much. Each Friday morning the children chose membership in a specific group and appointed a chairman. As part of their library trip on that morning, the chairman was to find a poem which each group could work into a choral presentation. On Friday afternoon the groups met and worked out their choral patterns. After half an hour, the groups presented their work to each other. Often the whole group decided to tape some of the presentations. After awhile the class had a whole tape of interesting poems to which to listen.

One particularly fine choral exercise was "Paul Revere's Midnight Ride," which the children "polished up" for a program at a parent-teacher meeting.

When the curtain opened the stage lights were lowered to blue, to give the suggestion of night. To the left of the stage was the Old North Church tower, constructed from orange crates and painted mural paper by a committee of boys. To the right of the stage two groups of the fifth graders stood, faces toward the audience, hands clasped behind their backs.

One group began to make the sound of the horse's hoofs galloping in the distance. Soon the other group began the poem to the rhythm of the horse's hoofs. "Listen, my children, and you shall hear, Of the midnight ride of Paul Revere." During the course of the poem, the red light flickered in the north tower. One boy had painted Paul Revere and his galloping white horse on the side of an old mattress box and had cut it out. In the blue light he galloped it across the stage. The result was very effective.

These children had a creative experience in planning their program. In this case the product was important, because they wanted to do something worthwhile for their parents. Mr. Howard added another dimension to his objectives for this presentation. Yet he realized that the creative thinking in this situation took place *before* the curtain opened on the evening of the parent-teacher program. Through the *process* he accomplished his objectives; the *product* gave the children the feeling of success which is always needed to motivate further creative effort.

Another way to provoke creative thinking with choral speaking is to give the children a poem which lends itself to many adaptations and allows them to explore various ways of presenting it. Here, again, is an opportunity for several groups to be working at one time and then share ideas after each has worked out its pattern for presentation.

Mr. Foote used the "Pop-Corn Song" by Nancy Byrd Turner for this purpose late in the fall when children had made popcorn for their Halloween Party.

The class worked in four groups, with eight children in a group. They came up with these four different ideas.

Group 1: Half the group (four) made the popcorn sound all through the poem saying "Pop-pop-pop-pop" continually.

The rest of the groups said the poem as follows:

All:	Pop-pop-pop	*Group of 4:* Pop-pop-pop
Person 1:	Said the pop-corn in the pan.	Pop-pop-pop
All:	Pop-pop-pop	Pop-pop-pop
Person 2:	You can catch me if you can.	Pop-pop-pop
All:	Pop-pop-pop	Pop-pop-pop
Person 3:	Said the kernel white and yellow	Pop-pop-pop
All:	Pop-pop-pop	Pop-pop-pop
Person 4:	I'm a happy, dancing fellow.	Pop-pop-pop
All:	Pop-pop-pop	Pop-pop-pop
All:	I can dance and skip and hop.	Pop-pop-pop
	Pop-pop-pop-pop	Pop-pop-pop
	Pop-pop-pop	Pop-pop-pop

Group 2: This group divided into three subgroups of 3, 3 and 2 in a group.

Subgroup 1 (3) members	*Subgroup 2* (3) members	*Subgroup 3* (2) members		
	Pop-pop-pop	(Pop-pop)	(Pop-pop)	(Pop-pop)
	Pop-pop-pop	(Pop-pop)	(Pop-pop)	(Pop-pop)
Pop-pop-pop	Pop-pop-pop	(Pop-pop)	(Pop-pop)	(Pop-pop)
Said the	Pop-pop-pop	(Pop-pop)	(Pop-pop)	(Pop-pop)
pop-corn				
in the				
pan.				

etc., until the end of the poem when they all stopped and then shouted in unison, "Pop-Pop!"

Group 3: This group used the entire class. All the children snapped their fingers to give the illusion of corn popping. Then each of six children spoke a line in solo while the rest clicked their fingers and said all the "Pop-pop-pop" lines.

Group 4: This group added dramatization to their interpretation. One person stood before the group and said the first 2 lines.

> "Pop-pop-pop
> Says the pop-corn in the pan"

At this each member of the group went into action behind her. Some jumped in short, jerky jumps; some moved in labored emphatic stomps, some ran lightly, while all said, "Pop-pop-pop" and then became very still while the speaker said, "Said the kernel white and yellow," when the action resumed.

Fingerplays

Closely allied with choral speaking is the use of fingerplays. Fingerplays may be used in chorus while the children use their fingers to "act out" the poem, or they may be used by a group or individuals. Fingerplays have all the advantages of choral speaking: children say words and become familiar with them in a meaningful context so they become a part of normal speech. The children benefit a great deal by fingerplay because they will often speak with a group when they will not speak alone.

There are many poems written especially to be fingerplays. Other poems have been adapted to use as fingerplays.

While fingerplays are very useful in getting words into a child's oral vocabulary, the truly creative part of using fingerplays comes when children write their own.

Here is an example:

Poem	*Action*
One little rocket	Left fist clenched, index finger
With a pointed nose	pointed up like a rocket. Place
On a launching pad	fist on flat right hand. Have the
Off it goes!	rocket go off into the air.

Choral Speaking with Music

Some passages from literature blend well to musical background. Teachers can persuade children to experiment with words and music to find these pleasant sounding blends. In some classrooms teachers often play a composition of beautiful music on a record as a background for reading poetry to children. "The Landing of the Pilgrim Fathers" takes on a new quality when read against a a background of "America the Beautiful."

Miss Norris had her sixth grade explore various possible combinations of words and music. At the Thanksgiving program the children dressed as Pilgrims and half the class recited "The Landing of the Pilgrim Fathers" while the other half sang and hummed "The Doxology" as a background. For other programs Miss Norris's group found the following combinations very beautiful:

Voice	*Music*
The 23rd Psalm	Singing and Humming "Battle Hymn of the Republic"
"Snowbound" by Whittier	"Jingle Bells" played and sung softly
"Have You Ever Heard the Wind?" by Stevenson	*Danse Macabre*

Let your children find their own combinations. Let them also find music to be played as a background for reading their own poems.

Sharon, age 7, selected "April in Portugal" to be played as a background to the reading of her poem:

Snow

The snow falls down to the ground
Until it covers the town
It is so soft and white
And sparkles in the morning light.

Raymond, age 9, had a group of boys hum "Home on the Range" while he read:

Cowboys

I wish I were a cowboy
Riding on my horse
Slowly over the plains.

The lowing of the cattle —
The singing of the cowboys —
The feel of summer rains —

The baking sun,
The cooling breeze,
The campfire in the night —

The moon's bright light,
The friendly dog;
The feeling all is right.

Music can help set conditions for creative oral expression in many other ways. Some teachers have been successful with these ideas:

1. Play music and allow the children to describe what it says to them.
2. Play a line of some piece of music on the piano (or a record player) and allow the class to make up words to go with it; then play the next line, etc., until they have written their own lyrics to the music.
3. Try the above in reverse. Select a theme such as *Elephants*. Ask a child to tell you something about elephants. After he does, create a line of music to reflect his thinking. Then ask another child to tell something about elephants, and so on, until a poem-song has been worked out which the entire class may say together.

The elephant walks heavy
   (heavy music)
The elephant is big
   (loud, voluminous music)
The elephant can dance
   (light, airy music)
He'll dance us a jig
   (jig music)

Helping children to blend music and words leads to helping them get feeling into their words, which, in turn, leads to creative experimentation.

Miss Jarvey, a third grade teacher, played three or four pieces of music on a record player. She then asked the class to select the one composition they considered to be the most beautiful. In this instance the children chose "Blue Star." Miss Jarvey asked each child to think what was the most beautiful thing in the world to him. When each child said he had an idea, Miss Jarvey had the children sit in a circle. In the center of the circle she placed a tape recorder and a record player. She then played "Blue Star" and recorded the opening theme on the tape recorder. Then she handed the microphone to the first child, who said, "The most beautiful thing in the world is my mother." While the child was speaking, Miss Jarvey turned down the volume of the record player. As soon as he finished, she increased the volume, and passed the microphone on to the next child. When he spoke, she again decreased the volume and so on around the circle until each child had recorded his idea.

In the playback she got, first of all, beautiful music, which softened when a childish voice said, "The most beautiful thing in the world is my mother," then swelled forth, and softened again as another childish voice said, "The most beautiful thing in the world are the stars twinkling in the sky at night," and so on. This created a very effective tone poem.

Variations of the idea may be employed on all grade levels using different themes such as:

1. The Saddest Thing in the World.
2. The Loudest Thing in the World.
3. The Softest Thing in the World.
4. The Ugliest Thing in the World.

On some holidays special recordings can be taped. On Halloween, for instance, the children may create a tape on "The spookiest thing in the world" spoken with *Danse Macabre* or "A Night on Bald Mountain." Fourth of July can bring about the question, "What is the noblest (or most patriotic, or finest) thing in the world?" recorded against military music.

Creative Choral Speaking

After children have used familiar material and have explored unfamiliar material, many teachers like to lead them into creating their own material for a choral presentation.

A teacher may take his cue from a poem or a short story, which one individual in the class may write. Following is an example of one such situation:

The Kite
(Grade 3)

Child: I sent my kite into the sky
Class: So high, so high, so high, so high
Child: I watched it toss and jump and leap
Class: And sweep, and sweep, and sweep, and sweep
Child: Until the sky was clean and bright
Class: So bright, so bright, so bright, so bright
Child: I brought it back from east to west
Class: To rest, to rest, to rest, to rest.

The teacher need not wait for this to happen, however. The collective minds of the children, all stimulated by a highly motivating situation can result in some unusual and exciting work, quite different from that presented by individuals. If the teacher is willing to accept children's work for the beauty and joy of it, whether it be in rhyming or free verse, free or structured prose, then all sorts of exciting things can happen in her classroom. Following are descriptions of classroom situations which demonstrate how some teachers have set conditions for their children to do creative speaking and creative thinking together.

Miss Parrott had a first grade in a suburb of a large industrial city. Her children were average middle-middle class and upper-middle class. It was December, and about half of her class was already reading in primers and first grade books. Christmas was coming. One morning, after a beautiful snow fall, Miss Parrott printed these words on the chalkboard:

CHRISTMAS IS COMING!

On the top of each of the other chalkboards she lettered: I can taste it! I can smell it! I can feel it! I can hear it! I can see it!

When the children entered the room many went to the chalkboard and read what it said. Miss Parrott encouraged these children to read it to those who could not read. As soon as the class was assembled she said, "Some of you read what was on the board this morning. Freddie, will you read it again for all of us?"

After Freddie read the titles, Miss Parrott said, "Let's work with this board first." She stood near the chalkboard panel which said, "I can taste it!" "Now, let's put on our thinking caps," said Miss Parrott, "and think of all the things we taste at Christmas that we don't taste any other time of the year. As you think of them I will put them here, even though all of you cannot read them yet. I shall read them to you and this will help me to remember your ideas."

Molly said, "We taste the cold air," and Miss Parrott wrote it on the chalkboard. Billy said, "Cookies," and Johnny said, "Gingerbread."

Miss Parrott continued until the children's ideas were listed on all the panels. Then she read what they had written:

> CHRISTMAS IS COMING! *I can taste it!*
> *We can almost taste the cold,*
> *when we take a breath of air.*
> *We can taste the cookies, gingerbread,*
> *and candy canes.*
> *There is nothing so good as popcorn balls*
> *and maple syrup on snow.*

CHRISTMAS IS COMING! *I can smell it!*
It smells like Christmas
Smell the pine of the Christmas trees.
Smell the cookies and the outdoors.
Everything smells like Christmas.

CHRISTMAS IS COMING! *I can feel it!*
We feel kind of Christmasy
We feel it from talking about it.
We feel the snow on our faces
We feel good and different!

CHRISTMAS IS COMING! *I can hear it!*
We hear the songs and poems
*   and Christmas bells everywhere.*
We hear the wind outdoors
*   and we hear the toys in the stores.*

CHRISTMAS IS COMING! *I can see it!*
Look at the presents being wrapped
See the children sliding down hill
*   and the skaters on the ponds*
See the crowds of people rushing around
And mother hiding presents so the
*   children won't peek.*

The next day Miss Parrott had printed this material on lined chart paper and the children read it. Miss Parrott then asked if it wouldn't be fun to say it together as a choral poem.

Sometimes teachers can structure a poem so that it falls into a pattern which lends itself readily to choral speaking. Capitalizing on the children's interest in rockets, Mr. Carney wrote this on the chalkboard.

One big rocket
Ready for a race
Going to be shot
Into Outer Space
Countdown
There goes Ten

There goes Nine

"Now," said Mr. Carney, "let's see what we can do with a rhyming poem. What rhymes with 'ten' that has the same kind of rhythm as the line, 'There goes ten?'"

The following poem resulted:

The Rocket

One big rocket
Ready for a race
Going to be shot
Into outer space

There goes ten
Get ready, Men!

There goes nine
Everything's fine!

There goes eight
Don't be late!

There goes seven
Aimed towards heaven!

There goes six
Down with the sticks!

There goes five!
Come back alive!

There goes four
Bolt the door!

There goes three
Are you ready?

There goes two
No more to do!

There goes one
Give 'er the gun!

There goes zero,
Come back a hero!

Ten-Nine-Eight-
Seven-Six-Five-
Four-Three-Two-
One!

   BLAST OFF!

This poem made a very effective choral poem with the blast-off finale! Many situations can be created to provoke creative oral composition by using numbers or colors to stimulate a kind of rhyming.

Chalk Talks

Chalk talks help develop in children: (1) good speaking vocabulary, (2) good speaking voice, (3) a concept of a logical sequence of ideas and (4) a creative imagination. Most children enjoy a chalk talk which has a climax. However, a climax is not absolutely necessary. Children enjoy hearing other children tell stories as they draw pictures. The addition of colored chalk adds variety to the presentation.

One form of chalk talk which stimulates oral creative expression is that which uses abstract color blocks as an agitator to creative thinking. The teacher uses colored chalk directly on the chalkboard or tapes large sheets of manila paper to the board and then proceeds to apply large blocks of color. The children are instructed to volunteer when the emerging design reminds them of something.

This is the way it went in Miss Sheckells' third grade. She took the colored chalk in her hand and started to make large circles.

"Boys and girls," she said, "I am going to put some pretty colors on this paper. When they remind you of something, you raise your hand and tell me." She applied yellow and red up to this point when Anne said, "It makes me think of a clown."

"All right," said Miss Sheckells. "A clown it shall be. And, while I am making a clown out of my colors, let's think of a poem or story that tells about him. I'll make him sad; maybe we could begin like this: Here we have a sad, sad clown."

She drew the mouth with the corners turned down and then put in a little, perky nose with black chalk. "What can we say for our next line?" she asked and Bobby said, "His nose turns up, his mouth turns down!"

"Good," said Miss Sheckells as she continued drawing on a clown hat and fancy buttons down his front. "Now what else can we say about him?" and she drew large feet on him.

"His feet are big," said Dale.

"That's fine, and we can put another idea with that line," said Miss Sheckells.

"Well, his hands are wide," said Marcia.

"Very good," said Miss Sheckells and she read the poem again. "Perhaps we can add one more line that rhymes with "wide"—any ideas? Why is he sad?"

Judy volunteered the answer, "His nose pulls off. I know. I tried."

FIGURE 5-12.   *Here we have a sad, sad clown . . .*

Here we have a sad, sad clown
His nose turns up, his mouth turns down.
His feet are big; his hands are wide
His nose pulls off. I know. I tried.

When Miss Sheckells tried the circles on another group she again had the clown idea offered, but with the results in Figure 5-13.

FIGURE 5-13.   *Once I made a funny clown . . .*

Once I made a funny clown
His mouth goes up
His nose goes down
With bells on his feet
And a bow on his neck

He tumbled down the street
By heck!

Before Miss Sheckells could get past the three circles to draw for another group, one child called, "It's a mouse." "All right," said Miss Sheckells. "Let's make a mouse." This was the response from this group as teacher and children created together.

FIGURE 5-14.   *Once there was a little mouse . . .*

Once there was a little mouse
He lived in a tiny house
He was as happy as could be
'Cause he was going on TV!

Using this pattern of color, Miss Senior got results like Figure 5-15.

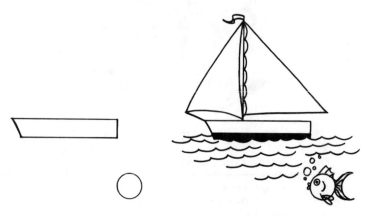

FIGURE 5-15.   *Once there was a lonely fish . . .*

Once there was a lonely fish
Way down in the sea
"Why doesn't something come,"
He said. "And play a while with me."
One day a great big boat went by—
The biggest he'd ever seen
"Oh I could play with it," he said
"If it were a submarine!"

In another classroom Douglas volunteered to make a chalk drawing. He went to the chalkboard and began to put spots of colored chalk over the paper. At the bottom of the paper he made a heavy line.

"Satellites," volunteered Kenny.

"All right, let's get ideas from each other. As Douglas draws we will write," said the teacher.

Figure 5-16 resulted.

Satellites

Satellites are in flight
Many colors—very bright
Oh, a magnificent sight
Polka dots in the night!

FIGURE 5-16. *Satellites are in flight . . .*

Sound Stories

Sound stories are very popular. Sometimes children or the teacher can find stories such as "Gerald McBoing-Boing" or "The Tiger Hunt," mentioned previously. Many other stories are equally as effective when sound is added to them. One library assignment for upper grade children might be to find a story suited to sound accompaniment.

Often the teacher can set up a beginning situation to create a sound story, and the children can take it from there. Putting such stories on tape contributes to their enjoyment because children hear the total effect better in the playback than they do while making up the story.

A sound story must be one that can have sounds added to it much the same way a round-robin story has words added to it. Think of noisy situations to get your clue: a visit to a factory, the circus, the carnival, a state or county fair, a living room with TV set, radio, hi-fi and people talking or a busy store. Start a plot by having a main character enter this situation, and add to the plot by adding sounds as the plot develops. Then the children in the room add the noises until the whole story reaches a climax.

Lap Stories

Lap stories are fun for all age levels. Instead of simply telling a story, the teacher sits down in the middle of a group where all can see and holds a simple piece of wall board in her lap. With a few props she tells or retells a story by acting it out on her lap board. The one way a lap story differs from any other story telling is that the teacher involves the children in the plot.

Flannel Boards

Telling stories by use of a flannel board is an excellent way for children to share words they know and to add new ones to their vocabularies. Commercial cutouts can be used for flannel board stories. Pictures from any old worn out books provide a wealth of material, if they are cut out and a small piece of flannel is pasted on the back so they will stick to the board. A new dimension in creativeness is developed, however, when children design and paint their own figures and symbols for use on the flannel board.

Flannel boards serve many purposes besides the telling of stories. Because children must *tell* about the materials they are putting on the flannel board, vocabulary may be developed in all subject areas.

Here are a few creative ways teachers have used the flannel board to develop vocabulary:

Miss Carmen asked her fourth grade children to give a third dimension to their flannel board stories by making the figures and objects from construction paper and designing them so they moved or opened. In presenting the "gingerbread boy," the children found that by bending one leg of the figures, they could give the appearance of running. They made the barn door open; the oven door opened so the little gingerbread man could be shut in; the mowers' pitchforks were separate from the mowers so they could throw them down, and a big gingerbread boy folded so first his arms and legs and, finally, his head disappeared.

Miss Creamer asked her sixth grade children to make simple flannel boards with four layers of flannel taped at the top so that the flannel could be flipped back over the cardboard backing. Then each child took his favorite book and picked out the four scenes from the book that he liked best. With wax crayons, he drew the scenery for each of the scenes in proper sequence on a sheet of flannel so he could tell his story in four scenes. These were used over a period of several weeks. Each child then gave his flannel board story as a book report to the rest of the class. Each child made the characters for the scene on construction paper backed with flannel (although fine sandpaper, blotters or flocking will also work) and built up each scene as he told the story, removing the characters and flipping the flannel as he went from scene one to subsequent scenes.

As part of a Christmas program, Mr. Fuller's fifth grade presented "The Small One" by Charles Taswell in the following manner: The children read the story and listed the eight major scenes on the chalkboard. They then signed up for the scene on which they preferred to work. Working in committees, they first made large flannel boards of the same size by taping outing flannel over cardboard cut from towel cartons. Then each group made characters, scenes and props to tell about its part of the story. The night of the program, the curtain opened to reveal the eight blank flannel boards resting on easels across the stage. Christmas music was playing softly in the background. A spotlight picked up a narrator standing on the side of the stage. The narrator began to tell the story and the spotlight moved to the first flannel board. Two children came forward from the back of the stage and proceeded to build their scene as the narrator told the story. Then the spotlight shifted to the second scene and down the line, until, at the end of the story, the footlights were brought up revealing a mural across the stage of the entire story. The children, grouped behind the pictures, sang a Christmas carol to end their portion of the program.

Original Flannel Board Stories

Real creativity is evidenced in using the flannel board, after the teacher has utilized it effectively with the children, as a motivator for their own creative work. The ultimate goal is to have children create their own stories and use their own ideas to present them.

Dramatizations

A very natural way for children to develop good oral expression is through dramatization. In the primary grades free play is an integral part of the child's life and he reflects the words he hears about him by using them in his play. New words may be introduced through situations set up by the teacher as the child matures, through:

1. Dramatizing favorite stories and poems and events.
2. Dramatizing problem stories.
3. Role-playing.
4. Writing and producing scripts.
5. Acting out telephone conversations, scenes, etc.

Inasmuch as the main purpose here is to develop meaningful vocabulary and good speaking quality, a finished product is of little consequence unless the dramatization is to be used for a production to be presented to parents.

Puppets

There are many kinds of puppets and many ways in which they can be used to develop good speaking habits and good vocabulary. In Figure 5-17 are some ideas for using them in the classroom.

Fist puppets can be made quickly. With the children crouched behind a table, they can hold the fist puppets into view and have them carry on conversations or create jingles to recite to the class.

FIGURE 5-17.   *Using puppets to develop oral expression.*

Here is a jingle a sixth grade boy said about his puppet as he made her jaws move rapidly.

> *There was an old lady*
> *I made her one day*
> *She liked to chew candy*
> *She had much to say*
> *She loved most to talk*
> *She talked like a jet*
> *And only would stop*
> *To light a cigarette*
> *(here he put a cigarette in her mouth).*

Paper bag puppets can be made quickly and used for rhymes, for dramatizing stories, or for solving problem stories (Figure 5-18).

FIGURE 5-18.   *Paper bag puppets.*

Stick puppets also serve to help children create ways to express themselves (Figure 5-19).

FIGURE 5-19.   *Stick puppets.*

A Kleenex box or small shoe box makes a small theater for two children to present shows to each other or to small groups (Figure 5-20). The tips of fingers can have faces put on them with colored chalk, colored pencil, paint or make-up, to represent puppets.

FIGURE 5-20. *John used small tissue boxes and shoe boxes to make stage settings for his finger puppets.*

Finger puppets can also be made with the fingers used as the legs, thus providing many opportunities for desk-top dramatizations (Figure 5-21).

FIGURE 5-21. *Finger puppet.*

Papier-mâché puppets provide excellent opportunities for all sorts of dramatizations. Children may be given boxes of junk or bags of materials which may be useful in making puppets, and encouraged to make the puppet using a variety of these materials.

PAPER MÂCHÉ PRESSED ON PAPER STRIPS OVER A LEMON OR SMALL LIGHT BULB

FIGURE 5-22.   *Papier-mâché puppets.*

Teaching them to make puppets will help them in perfecting skills. The creative puppet will be the one the child invents to make a character to help him solve a life problem with which he is closely identified.

Shadow Plays

Shadow plays provide another excellent way to introduce words into the child's oral vocabulary. Here are some ways shadow plays may be used.

Hang a sheet before the room. Place a bright light behind it.

Children can make simple scenery by using cardboard to create shadows, or simply by cutting newspaper and pinning it to the sheet to make shadows. Turn out the light to change the scenery. Be sure the children perform close to the sheet so that they will make clear-cut shadows.

FIGURE 5-23. *Red Riding Hood.*

Take a large carton such as a paper towel carton and cut a hole in it to represent a stage. Tape a piece of sheeting or unbleached muslin over the hole. Put a bright light behind the carton. Using the towel carton stage, encourage children to cut out cardboard figures and tape them to long wires. Wire coat hangers, when pulled straight, are excellent for this purpose. These figures can then be pressed against the muslin to create shadows without the operator's shadow showing. The operator must sit or stand behind the light which creates the shadow (Figure 5-23).

Figures can also be cut from cardboards with a tab on the bottom so they may be operated from beneath the carton simply by putting a slit in the back of the carton and pushing the figures up onto the screen, then moving them about by manipulating the tab.

A simple way to make scenery for this type of shadow box is to paint the scene with thick tempera paint or black flo-pen on to a heavy-grade Saran wrap. The scene can then be pressed firmly against the muslin and it will stick. When the light is turned on, the paint or flo-pen ink casts a shadow making a fixed scene against which the movable figures can act. This technique provides an easy way to change the scenery quickly.

Reading and Hearing What You Write

Mr. Gans felt that one way to improve speech (as well as writing) would be to have the children hear their stories and poems read aloud.

He made arrangements to have a portable cassette tape recorder in his room, with a supply of 15-minute tapes. Children who cared to were encouraged to take a story they had written, or a poem, and go into a quiet room or a quiet place in the classroom set aside for this purpose and make a tape of the story by reading it aloud into the microphone. They should then hear themselves reading. When the completed, edited writing was submitted to Mr. Gans, they could also submit the tape and Mr. Gans could listen to them read aloud while he read the story silently. Through this technique he was able to help the children with their speaking, reading and writing habits.

SUMMARY

In the years ahead it is likely that our children will be called on to speak often before large groups of people, either directly or by means of radio or television. During a recent presidential election the candidates talked to over 60,000,000 people at one time. The ability to speak effectively before groups and audiences is a needed skill in the space age. This is a skill which needs to be developed in the elementary school. Oral communication is the most effective, the most common and the first means of communication among men, and it is the basis for a sound program in reading, handwriting, spelling, word usage and creative writing. To learn to speak effectively means to speak creatively; inasmuch as words are put into new patterns for expressing ideas.

TO THE COLLEGE STUDENT AND THE CLASSROOM TEACHER

1. Many students say to me, "There are so many good ideas in your books on creativity, but if I try them in my classroom am I not stealing them—is this creative even though I get creative results?" I remind them that *adaptation* is one form of creativity— a low form, it is true, but probably the form most commonly used in classrooms. Discuss this problem with your colleagues.

2. One form of adaptation would be to take the *idea* of using pictures to develop vocabulary as it is reported here and brainstorm all the *new ways* that you can think of to use pictures for vocabulary building. One approach might well be to collect some very unusual pictures from magazines and other sources and then brainstorm some unique ways of using them to develop descriptive vocabulary.

3. If you are a classroom teacher, take a look at your own program in oral expression. Does it serve as a base for the other language arts? Does it grow up from the experiences of children or is it fed *down* from your experience as a teacher? Think of all the ways you can introduce new vocabulary words to children by providing experiences from which the words grow.

4. Here is an activity to try in class, whether it be in grade school or college.

Sell a book. Have students prepare a sales talk about a recent library book they have enjoyed, and one that might be enjoyed by others. Pictures, drawings of a particular scene or the book cover could be used to stimulate interest. A demonstration could be given concerning something learned in the particular book, or telling just enough of the story to whet the appetite of a prospective reader.

5. Observe a regular classroom in operation and note the number of times creative oral expression is suppressed in order to complete some written work. List all the ways you can think of where controlled oral expression might replace busy work or meaningless seat work.

6. What were the basic objectives of Mr. Howard's plan in the instance described on page 169? On what basic principles of creativity did he build the assembly program?

7. Should the program in oral expression be the same in a city slum area as in a wealthy suburban village? Why or why not?

8. Try this with your colleagues or with children in a classroom (Figure 5-24). Have the tail and two eyes on ditto paper and away they go. An oral story to explain Snickerdoodles.

Note the differences in the drawings and the stories that go with them.

9. Consider the stress the author places on the importance of oral expression and then think of the pros and cons for the use of workbooks in the school program. Think through several ways in which workbooks might justifiably be used in a program of oral expression.

10. Reread the episode of the show and tell period on pages 147–48. Note carefully how Miss Crane helped the class: (1) by pooling their individual vocabularies so the children learned new words from each other and (2) by introducing new words and

new meanings herself. Consider the definitions of creativity in Chapter I and ask yourself: Can the teaching of words be a creative act? Did Miss Crane help the children *learn* new words through discovery or did they *create* new words?

11. Look through the ideas suggested in this chapter and select some samples from them which could be used in an autocratic as well as a creative classroom. Discuss this statement: A teacher who does not understand the concepts of creativity may appear at times to be teaching creatively but in reality is doing little to advance the creative development of her students.

12. Demonstrate before your class some of the uses of the flannel board for creative teaching as shown by Paul Anderson in his book *Flannelboard Stories for Primary Grades* (see bibliography).

13. Visit your school library and try to find books which emphasize the oral program in language arts over the written program. How many present exercises for stimulating oral expression?

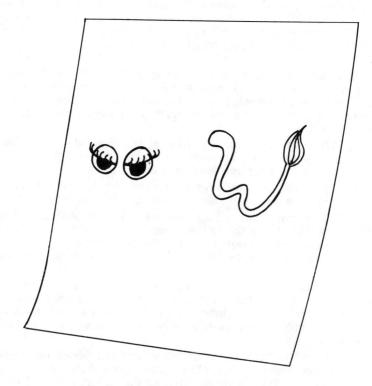

FIGURE 5-24.   *The birth of a Snickerdoodle.*

14. Brainstorm all the ways you can think of to tell stories creatively to children.

15. Read Batchelder and Comer's book of *Puppets and Plays* (see bibliography below) and Pierson's "Puppets, Teachers and Creative Dramatics" (see bibliography). Choose some aspect of one of these to demonstrate before the class.

16. For exercises in the clever manipulation of and play with words, see Westcott's *Word Bending with Aunt Sarah* (see bibliography).

SELECTED BIBLIOGRAPHY

Adams, Bess Porter. *About Books and Children*. New York: Henry Holt, 1953.

Anderson, Paul. *Flannelboard Stories for Primary Grades*. Minneapolis: Denison, 1962.

Arbuthnot, May Hill and Sheldon L. Root Jr. *Time for Poetry*. 3d ed. Dallas, Texas: Scott Foresman, 1968.

Bamman, Henry J., Mildred A. Dawson and Robert J. Whitehead. *Oral Interpretation of Children's Literature*. Dubuque, Iowa: William C. Brown, 1964.

Batchelder, Marjorie H. and Virginia Comer. *Puppets and Plays: A Creative Approach*. New York: Harper and Row, 1956.

Burger, Isabel B. *Creative Play Acting: Learning Through Drama*. New York: Ronald Press, 1966.

Byrne, Margaret. *The Child Speaks*. New York: Harper and Row, 1965.

Calder, Clarence R., Jr. and Eleanor M. Antan. *Techniques and Activities to Stimulate Verbal Learning*. New York: Macmillan, 1970.

Carlson, Bernice W. *Act It Out*. New York: Abingdon Press, 1965.

Crosscut, Richard. *Children and Dramatics*. New York: Charles Scribner's Sons, 1966.

Cullum, Albert. *Greek Tears and Roman Laughter: Ten Tragedies and Five Comedies for Schools*. New York: Citation Press, 1970.

―――. *Push Back the Desks*. New York: Citation Press, 1968.

―――. *Shake Hands with Shakespeare*. New York: Citation Press, 1967.

Grayson, Marion. *Let's Do Fingerplays*. Washington, D.C.: Luce, 1962.

Groff, Patrick. *What's New in Language Arts: Oral Language.* Washington, D.C.: American Association of Elementary-Kindergarten-Nursery Educators, N.E.A. Center, 1970.

Jacobs, Leland B. (ed.). *Using Literature with Young Children.* New York: Teachers College Press, 1965.

Koskey, Thomas. *Baited Bulletin Boards: A Handbook for Teachers.* Belmont, Calif.: Fearon, 1954.

MacCampbell, James C. (ed.). *Readings in the Language Arts in the Elementary School.* Boston: D. C. Heath, 1964.

McCaslin, Nellie. *Creative Dramatics in the Classroom.* New York: David McKay, 1968.

Murray, Ruth Lowell. *Dance in Elementary Education.* New York: Harper and Row, 1963.

Pierson, Howard, "Pupils, Teachers and Creative Dramatics." In James C. MacCampbell (ed.). *Readings in the Language Arts in the Elementary School.* Boston: D. C. Heath, 1964, pp. 151–60.

Pronovost, Wilbert. *The Teaching of Speaking and Listening in the Elementary School.* New York: Longmans, Green, 1959.

Rasmussen, Carrie. *Speech Methods in the Elementary School.* New York: Ronald Press, 1962.

Shaftel, Fannie R. and George Shaftel. *Role-Playing for Social Values.* Englewood Cliffs, N.J.: Prentice-Hall, 1967.

Siks, Geraldine B. *Childrens Literature for Dramatization.* New York: Harper and Row, 1964.

———. *Creative Dramatics: An Art for Children.* New York: Harper and Row, 1958.

Smith, Brooks, Kenneth Goodman and Robert Meredith. *Language and Thinking in the Language Arts in the Elementary School.* Chapter IV, Language in Communication. Boston: Allyn and Bacon, 1971, pp. 189–246.

Smith, James A. *Creative Teaching of the Language Arts in the Elementary School.* Chapter IV, Listening. Boston: Allyn and Bacon, 1967.

Tooze, Ruth. *Storytelling.* Englewood Cliffs, N.J.: Prentice-Hall, 1959.

Westcott, Al. *Word Bending with Aunt Sarah.* Mankato, Minn.: Oddo, 1964.

Williams, Helen V. *Puppets Go to School.* Philadelphia: Winston, 1955.

CHAPTER VI

Creative Writing

I Never Knew

I came and I cried,
I laughed and was happy,
I saw a man die and saw a man born.
I learned and retained knowledge,
I saw beauty and horror,
I heard beautiful music and sang.
I danced and was joyous,
I respected and hated,
I worshipped and believed.
I was ecstatic and depressed,
I was glad and I was lonely,
I loved and was loved.
I lived and I died—and Oh, God! what I'd
Give to do it over again!

SUSAN

TO THE READER

If you have any doubt about the statements of children's abilities to write on all subjects at any time and to do it well, this chapter should convince you. The poem at the beginning of this chapter, written by a bright child, is a sample of the deep feeling young people can express in their writing—and shows more clearly than all the writing I have done so far, how creativity can be expressed through writing.

The sole purpose of this chapter is to expound the place of creative writing in the logical sequence of language development and to hope that you have an enjoyable time reading the work of young authors.

INTRODUCTION

On page 38, one of the objectives for teaching the language arts is stated as follows, "Each child needs come to appreciate the beauty of language itself, the effective use of words and creative ways they may help him express his own original thoughts." The text goes on to say, "This is a study of language for language's sake. It is loving the rhythm of certain words; it is delighting in the way words are put together; it is using words and phrases to paint pictures. It includes the creative: the job of sorting, deciding and choosing the right word for the right spot. It means children evaluate words according to what they can do to make language forceful and effective. It means children write their own literature and recognize beauty in the writing of others. It is the building of appreciation for authors, poets and composers. It is the knowledge of that which lifts language from the commonplace to the beautiful."

This objective is best attained through a rich program in oral expression as described in Chapter V and a well-developed program in creative writing as set forth in this chapter. These portions of the language arts program might well be called "the literature of children."

Children rarely write what they do not say. Also prerequisite to a creative writing program is a sensible, meaningful program in reading. Such a program in reading is one that utilizes the oral vocabulary of children to make classroom charts, labels and stories *so the children may see their own words in manuscript or written form.* When the visual images of these words are stamped on the child's mind, he is ready to reproduce them in his own handwriting. He then has the tool he needs to write the beautiful things he has to say.

A reading program which follows a basic text where no supplementary provisions are made for permitting the child to see his own vocabulary in print is one which handicaps the child in his creative writing. In the example of the show and tell period narrated on pages 147–48 Miss Crane helped the children develop a descriptive vocabulary on the oral level, and then showed the children how the words looked by printing them on the chalkboard. These words were left there so all the children might see and use them.

In Chapter III the interrelatedness of language was discussed. Loban concluded that reading, writing, listening and speaking were all closely related. Children who were low in general oral language ability tended to be low in reading and writing achievement. Children high in general oral language ability tended to do well in gaining literacy skills. Loban also pointed out that reading and writing were related to sociometric position, and that all language ability and vocabulary correlated highly with success on group I.Q. tests. Because of the interrelatedness of the various forms of the language arts, it is essential that these be taught in an interrelated way. Translated into simple terms this means that in order to have an effective creative writing program, a teacher must have a strong program in oral expression, reading and listening.

When an individual writes creatively, he is communicating on paper in his very best way. As a communication technique the ideas he writes are predominantly important. Misspellings and imperfections in grammar are secondary considerations. Too much emphasis on spelling and grammar at this point checks the flow of ideas or frustrates the writer so that he abandons writing as a communication form. Because of this, spelling and grammar should not be taught during the process of creative writing, but should be taken care of in the editing which follows. Editing is necessary for the child to share his writing with others; it must be put in the common standard forms of English so that others may read it. A plan for editing the children's creative writing appears on pages 296–97. This plan works well for children who will share their writing with others. Some children write entirely for themselves, however, and when this is the case the teacher must respect the child's desire and teach necessary editorial skills in another manner, preferably through practical writing assignments.

Teachers set conditions for creative writing in several basic ways:

1. They provide for many experiences with smell, touch, sight and sound in the classroom or capitalize on the children's sensory experiences outside of school.
2. They help the children put these experiences into spoken words in beautiful, descriptive ways.
3. The provide the children with the visual image of the words so they learn to read them.
4. They help the children reproduce these words in handwritten form.

5. They provide the permissive, experimental atmosphere necessary to all creative endeavors.
6. They then stand off and let the child write.
7. *After* the child's ideas are on paper the way *he* wants them, the work is edited.
8. They keep in mind the creative process described in Chapter II.
9. They also keep in mind the principles of creative teaching described in Chapter I.

THE QUALITY OF WRITING

Teachers are often concerned with the quality of creative writing. This is a just concern but not a very important one on the elementary level. It is "just," because every child ought to function most of the time at the peak of his ability. Not to do so makes him feel unworthy and insecure, but it is relatively unimportant because quality is a value judgment and values among individuals differ. A child may rattle off a tiny gem which one teacher brushes aside because it doesn't rhyme, while another teacher may lavish praise on it. Quality in writing comes only after many experiments and struggles with the use of words. Children have to manipulate and explore words just as they do paint. Quality comes in painting after many stages of development. So it is in creative writing and the teacher must recognize each stage as a developmental one. Quality is an end result and teachers of creative writing are more interested in what the writing does for the child than in the quality of the product.

Susan, at the age of five, called a dandelion a "flower penny." At the age of seven, in the second grade she wrote: "At one time all the flowers grew in my lawn. But King Midas turned them all to golden dandelions."

At nine, in the fourth grade, she wrote:

> *In the morning when the yellow stars die*
> *Then they drop out of the sky*
> *In the morning the stars are gone*
> *They are dandelions on my lawn.*

Who is to say which is quality? The wonderful thing is that Susan's teachers have kept Susan writing and writing!

This is not to say that teachers should not be constantly working to improve quality in the creative writing of children, but it serves as a reminder that quality is difficult to judge. It is developmental and varies with the abilities and experiential background of each child. One of the best ways to improve quality in creative writing is to provide a planned, rich program in oral expression in the classroom. Teachers can work with each child to help him develop his own abilities. Every idea suggested in the last chapter and in this chapter is included because the author found: (1) the ideas kept children writing and (2) they helped improve the quality of creative written expression when used daily.

KINDS OF WRITING

There are basically two kinds of writing: the practical and the creative. Burrows, Ferebee, Jackson and Saunders distinguish between them as follows:

> . . . We recognize that there are two fundamental kinds of writing. One is practical, the other personal. There is a gratifying sense of power that comes to any individual when he can fulfill the practical writing demands of his own life, whether it be the first brief direction that goes from school or the lengthy treatise that terminates an original study. And even more telling in its expansive effect is the personal writing that wells up out of the depths of the spirit.[1]

Practical writing deals with those formal matters of communication which must be taken care of in order to function socially in a culture: the writing of invitations, formal business letters, notes of appreciation, thanks and the like. This is not to say that these types of communications cannot be creative. Indeed, they can, but the form and formality of the message is more likely to communicate the basic message because it is an accepted cultural form.

It is when we add a heart and mind to writing that it becomes creative. When children begin to coin words, when they manipulate and explore them, when they begin to draw analogies, when they see relationships in their environment and draw comparisons in word experiences, when they paint word pictures and become unique and novel in expressing themselves, we have creative writing.

Creative writing may well be illustrated by Sharon's description of her dream.

---

1. A. T. Burrows et al., *They All Want To Write* (rev. ed.; Englewood Cliffs, N.J.: Prentice-Hall, 1962), p. 2.

My Dream Knight and I

*I was walking on a rainbow when I met this handsome
knight. He was gleaming in armor of gold and silver. He
had two stallions. One was black the other was white. He
asked me to ride on the white horse. Then a mean knight
came up and hurt my love. After a long while he got well.
Then I woke up out of the daze, just as we were going to get
married.*

Sharon
Grade 4

Practical writing may best be illustrated by Nancy's letter.

Dear Dr. Smith,

You made me think that school is fun. I liked the story
about The Three Bears especially when baby bear said Burp!
I thought that was very funny. It was fun acting out things.
Hope you can come again.

Sincerely yours,
Nancy Graupman
Grade 3

This author feels there is a third kind of writing—one that com-
bines the two, as shown in this second grade letter from Jonathan
(see also page 13).

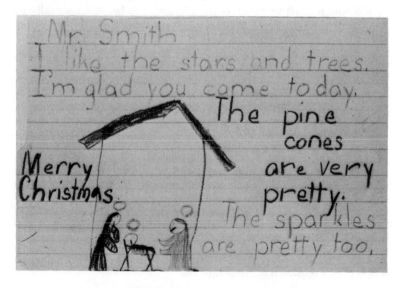

FIGURE 6-1. *Jonathan's letter.*

PURPOSES OF CREATIVE WRITING

Four basic purposes for creative writing follow:

1. It gives the child opportunity to express his own intimate thoughts and feelings concerning experiences with which he comes in contact.
2. It makes provisions for those children who possess literary talent to secure encouragement and appropriate instructions.
3. It arouses and maintains a sensitiveness to, an interest in and an appreciation of good literature.
4. It is more conducive to the development of language ability than are traditional procedures.

In this chapter we will discuss ways by which teachers may set conditions for developing creative writing.

NATURAL CONDITIONS FOR DEVELOPING CREATIVE WRITING

There are many situations and experiences in the daily program which provide a natural stimulation to creative writing. These should be utilized to the fullest. No matter how clever the teacher, she will eventually need to remotivate the children in order to give them added stimulation and impetus for writing. It is then that she resorts to other methods—contrived situations in which the spark is fanned so it flames in new colors and new word pictures.

Some problems which the teacher must consider in setting natural conditions for developing creative writing are as follows:

1. *What are the characteristics of good topics for creative writing other than open-endedness?* The topics should, obviously, be on the interest level of the children for whom they are chosen. They should be challenging, unusual or as original as possible. A topic such as "The Cow" is less likely to challenge a child than a topic such as "The Singing Cow" or "The Cow Nobody Loved." When a teacher suggests topics there should be many options for the children except in unusual cases where all write on one topic. And, a child should always be allowed to write on a topic of his own choosing rather than the options presented by the teacher. Teachers can get clues for topics by listening to the conversation of the children, especially when they first come to school in the morning and while they are at play on the playground. Topics should be selected which deal with all the senses and which can be highly personalized by each child. This chapter offers many ideas for choosing a wide range of appealing topics.

2. *How can the teacher present the topic in a motivating way?* In all the illustrations given in this volume, care has been taken to emphasize the fact that most creative writing should grow out of the interests and experiences of the children. When the teacher capitalizes on children's interests, the "natural" conditions mentioned above are in effect and little preparation or motivation is needed. Consider how naturally the teachers who utilized a "teachable" moment led the children into a creative writing situation in the presentation of the May Day program as told on pages 28–29 and the classic oral expression period by Miss Crane described on pages 147–48.

Samples of strategies which were contrived by the teacher to stimulate a creative writing situation were exemplified in the account on page 35 of Miss Brown's utilization of sounds to motivate children, in the way the teacher on page 143 used words such as *happiness* to stimulate creative ideas, by the manner in which teachers used pictures in Chapter V, in the story of "The Blindmen and the Elephant" on page 165 in which Miss Gentry carefully planned a motivation for her lesson, and in the rocket poem lesson created by Miss Parrott on page 177. All of these are samples of strategies used by teachers to present various topics in interesting ways. Many more examples follow (see pages 213, 219, 227, and 230).

3. *How does the teacher deal with the non-self-starter?* A reference to page 24 will show that the author stresses that part of the creative teaching process is the withdrawal of the teacher at a certain time which allows the children to go ahead by themselves. A shifting of roles takes place at this time. The teacher plays a subordinate role as guide, helper, encourager and supporter rather than leader. Because most children will begin to write if highly motivated, at this time the teacher is freed to work with those who do not immediately go to work. The teacher should wait awhile, recognizing that these children may be in their incubation period and realizing also that some children need longer incubation periods than others. If a group of children does not appear to be motivated, she may go quietly to each one and ask each child to meet with her in a group in the rear of the room. If only one or two are not responding, she may sit with them and talk quietly to them.

In either case, the teacher must respect the fact that a "creative" mood may be very necessary in order for some children to write and they will produce little of worth if they do not feel properly oriented.

Some options are suggested here for ways of dealing with the children who have difficulty getting under way.

Listen to each child's reason for not writing. If he says he doesn't feel like it, have other tasks from which he can choose such as finishing another assignment, reading a book or story, helping with some classroom task such as making a vocabulary chart for the following week, etc.

If he is having trouble getting started but wants to write, ask such questions as: (a) "Can't you find the right words?" (If this is his problem, help him by suggesting words or making word lists together.) (b) "Is there no topic which interests you?" (If this is his problem help him to choose a topic or suggest he write on how he feels now—when someone has asked him to do something he does not want to do.) (c) "Would you like to write alone, later?" (If this is his problem help him to arrange his schedule so that he may work at something else now but may go off in a corner sometime later to write by himself.)

4. *How does the teacher adjust to different writing speeds?* Obviously, all children will not finish their creative writing together. Some will want days, others will need only minutes. In open classrooms where children have learned to schedule themselves for most of the day this is no problem. In more traditionally organized classrooms it is wise for the teacher to follow any creative writing "period" by a work period where children may go to work on their own and work at assignments they can complete themselves and in comparative quiet, thus giving the majority of the class the opportunity to complete their writing undisturbed.

In some instances teachers have scheduled self-instructional periods immediately after creative writing. Others have no set creative writing period but allow the children to write any time they feel moved and have free time during the day. The children, in this case, sometimes experience a session together where motivation is gained, then most of the children go to work while group 1 meets with the teacher for reading (or some other) instruction. The fault of this plan is that the high motivation which is established may well be diluted or lost by the time group 1 gets around to writing.

Other teachers have planned creative writing periods before reading periods, library periods, study periods and the like so that children may run over the time allotted with a minimum of confusion and disorganization.

5. *How is the editorial procedure conducted?* It has been mentioned that one sound idea for editorial procedures may be found on pages 296–97.

6. *What about recopying?* No author writes his first draft in a beautiful and flawless manner. He works and rewords his product until he is satisfied with it. Then it is ready for the typist or the

publisher and as a social courtesy he types or writes his manuscript in such a manner that it looks its best. To be realistic about writing manuscripts, children (junior authors) should be allowed the privileges of senior authors and should be encouraged to write their first drafts in such a manner that they can be worked over, edited and chopped up. Once.the writing reads exactly as the child and his editors want it, it should be copied in the child's best handwriting (or typed) to be posted on a class bulletin board or published in a school newspaper or magazine.

7. *Should children share their creative products?* Only if they want to. Some of the most beautiful writing I have had from children was that slipped under my door at home or in a drawer in my desk at school. It was obviously to be shared with no one but me. I respected the child's wishes and we shared a secret together. To handle this situation without causing embarrassment to the child, I always kept on my desk two letter boxes, one labeled "To Be Shared with the Class," and the other labeled "For Mr. Smith." I explained early in the school year that the children who had something to share with the class in any way—that is, something to put on a bulletin board, something to read or something to use in the school paper—would put it in box 1, but those who had written something just for me—an arithmetic assignment, a handwriting practice sheet, a poem or a story—would put it in box 2. In this way I was able to respect the child's wishes and keep him in my confidence. Using the file folder system described on pages 296–97 also enabled me to communicate with him without speaking to him before the entire class.

Part of the joy of creating is sharing the product. Sharing periods should be planned except for such instances as those mentioned above. Sharing periods can take on many creative forms, however. Instead of a child reading his creations before the class, he may want to read them on a tape while a buddy supplies sound effects or music; some may prefer to dramatize their products or present them in choral speaking. The presentation may be as creative as the product.

NATURAL WAYS TO MOTIVATE CHILDREN TO CREATIVE WRITING

1. Writing autobiographies.
2. Keeping diaries.
3. Writing poems or stories of children's experiences.
4. Writing jokes.
5. Making up tall tales.

6. Writing pen-pal letters.
7. Making poems for birthday cards, mother's day cards.
8. Writing announcements for reading over the loud-speaker system. In some schools, each grade has the responsibility for the first ten minutes of every day to use the loud speaker to pipe messages, announcements and an opening exercise into each room.

Some Ways to Bring Creativity to Ideas You Already Are Using

1. Label pictures brought in by the children as they are mounted for the bulletin board. Instead of labeling a picture with an obvious caption such as "The Snow Storm," work with the children to get words which catch the exact flavor of the picture. One first grade child wrote this of a picture depicting a heavy snowfall:

IN YOUR CLASSROOM HAVE A *WRITER'S CORNER* SET OFF FROM THE ROOM BY A SCREEN

WRITE RADIO, TELEVISION AND SCREEN PLAYS

KEEP A *VOCABULARY CHART* ENTER ALL NEW WORDS WHERE CHILDREN MAY *SEE* THEM

KEEP *DICTIONARIES* AND BOOKS ABOUT *WORDS* EASILY AVAILABLY

FIGURE 6-2. *Ideas that set conditions for creative writing.*

FIGURE 6-3. *A fourth grade edits its creative writing for a school yearbook (pages from the yearbook below and right).*

*Last night I went to
sleep and I awoke in
a silent, white city.*

2. Little children can dictate stories to the teacher who can type them with a primary typewriter or put them on chart paper. When the teacher reads the story back to the children it can be illustrated as a reading chart or bound with others to make big books.

3. Build word charts by taking a well-known word and making as many words from it as possible. After a driving rainstorm, a fourth grade constructed this chart of words.

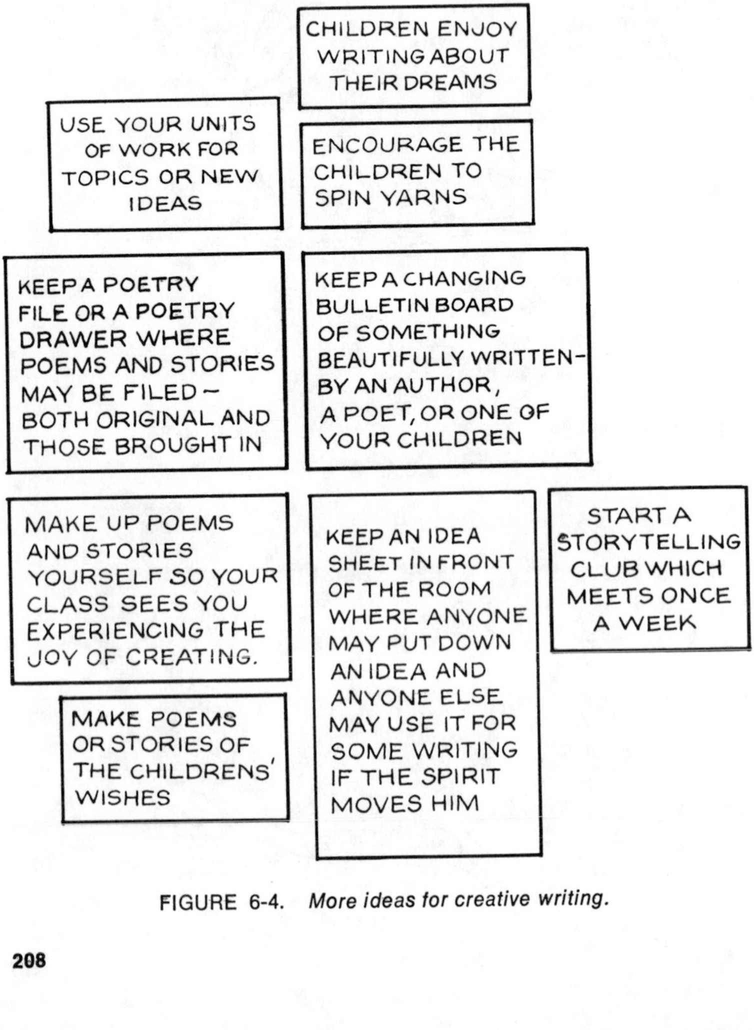

CHILDREN ENJOY
WRITING ABOUT
THEIR DREAMS

USE YOUR UNITS
OF WORK FOR
TOPICS OR NEW
IDEAS

ENCOURAGE THE
CHILDREN TO
SPIN YARNS

KEEP A POETRY
FILE OR A POETRY
DRAWER WHERE
POEMS AND STORIES
MAY BE FILED –
BOTH ORIGINAL AND
THOSE BROUGHT IN

KEEP A CHANGING
BULLETIN BOARD
OF SOMETHING
BEAUTIFULLY WRITTEN–
BY AN AUTHOR,
A POET, OR ONE OF
YOUR CHILDREN

MAKE UP POEMS
AND STORIES
YOURSELF SO YOUR
CLASS SEES YOU
EXPERIENCING THE
JOY OF CREATING.

KEEP AN IDEA
SHEET IN FRONT
OF THE ROOM
WHERE ANYONE
MAY PUT DOWN
AN IDEA AND
ANYONE ELSE
MAY USE IT FOR
SOME WRITING
IF THE SPIRIT
MOVES HIM

START A
STORYTELLING
CLUB WHICH
MEETS ONCE
A WEEK

MAKE POEMS
OR STORIES OF
THE CHILDRENS'
WISHES

FIGURE 6-4.   *More ideas for creative writing.*

Rain

rainstorm	rainfall	raincoat
rain water	rainy	raindrop
rain check	rainbow	

4. Place something soft, or something rough, or something sticky in a bag. Pass it around and encourage the children to put a hand in the bag and feel it. Then have them write about how it felt.

5. Have the children make a string painting. (This is a painting made by dipping string in paint and laying it on or folding it on paper.) Have them write what they see in the abstraction.

6. *Get well cards:* Children can make their own cards, write letters or prepare surprises for a sick classmate who is absent. A chart is made of the number of days the student is apt to be absent. An envelope containing a number of the cards is mailed every day, so the sick child receives a packet of cards every day he is away from school. These cards and letters can be a strong motivation for some very creative writing.

7. *Passing notes:* The teacher can capitalize creatively on the children's natural desire to pass notes to each other. A mailbox can be constructed from an old carton—especially one which has separate sections (such as a paste carton). Children are then assigned a box, and are encouraged to write notes to each other and to the teacher and to mail them. The notes are distributed just before the children go home. This gives the teacher a chance to write special notes, assignments or suggestions to children who need them most.

8. Have each child write a description of another child. The description should include five clues. Then the composition is read to the rest of the children who try to guess who he is describing.

9. Have each child write about himself—physical appearance, likes, dislikes, hobbies, etc., but his name should be written only on the *back* of the paper. The descriptions are then read and posted on the bulletin board so that all may guess the subject. Looking on the back is permitted only as a last resource.

TOPICS FOR CREATIVE WRITING

The joy of being creative is that you can write about anything or nothing, and in most any manner you like. You can write serious

WRITE A *WORD PICTURE*
OF THE KIND OF MUSIC
WHICH COMES FROM EACH
MUSICAL INSTRUMENT OR
THE ORCHESTRA AS A WHOLE

TALKING POEMS
WRITE AS THOUGH
YOU WERE TALKING
TO SOMEONE

WRITE POEMS OF
WONDER
AND F E A R

PLAN TO MAKE A
CLASS YEARBOOK

POEMS AND STORIES CAN
ALWAYS BE WRITTEN ABOUT
HOLIDAYS AND *SPECIAL DAYS*

FIGURE 6-5. *Children can dramatize stories they love. Also, the teacher can present the children with a situation and they can plan an impromptu dramatization using a few simple props. Here a girl has been accused of cheating on an exam. Empathy and feeling was strong and helped introduce emotion words in meaningful context.*

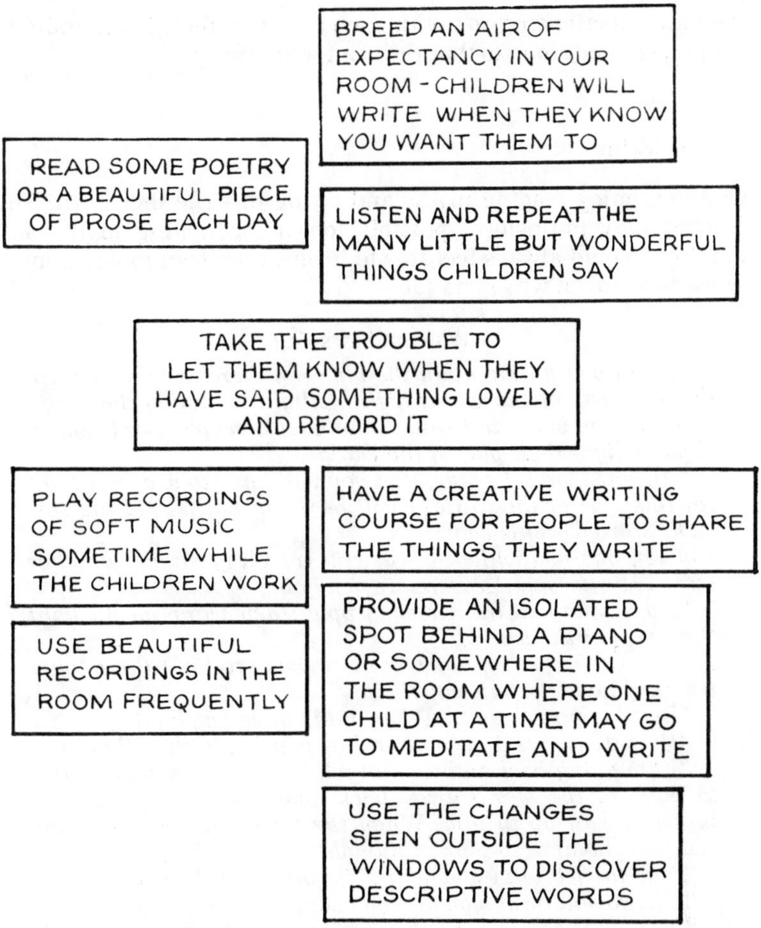

BREED AN AIR OF
EXPECTANCY IN YOUR
ROOM - CHILDREN WILL
WRITE WHEN THEY KNOW
YOU WANT THEM TO

READ SOME POETRY
OR A BEAUTIFUL PIECE
OF PROSE EACH DAY

LISTEN AND REPEAT THE
MANY LITTLE BUT WONDERFUL
THINGS CHILDREN SAY

TAKE THE TROUBLE TO
LET THEM KNOW WHEN THEY
HAVE SAID SOMETHING LOVELY
AND RECORD IT

PLAY RECORDINGS
OF SOFT MUSIC
SOMETIME WHILE
THE CHILDREN WORK

HAVE A CREATIVE WRITING
COURSE FOR PEOPLE TO SHARE
THE THINGS THEY WRITE

PROVIDE AN ISOLATED
SPOT BEHIND A PIANO
OR SOMEWHERE IN
THE ROOM WHERE ONE
CHILD AT A TIME MAY GO
TO MEDITATE AND WRITE

USE BEAUTIFUL
RECORDINGS IN THE
ROOM FREQUENTLY

USE THE CHANGES
SEEN OUTSIDE THE
WINDOWS TO DISCOVER
DESCRIPTIVE WORDS

FIGURE 6-6.   *Starter offers for creative writing.*

stories or nonsense poems. You can try limericks, riddles or book reports. All that is really needed is that skill of writing, a good open-ended situation and creative conditions under which you may work!

On the following pages I have listed many topics used by teachers everywhere to excite children to write. The results of their choices are evidenced in the sample writings accompanying the topics.

The secret of stimulating effective creative writing is simple: (1) encourage children to write about *their* experiences—and they are experiencing *something* every day of their lives, and (2) set proper conditions so that they can write freely.

Writing Myths

Children enjoy reading myths and trying to write their own. The teacher may brainstorm possible topics for writing myths and children should always feel free to invent their own topics. Jimmy chose to write on why stars fall.

Why the Stars Fall

Once upon a time up in the blue sky there lived a star. He lighted parts of the world with his light. One day the moon came to the star, and said, "The Greek people want you to come to light their part of the world."

"Alright," said the star, "but you will have to use your light for this part of the world. I will be going now," said the star as he started on his way.

Then one day while he was still traveling he met another star. The star said, "Where are you going?"

"I am going to the Greek people, they want me to light their part of the world."

"The Greek people don't need anybody to light their country, they have the sun now."

"But the moon said that they didn't have any light."

"He was just trying to get rid of you," said the other star.

"I am going back to him and tell him that he can't do this to me," so the star started back again. When he saw the moon he ran up to him. When the moon saw him he said, "Oh are you here so soon? I thought I got rid of you."

"No, not yet, but I will get rid of you," said the star.

"Oh, do you think you are big enough?"

"Yes," said the star. So they started to fight. The moon still had the light and it was still very hot, so the moon threw the hot light at him and it hit the star. The star caught on fire and then to make matters worse the moon came over to the star and pushed him. He fell down from the sky toward the earth he went, down, down, down until he burnt out. Ever since that time people speak of falling stars.

Myth of Greece

I am going to tell you a story about a country which makes me feel hungry, everyday I think of it. It is called Greece.

One day an old woman was expecting royal company. And all she had in the house was a pan of bread dough and a can of grease. So wanting to make something special, she fried pieces of the dough in the grease and coated them with sugar. These looked like large brown nuts, so she called them doughnuts.

That is how Greece came to be the first country to make doughnuts.

Writing to Music

Teachers have often played mood music and asked children to write about it. It is generally a fruitful idea as indicated by these poems.

Record: La Mer
Response: Marcia, Grade 4

La Mer Music

I feel like I am at the seashore alone. The waves are going in and out. While I was sitting there the waves made a loud noise. As the waves came in they crashed. And the noise went back to the ocean.

Record: La Mer
Response: Kathy, Grade 4

How I Feel

It's in old poor China Town at night. The winds are playing little tunes; the ocean comes up and hits the little China Town docks. The sky should be getting lighter but it gets darker and darker. When China Town wakes up the waves are slapping against the rocks blowing spray everywhere. Everyone is terrified, the people of China Town are running out of their houses atop the steep hillsides. The ocean is very rough now. The cliffs on the hillsides are breaking now. The clouds are getting blacker. The storm breaks and the thunder and lightning come down like never before. "Watch out, watch out," the waves seem to be saying. There is a great flood. Just then a huge wave strikes the village. It is the last one. And rising in the sky is a beautiful rainbow.

Writing Mini-Poems

A highly motivating device for beginning poetry is to engage the children in writing mini-poems. Like haiku, mini-poems are short and expound one idea in a simple way. Unlike haiku, they are unstructured. The following mini-poems came from a first grade.

Ear muffs are fun to wear
If you want to take care,
Of your ears!

Bells go jing-a-ling
And all the people sing.

STEVEN ALEX and
BRIAN FITCH

We like to ride in a snowmobile,
Sometimes we get to turn the wheel.
It's fun to ride in a snowmobile!

I like to roll,
In the snow,
I like to roll
Down hills,
I like to roll
In the snow,
But sometimes I get chills!

SUSAN DOUBLEDAY

Foam

Little rain drops,
I saw you yesterday,
Running down the trumbling
summer waves.

SHIRLEY WIGGAND
Grade 4

Famous Men

Famous men or famous people inspire some children to write. Often national heroes provide a strong motivation for some children to express their feelings, but historians, poets and athletes also do it.

Longfellow's Work

As he sits in his home
Working night and day,
He makes up poems
To make children gay.
As he strokes his beard

> *To think up a rhyme,*
> *He does this fast*
> *And goes to the next line.*
> *His poems make sense*
> *And are interesting too*
> *His parents were proud of him*
> *As yours would be of you.*

DONALD PANKO
Grade 5

Science Topics

One spring day I went to visit a third grade. I was planning to do a demonstration lesson in creative writing for some teachers in the school. When I arrived the children were in an unbelievable state of excitement. A butterfly had just emerged from a cocoon Dale had brought to school three weeks before.

To attempt to divert their attention to anything I had planned was unrealistic so I took advantage of their high motivation and used the butterfly as the base of my creative writing lesson. Within ten minutes the following poem appeared on the chalkboard.

The Big Surprise

> *One day about three weeks ago,*
> *Dale brought in a cocoon to show.*
> *It was brown and withered and dry.*
> *Would a butterfly hatch?*
> *We thought we'd try.*
>
> *What a surprise on the first day of spring,*
> *A butterfly came out and spread his wing.*
> *And made us think of a flower in bloom,*
> *And we did have a surprise in our very own room!*
>
> *On his wings were two velvet eyes,*
> *It looked like a caterpillar had on a disguise.*
> *How could he spin himself into a leaf,*
> *And come out colorful as an Indian chief?*
>
> *What a surprise for Mr. Smith in spring,*
> *To see a butterfly spread his beautiful wings.*

After I left the classroom, many children continued the creative writing begun that day. They sent me copies of their poems. I have included some here:

Butterfly

Butterfly, butterfly,
How do you fly?

Spread out your wings,
Open your eyes,
Lift up your feet,
And start to fly.

DALE C.

How Do You Know?

Oh butterfly with yellow wing,
How do you know when it is spring?

How do you know when to hatch,
And on your wing, a purple patch.

I hate to see you fly away,
But you'll come back some autumn day.

CAROL B.

Current events in science can be a source of inspiration to some children.

The Backside of the Moon

The backside of the moon,
*   Is really a scary place,*
While you're looking down upon,
*   the moon's colorless face.*

It is almost like a beach,
*   with footprints in the sand.*
And you're still looking at
*   this vast untaken land.*

You are unable to get in touch
*   with the people at home you know.*
Unable to let them see
*   this big, mysterious show.*

SUE O'SHAUGHNESSY

Mystery Stories

Divergent thinking is the base for all creative acts. It is promoted by open-ended situations which demand *many possible* answers or a few logical answers rather than one *correct* answer. Mystery stories are creative, divergent thinking, open-ended situations where facts are continually being reworked into new possible solutions. Highly creative children enjoy writing mystery stories.

Alvin drew the picture below and Audrey wrote, "The Mystery at the Old Mill" to go with it.

FIGURE 6-7. *The Old Mill.*

Impossible Things

Sometimes things you don't see make interesting poems.

Did You Ever . . . ?
Did you ever,
See a snail
Carrying a pail?

Did you ever,
Cross half a tomato
With half a potato?

Did you ever,
Ride across a moat
On the back of a goat?

Did you ever,
Try to knit
Wearing a mitt?

Did you ever,
Fall on an egg
And break your leg?

Did you ever,
Rock in a chair
With a bear?

Did you ever. . . .
NEVER!

LISA MCSWEENEY

Nature

Children enjoy writing about all aspects of nature, and will often illustrate their creations.

Birds

"Think," said John.
"Think," said Jane,
Sitting on the garden fence.
Talking one day.
Think about the birds;
The way they grow.
They don't have long legs
At all, you know.
They don't have big ears
At all, you know.
Aren't birds funny
The way they grow!

BRIGETTE FOEDER
Grade 3

FIGURE 6-8. *"Birds" by Bridgette.*

Spring

Along with flowers comes the rain,
Pitter patter on my window pane.
The birds are building their nests
After a long winter's rest.
And when we see the green grass grow
Spring is here, we know.

CYNTHIA CORRENTE

Rhyming Endings

Rhyming endings are much fun for children. Rhyming sounds at the ends of words can be placed at the top of a card, and the children, collectively or singly, can brainstorm for words that sound like the key word.

In a second grade room I saw these charts made and used by the children:

found	place	Billy	day
ground	face	silly	play
pound	disgrace	chilly	say
around	race	frilly	gay

mound	pace	hilly	lay
sound		Milly	May
		Willy	pay
			ray
			way

Some of the poems resulting from use of these charts follow:

Rain

Today it's raining all around
See the puddles on the ground
After the rain goes away
We can go outside to play.

My Horse Billy

My horse gallops all around
My horse acts just like a clown
Even if he does act silly
I still love my horse Billy.

The Funny Clown

A clown jumps from place to place
With a funny painted face.
He gets himself in a fix
When he does his funny tricks.

Other types of phonics poems can be contrived by using the sounds which children use to communicate but which are not words, such as *grrr* to show what the lion says or *clang, clang* such as the fire engine says.

Spring

Spring is a wonderful month!
Hippty, hippty, hump!
It's so much fun,
'cause you can play and run.
Hippty, hippty, hump.

BONNIE
Grade 3

Children in a sight-saving class who rely on an acute hearing ability are often very sensitive to sounds, more so than the average child. One sight-saving class brainstormed for words that described the apple then sent me the list with the "sound" line at the end.

The Apple
The apple is: wholesome, juicy, sweet, red, rosy, ruby, tarty, tangy, lively, meaty, yummy, candy sweet, ripe, scrumptious, crunchy, crisp, munchy, cidery, pazaze, fruity, healthy and furthermore. . . . .
CRUNCH!! MUNCH-CHOP-SLURP SMACK!

Nonsense Rhymes and Stories

Clever, creative ideas may be expressed in nonsense rhymes as observed below:

> *Once there was a shoe*
> *Who said "I always walk with you."*
>
> > PAM
> > *Grade 2*

> *I once saw some llamas*
> *That were in pyjamas.*
>
> > CATHY
> > *Grade 3*

Social Studies

Topics in the social studies often supply enough interest so that some good writing may result:

What America Means to Me
America is a free country
You say anything you please!
You worship as you please.
You speak what you think is right.
In America you do anything you like.
Some people think you can break laws like: killing,
*   shooting, breaking windows, stealing, robbing.*
These are easy rules to follow,
But every thing else you can do.
You can go to school and get an education instead of some-
*   one saying "Get out, this is just for rich people. Or if*
*   you're walking on the sidewalk no one stops and tells*
*   you to walk in the street.*
Nobody really knows what the Statue of Liberty means, I
*   think it means this:*

This is the land of the free. The land of Good Will—
Where all people are treated equal.
For no man is different, the rich or the poor.
God bless America the land of the free.
Where all men are treated equal and fair.

PETER
Grade 6

Changes

Boy, have times changed!
Remember those Western days.
When stagecoaches were stopped.
And taken somewhere else.
Now, we are flying over bays.
Being hi-jacked to Cuba and not
Getting back for days.

The train took over the stagecoach.
The plane took over the train.
The rocket will take over the plane.
And who knows what will take
Over the rocket?

MARK STRICKLAND
Grade 6

Washington's Attack

The Hessian soldiers across the Delaware,
  Were by their fires and warmly clad,
While Washington's soldiers tried to keep from freezing.
  And used what clothes they had.

It was taking a great dare,
  Washington's soldiers took that night,
To cross the freezing Delaware,
  But they knew that victory would be bright.

And then with a sudden surprise,
  Washington's soldiers came upon them,
And you could hear the shouts and cries,
  Then, Victory, Victory was the cry of Washington's men.

GORDON CLEGY
Grade 5

Words for Tunes

Although writing new words for established tunes is not the highest form of creativity it is, nonetheless, a simple form of creativity and can be a springboard for more sophisticated types of writing.

This poem, composed in a third grade, was a great source of enjoyment to the class.

Halloween Ideas

(*Song Tune: "Sing a Song of Sixpence"*)

First you take a pumpkin
 Orange and round and fat
Then you cut the top off
 That makes a hat.
Take a knife and hollow out
 mouth and nose and eyes.
There a Jack-o-Lantern stands
 A very great surprise.

Everyday Things

That children like to write about everyday things can best be shown by allowing the children's poetry to speak for itself.

Grandma's Knitting

Grandma is sitting
Doing her knitting
Kitty has the yarn
I hope she'll do no harm.

Scott
Grade 1

Fire Drill

When we have a fire drill,
You'll be safe if you will
Always be alert and ready
Keep the line moving steady.

Warren
Grade 2

Pussy Willow! Pussy Willow!
Pretty! Pretty! Pretty!
Kitty! Kitty! Kitty!
Come out, come out
And play with me—
No! I have more fun
Playing on the willow tree!

Sayra
Grade 1

Humor

Creative children have a wonderful sense of humor. Their humor at times may vary greatly from the humor of adults, but if we understand their humor, we enjoy it. In the classroom, common use of oral and written humor can do much more than build good rapport between teacher and students. It can develop creative imagination in expression and a certain amount of wit. Wit is a result of good thinking plus an opportune moment. Witty remarks and a good sense of humor provide a means of creative communication and promote a type of social relationship in the classroom that no other form of expression can accomplish.

Paul and Patricia, ages ten and eleven, were infatuated with each other. One noon hour, while eating their lunch directly after a class discussion of Yellowstone National Park, the teacher overheard this conversation:

Pat: Paul, you know you remind me of Old Faithful!
Paul: Yeah, why?
Pat: Just a little squirt!

The children within hearing distance guffawed at this, but Paul hesitated but a minute and retaliated with: "Oh, wise guy-ser, huh?"

Such wholesome, challenging interplay of words sharpens the child's ability to speak and express himself. The sense of humor in children is a joyous thing to be protected and encouraged. All creative children have it.

Teachers can promote humor in a variety of ways. Many funny stories should be read together and enjoyed. Funny situations should be dramatized. Good jokes, geared to the level of humor the child appreciates, should be shared daily. And the funny things children think should be written on paper or painted.

In other parts of this volume the humor of children has been shown. Here are a few samples from the middle grades.

The Ghost

The ghost is creeping
Up the old broken steps
Of the old dark house
Wakening all the ghosts
With a yell—and—
Oops! he fell!

EILEEN
Grade 4

Interlude

A cold, dark night—
The moon above
A sigh—
A de—ep breath—
Ah ——— love?
No. ——— Skunk!

JIM
Grade 6

My Garden

In my garden I grow many flowers
There is a bug that will kill all my flowers
In three or four hours,
I wish I could do something about that bug.
I think I will ask the maid
For a can of RAID.

EILEEN
Grade 4

Poetry as Imagery

Gold

Standing high on a hill
Looking down upon all
Stands a tall and handsome tree
Letting fall her golden leaves
They lie at her feet
Making a golden path
For all to see.

PHYLLIS D.
Grade 6

Sleet Storm

White fingers waving to the freeze—
Heavy trees on bended knees
Road of glass, sky so gray
Such a gloomy, lovely day!

MARION B.
Grade 6

Expressing Emotions

Most children choose one art form as their particular means of emotional release. Whatever the form, the teacher should encourage each child to develop his potential in this area in his own way, for he will find enjoyment and satisfaction through the use of this medium throughout life. That many children do secure emotional release through their writings is evidenced by much of the writing reproduced above and below.

Some teachers take a great deal of time to develop the "feeling" concept because good literature creates a feeling or mood in the reader. Children discuss how they felt when the fire bell rang, or when they were late, or their reactions to their first airplane ride. Vocabulary to express these feelings is developed by the teacher and children working together. When children write, it is with poetic charm.

When a teacher recognizes and encourages release of tensions, anxieties and frustrations through any sort of media, she is guiding her children to an emotional maturity they cannot gain when their problems build up within them to hostile feelings toward the world. Hostile feelings, feelings of fear and aggressiveness or feelings of insecurity need not result in negative behavior. Channeled into constructive forms of expression, they can produce good for the individual and his society.

The classroom abounds in natural situations from day to day where constructive forms of expression may be developed. Children who are encouraged to write will soon write everything that they feel.

CONTRIVED METHODS OF SETTING CONDITIONS FOR CREATIVE WRITING

The teacher must plan many ways to bring new words to the child's oral vocabulary and make them an integral part of his common speech. To build a colorful yet common vocabulary, teachers will need to go beyond the use of the natural ways of developing creative writing and contrive ways to put new colorful words into the oral and written vocabulary of their students.

The WRITE Way to Teach

Just as children enjoy playing and experimenting with words on an oral basis, they must experiment and play with words on paper.

Here are some interesting ways to help children become experimental with words.

How would you say it? From the time that children first learn to read they come across phrases which appear again and again in their reading to the point where they almost become meaningless. Groups of words like "the starry sky," "pretty as a picture," "the silvery moon," "sweet as a rose," "the desert sands," "the whispering pines" and others are hackneyed and trite.

From their early years, teachers can alert children to novel and colorful ways of expression by drawing attention to these phrases in their books and asking children to collect them. The teacher can then put an envelope on the bulletin board with the phrase, "How would YOU say it?" printed on it. Below it she can place a pile of five by eight cards. As children find these phrases, they come and write them on a card and place the card in the envelope. After several have been collected the teacher may use them as a springboard for a discussion on different ways of saying them. These new ways can be written on the back of each card. Then the teacher can encourage children to write the new ways of saying the phrases whenever they like—thus providing a stimulating independent activity. The new phrases will later appear in their creative writing.

On the back of a card which said, "the starry sky," a fifth grade girl wrote, "There in the heavens, the GREAT JEWELER spread all his diamonds on black velvet."

In a second grade a child wrote on the back of a card which said, "Pretty as a rose"—"As pretty as a newly washed baby."

A nine year old cub scout, recently returned from a camping trip, wrote this for "the silvery moon": "The moon was a flashlight in the sky."

Billy, in grade 3, took "sweet as a rose" and turned it into "sweet as peppermint fudge." When the teacher said, "Well, that's good but I never had peppermint fudge," Billy responded, "Well, neither did I, but I bet it's mighty sweet!" Billy is a scientist!

One excellent way to build a sensitivity to unusual words is to make a special chart. One fourth grade placed on this chart only big words which everyone in the class understood:

our $64,000 word chart

stratosphere
conscience

uncanny
abstract
realistic
astronaut
historical
eradicate

Make collections of happy sounds, sad sounds, loud sounds, friendly sounds, angry sounds and annoying sounds. These often turn out to be delightful poems. Here are a few samples:

Happy Sounds	Loud Sounds	Angry Sounds
Tee-hee	Ouch	Grrr
Ha-ha-ha	Eek	S-s-s-s
Ding-a-ling	Bam	R-r-ruff
Tra-la-la	Boo	Bop
Tinkle-tinkle	Click-clack	Biff
tra-la-la	Chug-chug	Bam

Writing Jingles

Using a standard reading pocket chart and some five by eight cards, have half the room write nouns (or words that tell things) and the other half write verbs (words that do things). Let one child put a verb in the chart. Leave a space before and after it big enough to hold other five by eight cards. Then ask for a verb that rhymes with the first one. Match verbs in this manner until several rhyming verbs are placed on the chart. Then have the children who wrote nouns insert them before the verbs where they make sense. In one first grade this is what happened:

Bubbles	pop	Rabbits	hop
Babies	cry	Flowers	die
Horses	prance	Children	dance
Worms	wiggle	Girls	giggle

This idea was adapted from a suggestion made in *Helping Children Write* by Mauree Applegate, Evanston, Ill.: Row, Peterson, 1954.

Writing Haiku Poems

Haiku is a form of Japanese poetry which is structured in the following pattern: the first line has five syllables, the second line has seven syllables and the last line has five syllables. Haiku is generally written about the seasons or about some simple bit of nature. It does not rhyme and is usually a beautiful idea expressed in this simple rhythmic pattern. Haiku is a good illustration of the fact that creativity does not mean that children must have complete freedom in which to create; creativity can take place (and does, in truth, most of the time) in structured situations.

Children will turn out haiku poems by the yard—from first grade through adulthood in fact. A simple way to start the young child is by giving him a dittoed paper wherein the syllables are indicated (or "beats" when I am talking to first graders) for each line.

Share with me one of the haiku poems children have submitted to me.

Pretty Wishing Star

Up there where you are
A pretty bright twinkling star
Don't go away, star.

LAURIE G.
Grade 3

Writing Cinquain Poetry

Cinquain poetry is an extension of haiku which children enjoy very much. Because it is structured it also demonstrates that creativity can be developed with restrictions.

Cinquain is easily presented when children are given a dittoed sheet marked as follows:

_____	(a word)
_____ _____	(2 describing words: adj.)
_____ _____ _____	(3 action words)
_____ _____ _____ _____	(a statement or 4 more adj.)
_____	(a synonym or describing word)

Or, the material may be presented as follows: On line 1 write a *topic*, on line 2 write two words that *describe* that topic, on line 3 give three words which tell *what* your topic does, on line 4 write four words that tell *why* or continue to describe it, on line 5 write a word that means the *same as* or *describes* the topic.

Here are some cinquains that Mr. Moses's class shared with me.

Feathers
Soft, light
Falling, blowing, flying.
How I like feathers
Nice.

TERRY WEILAND

Girls
Kissable, pretty,
Hopping, skipping, playing
Mean, dumb, nice, teasing
Girls.

TONY LIGOCI

Boys
Handsome, cute
Kissing, looking, watching
I love some boys,
Wonderful

CASOLEE FORGETS

Pipe Cleaner Compositions

Miss Barter, grade 2, gave each of the children two pipe cleaners and asked them to make something of them, then staple them to the top of a sheet of paper and write about them. Holly made a rabbit.

The Easter Rabbit

Once there was a rabbit and he wanted to be an Easter Rabbit. He didn't know how to get the eggs and so he was crying. But while Bunny was crying he kept one eye open to see if anyone was coming.

Buzz, buzz, buzz,! Honey bees were flying by on the way to their hive. As they flew, their wings made a soft buzzing noise. Then he went on walking all by himself.

A bird said, "Why are you crying?" The rabbit said, "I want to be an Easter Rabbit."

"A crybaby will not be an Easter Rabbit," said the bird. Be gay and sing and be happy. The rabbit sang and sang and was very happy.

HOLLY WILGUS

Jimmy made a dog:

My Dog

I have a white dog.
I call her Girlo,
She is so slow.
She's as slow as a burro.

But when she runs.
She is so fast.
I can hardly see her.
As she goes past.

JAMES LAW

Creating a Mood for Creative Writing

Special moods may be set as part of the conditioning for creative writing. Generally, writing done while children are in the mood produces groups of words not commonly used under other circumstances.

There are many ways a teacher may create moods:

1. By supplying various sounds.
2. By playing music.
3. By reading poetry or stories.
4. By drawing the shades.
5. By using an affected voice.
6. By dramatizing a scene.
7. By using a film.

Read Mary O'Neill's *Hailstones and Halibut Bones* to the children as a good example of setting a mood for creative writing. Most teachers find that poems seem to come naturally with children as a result of listening to this charming book.

Using music to set moods. The teacher can select musical recordings and ask the children to write what comes to mind as the music is playing. Later, these can be read while the music is played softly and the combination taped. During the playback, children will see how a mood can be created by the blending together of music and words. Unfamiliar music generally solicits more creative responses than familiar music in that children have no preconceived notions about unfamiliar music. Some popular recordings, as well as classical recordings, are excellent for this type of activity. The following are good:

"Tara's Theme"	Theme from *Helen of Troy*
"Summer Place Theme"	*Pictures at an Exhibition*
"Blue Star"	*Nutcracker* Suite
"Tracy's Theme"	

An elaboration of the activity in the chapter on oral expression (see page 172) may be carried out with the children writing poems on: "What is the most beautiful thing in the world," the saddest thing, etc. If the resulting poems and prose are especially sensitive to the music, children can read them to each other with musical backgrounds or tape them with the music. Lower the volume on the record player as each child reads his poem into the tape recorder but turn it up for a minute or two between the poems.

Using dramatics to set moods. Mood for creative writing may be established by use of dramatics.

Miss Frances, a sixth grade teacher, had a group of children meet with her before school one day. They planned to stage a scene which was kept secret from the rest of the class. In the middle of the morning, one of the members of the group who had left the room opened the door of the classroom and came rushing in.

"We're all excused," he exclaimed. "No school—we can all go home."

The three other members of the group immediately jumped to their feet and shouted. "Hurrah, we're going home." Before the stunned class could follow suit, Miss Frances said, "Boys and girls, this was a joke on you. Now we want you to write what you think happened and what you think you saw."

The resulting papers were fun to read. The variety of versions of what the children *thought* they saw was amazing.

Open-ended dramatics are a good stimuli for group or individual writing. The children give a play which stops before the climax and the other children, either individually or in groups, write the ending.

The class can also be divided into groups and each group given a paper sack with five unrelated objects. For the rest of the class, the children plan a skit in which they must use all five of the objects in the bag. Bags of objects may be kept in a closet and given to individual children in their free time to write stories which incorporate all five objects. It is interesting to see how the individuality of children shows in their writing about the same five objects.

Puppet plays, shadows plays, lap stories and role-playing all provide excellent opportunities for dramatic writing.

Using Specific Senses for Creative Writing

Literature, both prose and poetry, appeals to the reader when it touches his heart as well as his head. The "feeling" of a passage makes it memorable. Attempts to appeal to the senses of children help to develop "feeling" in their writing. Sometimes it is advantageous to dwell on one sense alone.

The sense of smell. Blindfold four or five children and let them hold your hand while you go to the office for something. Take them by a devious route and when you return let them: (1) tell where they have been and (2) how the smells they experienced made them feel. They will recognize the twang of the ditto ink as they went by the principal's office, the odors of cooking foods when passing the cafeteria, the smell of detergent as they passed the janitor's closet, your own perfume and the smell of perspiration in the gym.

Place objects, such as horse-radish, mustard, vinegar, ginger, vanilla, etc., on a tray. Blindfold the children and let them smell each item. Not only should they identify it but they should tell how it feels to them.

Mary Lou said, after sniffing horse-radish, "It felt as though I stuck my nose into a porcupine."

Peter, age 9, said about vinegar, "My jaws itched to be away from it."

Marcia, age 12, said about cloves, "They make me think of old things, like chandeliers, hoop skirts and pretty music. I felt old and long ago."

Children will also have fun collecting smells they like and putting them in poems, either collectively or individually.

One fourth grade wrote this one.

Smells We Like

I like the smell of an open rose.
I like the smell of fresh washed clothes
I like the smell of apple pies
I like the smell of tintex dyes!

A sixth grade wrote this about smells:

Smells

A smell can make you feel good . . . like:
The salty smell of the sea,

> *The fresh smell of the air,*
> *The smell of buttered popcorn*
> *For sale at the county fair.*
> *A smell can make you sad . . . like . . .*
> *The smell of funeral flowers*
> *The smell of a hospital hall.*
> *The smell of dying roses,*
> *A musty coat hung on the wall.*
> *A smell can make you lonely . . . like . . .*
> *The sickish smell of the hospital.*
> *The wet, damp smell of night.*
> *The smell of the fireplace burning*
> *On a frosty, icy night.*
> *A smell can make you glad . . . like . . .*
> *The smell of cooking dinners,*
> *The cold, crisp air of fall,*
> *And when mother's baking cookies*
> *Send their fragance down the hall.*

In a sixth grade, a teacher used two charts where children wrote phrases which they used in poems and stories written during the week. One set looked like this:

Smells Boys Like	*Smells Girls Like*
Fresh-baked bread	French perfume
Smoky campfires	Boiling soup
Wet, wet woods	Department stores
Hot apple pies	Hot apple pies
Hot buttered popcorn	Hot buttered popcorn
Fresh pigskin footballs	Newly washed babies
Hot pizza pies	Hot chocolate
Black, boiling tar	Lemon yellow lilies
New automobiles	Clean houses
After shave lotion	After shave lotion

Children can also draw analogies by stating their favorite smell on a card and adding what it reminds them of. Some fifth graders wrote these:

> *I like the smell of my mother's cologne*
> *It's like roses*
> *I like the smell of clean sheets*
> *It's like catching the wind and sun in a cloth.*
>
> *I like the smell of popping corn*
> *It reminds me of:*
> *Carnivals*

Circuses
Scout camp
And—evenings around the fireplace with my family
  —all buttoned in from the winter storm.

Children can also write sentences of smells, leaving blank a place to put in a descriptive word, such as:

1. The ———— smell of smoke.
2. The ———— smell of hot apple pies.
3. The ———— smell of pine trees.
4. The ———— odor of the skunk.
5. The ———— smell of gasoline.

A sixth grade teacher introduced many new words in this situation in trying to help the class find exactly *the* word which would express their feelings. After much discussion, they chose these phrases. Later, in their writing, they chose many of the other words which had been suggested.

1. The pungent smell of smoke.
2. The yummy smell of hot apple pies.
3. The tantalizing smell of the pine trees.
4. The nauseating odor of the skunk.
5. The haunting smell of gasoline.

Some excellent dictionary work resulted from this work with words.

The sense of hearing. Such trips as those mentioned above may be followed by "hearing" trips. Children can close their eyes and listen to sounds and try to guess where they have been. Also, open the windows on a warm day and let the children listen to the noises in the street. Then they can make up a story or a poem about what they have heard.

The sense of sight. Almost all the suggestions in this section rely on the sense of sight. There are many ways children can sharpen their observations to put what they see into words and eventually into their writing.

One project that has helped children to really see and compare is *The Window Trip.* From wherever he is sitting in the room, the child chooses a window. He notices carefully the scene which the window frames. He then thinks about the picture framed by the window, the way it makes him feel, how it makes him think. Then he writes about it and the teacher files the poems and stories. A few months later, he sits in the same place and writes about the same window. This he does about four times during the year. In the spring, the four observations are written into a booklet. The difference in the descriptions helps the children to see how different words help to describe the same scene at different times of the year. Even if the view out the window is a wall with a vine, it changes with the seasons, the light and the weather.

Sometimes a sign on the bulletin board can sharpen observation. The teacher says, "What do you see out our windows? Write it here." She provides five by eight cards for the children to write on and envelopes into which they may deposit their ideas.

This is what one child wrote about her "window picture."

*When I look out of my window
I see the pretty trees
With their nice green leaves—
It's summer then.*

*When I look out of my window
I see the pretty trees,
The trees are all dead—
It's winter then.*

*At night I go to bed
And when I wake up in the morning
And look out of my window
I see the pretty white snow.*

*When the snow has melted away
Then I can see the pretty
Green grass again—
It is spring, then.*

JANE
Grade 3

Other cards which can be used to motivate children to explore the senses are:

1. How does it feel to be green?
2. How does a Christmas tree feel when it is cut down?
3. How tall is truth?
4. What color is happiness?
5. Why is hurt like hunger?
6. What is electricity?
7. What is the taste of sorrow?
8. Where is hunger found?
9. How old is honesty?
10. What is happiness?

Often poems, stories, or little essays with strong, emotionally toned words result when children are persuaded to put their gripes or dislikes into words. Here are two examples of writing which resulted when a teacher asked the children to write about colors.

Purple

Purple is fruity,
Grapes are purple,
It's the color of lady's finger nails,
Also Granny's old fashion grape jam,
And bruises on a leg.

Purple is the binding of a book,
Also the eyes of a Teddy Bear,
Purple is yarn to make a picture,
And a flower called a Pansy,
Purple is a colored basket,
With designs on it.

JANE
Grade 5

Red

Red is a color in the sky.
Way up so high
The breast of a robin
A sweet cherry
A blazing fire
And a strawberry
Red's, turning leaves
A heart
A dainty
Cherry tart
Our blood
And some hair
Our lips
And steak that's too rare
Tulips and
One kind of crayon
Cherry juice and
A raspberry stain
Red's real bright
It's out of sight.

TERRY C.
Grade 7

Other Ways to Help Children Explore Feelings

1. Place a set of "I wonder" cards in an envelope on the bulletin board. Children may draw a card and write about it at any time.

I Wonder

I wonder how it feels to be an astronaut?
I wonder what a rainbow sees?
I wonder how Columbus felt when he saw America?
I wonder what kangaroos are thinking?
I wonder what it would be like to own ———?
What is poetry? fear? ice?

2. Similar to this are "How did you feel" cards:

How did you feel the day you discovered you were lost?	How did you feel the time you hit your brother?
How did you feel when you stepped on a snake?	How did you feel when your kitten died?
How did you feel when you were late for school?	How did you feel when your best friend moved?
How do you feel when you hear beautiful music?	How did it feel to have a shoe full of sand?

3. Choose a "feeling" word. Discuss it with the children. Apply it to a time of day. Encourage the children to write, using the word, and repeating it as often as possible in a poem or short story.

The word *warm* is a good example. The children decided to apply it to nighttime. Here are the words they put with it:

warm	fire
warm	house
warm	mother
warm	cocoa
warm	popcorn
warm	sleepers
warm	bath
warm	blankets
warm	bed
warm	kisses

Here is a poem that came from the list:

> *Warm is a wonderful word*
> *I like to be warm,*
> *Warm, Warm.*
> *I like to say warm,*
> *Warm, Warm.*
> *Warm at night*
> *Warm fire, warm house,*
> *Warm cocoa, warm tummy,*
> *Warm mother, warm kisses,*
> *Warm blankets, warm bed.*
> *Warm, Warm, Warm.*
> *Warm is a wonderful word.*

Using Questions

Children are full of questions. Often the teacher is too busy to answer them. To discourage children from asking questions is to deny them the right of creative growth.

One way to make use of these marvelous, ingenious questions children ask is to have them write them on paper. Tack an envelope to the bulletin board. On it, in heavy print, say "Our Whys." Then encourage the children to come and write their questions on three by five cards and put them in the envelope. Each week, a certain time should be allotted to discussions of these questions.

Another way to use them is to write poems about them. After a while, you will notice that some of the questions rhyme. Some day arrange those that rhyme into poems, and put them on the bulletin board. Children can then be encouraged to write why poems about their own questions.

Here is a poem written by a fifth grade about the many questions they collected:

> ### Our Why Poem
> *Why must I always be good?*
> *Why do woodpeckers knock on wood?*
> *Why do sisters push and poke?*
> *Why is there smoke?*
> *Why do we eat with forks and spoons?*
> *Why the moon?*
> *Why can't we have pie at every meal?*
> *Why does flannel have an itchy feel?*
>
> *Grade 5*

Using Surprise Ideas

1. Use ideas that are simply illogical ones needing a logical explanation.

Write About These

a. You open the cellar door, and there, on the floor, stands a donkey!

FIGURE 6-9. *"Pretend" ideas.*

b. You go to see your dog's new puppies, and there, under her, is a rabbit.

c. Right in the middle of an exciting adventure you wake up with a start—it was all a dream!

d. You hurry to your room to dress for the party. Your new dress is hanging in the closet so you rush to open the door. Inside it is a 6 foot rabbit . . .

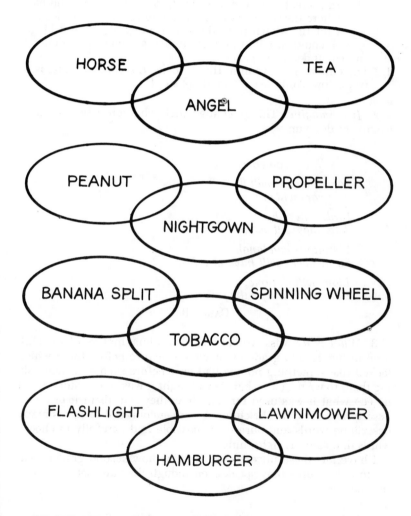

FIGURE 6-10. *Take three unrelated words and make them into a story. It can be a sensible or silly story.*

What Happened?

a.   What happened the day you fell in the mud puddle?
b.   Mrs. Fleming was all dressed up in her beautiful new clothes the evening she arrived for our party. She looked very pretty. Mother had told me I could help serve the punch. I was very proud as I entered the living room with the tray full of glasses —and then it happened. I stumbled and . . .
c.   I heard a great roar and a boom. Quickly I ran into the back yard where the noise came from. There I saw a queer looking object floating down from the sky. It grew bigger and bigger until I could see it was a giant flying saucer. Suddenly it landed, and a door opened . . .
d.   The cliff was before him. He could see the valley hundreds of feet below. And the car would not stop!

2. *Just imagine:* Things change their characteristics, such as fish fly, birds swim.

Someday

Someday pigs will fly,
And cars will cry.

Birds will talk,
And flags will walk.

Elephants will laugh,
Short necks will have giraffes.

Lions will be tame,
But people will be the same.

CAROL B.

3. *What is it?* Miss Arnold teased the imagination of the children in her second grade by placing a picture before them which looked like something no one had ever before seen and then asking them to write: (a) what they thought it was; (b) a story about it; (c) what it was used for; (d) how they felt about it or (e) a description about it. The children were encouraged to use as many describing words and phrases as possible and carefully to choose words that said the right thing.

I have left these uncorrected to show how second graders will try to write words they speak even though they are not certain of the spelling.

I think it is something from a wedding. Some one got married. And you went to the wedding. You looked at it.

Then you thought for a moment. I will try to make that. So you did make it. BUT! It wasn't the same it just was a little just a little different. Just a little different. NOW I talking about something elese. I think it is a gient tooth pick. I know tooth picks don't have ribbins on it. But it is big like a toothpick.

And that is all I say. The End.

VICKI

I think this is a miceriphone. Because it is tall and you can talk in the top of it. Or maybe it is a elevateor. Because that red thing you can put your hand in and push the people up. It could be a giant's umbrela. Because when you turn it upside down it looks like a umbrela. It could be a giant flag. If you turn it upside down. It could be the Empire state building. The End.

Unrelated Ideas

Miss Irwin made up cards with the names of ten objects on each— many of them unrelated. The children drew a card and wrote a story using all ten of the objects in the story in such a clever way that the remainder of the class could not guess the words. Here is Michele's story. Can you tell which ten words were on her list?

The Tower

My name is Janey Larkin and I attend the Elementary School in Craneville, North Dakota. I like school very much, but seem to have a bad habit of getting into trouble during some of my classes. Last week, for instance, I really had myself quite a time.

It happened last Monday morning. My sister tossed me two apples which I stuffed in my lunchpail. Then I grabbed my books and started for school.

During Social Studies I was very much interested but during Reading I began to feel restless. While the teacher was giving us a lecture on how to read quietly, I started fooling with my book. Then I got an idea. I could build a tower with my school supplies.

I started with my two Reading books, their pages face down. Next I found my Social Studies book and placed it neatly across the two Reading books. I was wondering what I could add to it, when my hand struck a small box inside my desk. This I balanced on the Arithmetic book which was placed on top of the Social Studies book. Next I took the two apples from my lunchpail and put them on top of the box.

243

Finally I found just the thing I needed for the top—a roll of tape. I had just finished balancing the tape when I heard a faint giggle. It was Mary Ann.

Then I noticed one of the bottom books was slipping. Crash! The book fell, and so did the rest of my tower.

I slowly looked around and saw that all the kids were laughing—but not the teacher. Somehow the look in her eye seemed to tell me that I would be spending the rest of the period in the hall.

MICHELE
Grade 6

Personification

Many teachers teach the concept of personification through the writing of poetry. Debbie personifies the sea in the following essay. Debbie lives in a seaport city and the sea means a great deal in her life.

Her Majesty

The beauty of the waters of the earth is deceiving. The female that she is, she takes pride in her foamy delicate lace she makes for the shores of her neighboring countries. She is proud of her strength when she shows in her anger a threat to life. In her passion, she lures humans out to sea, then keeps them, not knowing someone loves them at home. In her jealousy she rages to her most disastrous wave, taking revenge on humanity.

She loves to show her playfulness and kindness, too. Sleek boards tickle her back as she gives millions a source of relaxation.

She is landlord to millions of plants and animals, and the little ones are amusing to children. To a seaman's ears her soft cooing is the most beautiful of symphonies, and herself the most beautiful of paintings. In her glory she is majesty to the heavens, in her anger, the tyrant of the world.

DEBBIE BELKOSE
Grade 7

Unusual Topics

Ask the children to select any one of many topics (and always allow them the alternate of choosing one of their own instead) and write, or paint about it. Here is a list I copied from one teacher's chalkboard.

An Adventure in a Bottle of Ink
The Cracklebackle
Changes
The Story with No Ending
A Nest from Nowhere
Devil Dog
The Thing in the Cellar
The Balancing Act
A Cold Homecoming
Why the Robin Has a Red Breast
Newborn Life
The Moon Laughed
A Jet Zoomed
A Dandelion Spoke
A Star Winked
The Rainbow Melted

Role Projection

The role projection technique appeals to different children in different ways. Bill pretends he is a player on the Giants baseball team in the story below. The unusual ending adds a unique flavor to this story.

Giants Vs. Cards

It was in the first inning in the ball game when the Cards heavy hitter came up. I was in left field moving out. Jim pitched. Strike one. Ball one. Ball two. Strike two. Jim pitched a curve. Crack! It made a line in left. I caught it shot it into second and he was out.

After the Cards got their ups, we got ours. Ray Rood was up first. Bob Nash was pitching. Rood walked. Two others struck out. We got a walk. There was a line drive into center. Rood got in. Now men on second and third. More walked or hit. Then I was up. I struck out.

Next inning I played in left. Then Bob got his ups. He hit one up first base line. First baseman picked it up. Bob quite didn't make it.

When the Giants were getting their ups, somebody hit a ball into the water. I went to go get it.

When the Cards were getting their ups, I was using a practice ball with Ray Rood and Fred Macarone.

When the game was in the third I walked.

As soon as the game was over everybody said "Nice game." The score was fifteen to ten. We lost the game.

BILL
Grade 5

Endless Topics

Children can be easily motivated to write about practically anything. Witness the following topic chosen voluntarily by a fifth
grade child.

The World

The world is not perfect for all the people.
Some live to see just war.
Some are very poor.
Some people are rich.
With clothes all beautiful—every stitch
Some are just hippies with beards that grow.
Some have hair so long that you can't tell if it's a boy or girl.
Some girls wear mini dresses and fishnets too.
I'm glad I'm me and you're glad you're you.

SUSAN SQUIRES
Grade 5

STARTERS FOR CREATIVE WRITING

1. Insight into children's personal problems can often be gained
by such suggested titles as "If I Had Three Wishes" or "Things
That Make Me Unhappy."

2. In an appropriate place keep a "Let's Write a Story or Poem"
box which contains pictures, materials, first lines of stories, haiku
and cinquain dittoed sheet blanks and all kinds of things that
can serve as stimulants to write.

3. *Situations:* Write a story or poem about them.

a. You are walking down the street when you hear a big wind
    blowing. Suddenly, the next thing you know you're in a
    strange bed and . . .
b. Your mother's appearance has changed—she looks twenty
    years younger . . .
c. You go downstairs for breakfast one morning and find the
    house deserted. So is the street and neighborhood. You can't
    find anyone anywhere . . .
d. You have a secret wish that you haven't told anyone . . .
e. If you could be an animal for two days, what animal would
    you want to be and why?
f. What will the North Star see happening on earth tonight?
g. You are a newspaper reporter rushing back to the office with
    the greatest scoop of the year.
h. During the winter a hibernating bear dreams about . . .
i. Men from Mars came down to earth and . . .

j.   You are a block of stone that will be carved into a statue. Many people look at you as a statue. What did you think when you were being made? What do you think when people go by? What are you like?

k.   You won a contest for the most unusual toy. What is it like? What does it do?

l.   You are opening a store. What are you selling? What does the store look like?

m.   Four turtles are going on a voyage. They travel on land, sea and air. Tell me their adventures and what they find at the end.

n.   Walking home from school, all of a sudden, a hand comes up through a crack in the sidewalk . . .

o.   You and three friends are stranded on a mountain. There's nothing around but snow and the wind blowing. Suddenly a phone rings!

p.   Due to a magic spell, you were put in the bottom of a bottle of Coke. How do you get out? Who saves you?

q.   Everything you touch with your pinky finger turns into a daisy! What do you do? What are some of the things that happen to you? How did this happen?

r.   Pretend your fingers are a family and write about what would happen if one didn't get along with the other four. What would be the consequences?

s.   You are a person in America who cannot speak English.

t.   The huge crate was in the doorway when you arrived home. It looked very mysterious with all its foreign stamps. Someone had already pried the nails loose, so all you had to do was lift the top up to see what was inside. You reached out your hand . . .

u.   You are up in the clouds on a mission over a foreign land. It is a beautiful morning. You see enemy planes coming toward you. What do you do? How do you feel? What happens?

4. All you need is three or four magazine pictures, the more unrelated the better. Use bold abstracts, action pictures, appealing pictures of animals or children. Tape pictures to chalkboard. Let all see and study them.

Then turn your children's imaginations loose, tying together such unrelated things as a picture of a waterfall, a space capsule, and a pair of shoes. Twenty minutes is long enough for writing.

Another day, let children make their own picture selections for a new story. Use these ideas two or three days in a row.

5. Classroom activities to provoke creative writing:

a.   Give each child a puppet and let him write whatever the puppet tells him.

b.   Give each one a word to write about. For example: *blub*.

c. Have the group write a book—each one writing a chapter.

d. The teacher brings in an unfamiliar object. Have the children write about what it is, where it came from and what it could be used for.

e. Bring in old hats or clothing for them to elaborate on verbally.

f. Bring in a piece of material and ask them what it could be and how it came to be that.

g. Give them an action word and have them build a story around it.

h. Bring in a stuffed animal for them to write about.

i. Show them a picture of a sad or happy person and ask them to tell a story on how he got happy or sad.

j. Show them a picture of the universe and ask them to create a story of their experience in outer space.

k. Show them an old hat. Put it on your head and ask them to write a story of what happens.

l. Show them a nature picture to create a story about.

m. Bring in a live animal to write about.

n. Stir their imagination with a picture of an abstract object.

o. Show a particular slide or slides that will interest them.

p. Have the children draw a picture and then tell the story behind it.

q. Take advantage of a coming holiday by having the children write one sentence about it. Have one child start it out, then pass it on to the next child.

r. Hand out words cut out of magazines. Have children use these as ideas and then write about them.

s. Imagine if you could receive just one present for Christmas, what would it be and why?

t. Imagine a man comes up to you and says you *must* spend the $100 he gives you in one day or you will die.

u. Have the class think of all the images and ideas suggested by one word (autumn, night, summer, beauty) and write them on the board.

v. Describe abstract words through images, for example, "Joy is a chocolate ice cream cone in the hand of a three year old boy."

w. Take a verb such as *walk*. Make a list of words that convey the idea of *walk* but are more exact (*saunter, march, strut, stagger*). Have the children act out the words.

x. Guess stories from book covers.

y. Write stories from books children like, for example, more experiences of Tom Sawyer as the child might imagine it.

z. Create a story bureau. Pupils of intermediate grades write stories for pupils of primary grades. All stories are bound into a large book and made available to primary teachers. A story chosen by the teacher to be read to primary class may be read by the author.

6. Try these beginnings for compositions:

a. If I could go to the moon, I . . .
b. If I were an animal, I would be . . .
c. Now you mustn't fool mother nature . . .
d. A funny game is . . .
e. In the land of ladybugs . . .
f. Anger is . . .
g. If I were ten feet tall, I . . .
h. One day my dog looked at me and spoke . . .
i. I was on my way to a party when . . .
j. One day the sun never came out . . .
k. One night when I was all alone . . .
l. I never believed in magic until . . .
m. If you can keep a secret, I'll tell you about . . .
n. Remember when . . .
o. If I had wings . . .
p. I rubbed my magic ring and . . .
q. I am a blood cell in the body of a great athlete . . .
r. The hardest decision I ever had to make was . . .
s. A "Gribble" is . . .
t. I never believed in reincarnation but . . .

7. *Titles for starters:* Try the following titles on a story board to get children started. Place the titles on strips of paper so you can keep changing some each day and use them more than once.

a. It Takes a Real Dummy for This Job.
b. Take a Deep Breath.
c. This Tape Will Self-destruct in 60 Minutes.
d. The Year That Homework Died.
e. The World's Largest Friend.
f. My Special Miracle.
g. Tomorrow.
h. When My Bugaboo Grew.
i. My Square Bowling Ball.
j. A School Without Tests.
k. When I'm President.
l. If We Had Fleas.
m. Ugh!*-!
n. What Is a Lonely Beach?
o. If Heels Could Talk.
p. Smoke.
q. A Tense Moment.
r. The Upside-down Cake.
s. The Sad Sack.
t. The People-Eaters.

8. Some ideas that may get them going:

a. Tell how a caterpillar feels crawling over the palm of the hand.
b. Children tear black paper into many shapes or silhouettes and write what they suggest to them.
c. Write what the raindrops in a puddle look like.
d. Describe a windy day.
e. Write "tall" tales about people or happenings.
f. Concoct new animals by joining two others—elecamel, kangarabbit—and make up a story with the new animal as a hero or villian.
g. Write conversations between the shoes of noted people.
h. After a discussion of secret fears, the children write about their greatest fear.
i. Pretend a huge skelton in the museum comes alive and tells an adventure out of its past.
j. Write about the spills and thrills of sledding, skating and skiing.
k. Listen to a story about a child with one outstanding characteristic such as generosity or talkativeness, then write a story about why the child would or would not make a good neighbor.
l. Write about things around the house that mysteriously disappear: Where's my baseball bat? Who ate the extra piece of cake?
m. Make up the good advice a mother pet would give her baby before it goes out into the world.
n. Write a yarn for the Spinners Club. All members write a story and keep a notebook of stories.

SUMMARY

"We have something to say," speak the children.
"Say it," says the teacher.
"We have something to write," speak the children.
"Write it," says the teacher.
And the language of the children falls on the ears of the teacher or it appears on her desk in piles of neat or untidy papers. She picks them up one by one—

"My Poem" by Betty
"A Summer's Day" by Sharon
"Henry the Hood" by Alex
"Three Hundred Pounds of Peanut Butter" by Alice
"Millions of Bedbugs" by Jody

Their words tumble forth for they *do* have something to say. Teachers, help them to say it!

TO THE COLLEGE STUDENT AND THE CLASSROOM TEACHER

1. Ask the children to collect pictures of common everyday places such as a village or city street, a field, a park, a road. Have them write how the picture will look a long time in the future. Also, how did it look a long time ago? This activity can be enhanced if they accompany their writing with drawings. In some instances the drawings may become very realistic when a transparency is laid over the picture and the changes are actually drawn over the existing scene.

2. Take a group of sildes on various subjects, related or unrelated, and show them with stacatto quickness to the children; then ask them to write their impressions of what the presentation meant to them. The idea—saturation technique—will be enhanced if you play rock or honkey-tonk piano music while this presentation is going on.

3. Try writing some cinquain or haiku poetry. In my college classes I ask each person to spend three minutes interviewing the person on his left until he feels he knows something about him and then to introduce him to the remainder of the class with a haiku or cinquain poem.

4. What background of experience do you imagine the young girl who wrote the poem at the beginning of this chapter had? Do you think she was of average or above average intelligence. Does she have good imagery?

5. Collect baby pictures from magazines or calendars. Paste them on white paper and then give one picture to each class member. Each member will then add an expression or caption of something which has happened in class which the picture suggests. Share your pictures and sayings. Can writing captions be creative?

6. Look up some of these topics and report on them (to the rest of the class if you are a college student).
a.   Children's humor
b.   Imagination
c.   Children's thinking

7. If you are a teacher, keep a collection of the imaginative, clever or beautiful things children say during the course of a week. In what creative ways can you use this material? If you are a college student, note the same thing about your contemporaries. Do some people consistently say things more beautifully than others?

8. If you are a teacher, revamp your language arts program so that much of your teaching stems from the creative writing of children. First, try to set conditions to get creative writing each day. Establish a creative writing corner, work with the children in arranging attractive bulletin boards, set up an editing file as suggested on pages 296–97 and think of many ways to motivate the children to write. Analyze their papers and make tabulations of their errors and misspellings. These tabulations could form the basis for your grammar program. Creative writing should be the basis of the school program in written expression.

9. Try writing something creative or try working with some media you have never used before. As well as you can, analyze the processes you go through. Do you better appreciate the efforts of the children who wrote materials for this chapter once you have tried to create something yourself?

10. The material in this chapter is ungraded in most cases. Take any five ideas and suggest ways they might be adapted to any grade level.

11. Read one of the starred books in the bibliography. Share these books in class by discussing them and reading passages aloud. Are the children in these books being helped to develop their creative powers or are they being exploited?

12. Select a *Starter* from one of the suggestions on pages 246–50 and write to finish it.

13. Make up words to a class song and put it to music.

14. Several books and materials are being manufactured to develop divergent thinking, creative thinking and creative writing in children. I have put an asterisk before some of the most exciting books in the following bibliography. Get some of these and study them; share them with your colleagues.

You will also be interested in Torrance's records *Sounds and Images* and *Commander of Communication*. Send for a set of these (Ginn and Co.). Listen to them or better yet try them with children—and react to their value in developing divergency in thought.

SELECTED BIBLIOGRAPHY

Anderson, Paul S. *Language Skills in Elementary Education*. New York: Macmillan, 1964.

*Applegate, Mauree. *Helping Children Write*. Evanston, Ill.: Row, Peterson, 1954.

Arbuthnot, May Hill (compiler). *The Arbuthnot Anthology of Children's Literature*. Chicago: Scott Foresman, 1953.

Arbuthnot, May Hill and Dorothy M. Broderick. *Time for Stories.* Dallas, Texas: Scott Foresman, 1968.

*Arnstein, Flora J. *Children Write Poetry: A Creative Approach.* New York: Dover, 1967.

Brewton, John E. and Sara W. Brewton. *Index to Children's Poetry.* New York: H. W. Wilson, 1942. First Supplement, 1954; Second Supplement, 1969.

Burrows, Alvina T., June D. Ferebee, Doris C. Jackson and Dorothy O. Saunders. *They All Want To Write.* Englewood Cliffs, N.J.: Prentice-Hall, 1962.

Carlson, Ruth Kearney. *Literature for Children: Enrichment Ideas.* Dubuque, Iowa: William C. Brown, 1970.

Chambers, Dewey W. *Children's Literature in the Curriculum.* Chicago: Rand McNally, 1971.

———. *Literature for Children: Storytelling and Creative Drama.* Dubuque, Iowa: William C. Brown, 1970.

Colwell, Eilsen. *A Storyteller's Choice.* New York: Henry Z. Walck, 1964.

Farris, Herbert J. "Creative Writing Must Be Motivated." In James C. MacCampbell (ed.). *Readings in the Language Arts in the Elementary School.* Boston: D. C. Heath, 1964, pp. 261–62.

Greene, Harry A. and Walter T. Petty. *Developing Language Skills in the Elementary Schools.* 4th ed. Chapter 8. Boston: Allyn and Bacon, 1971.

*Lewis, Richard. *Journeys: Prose by Children of the English-Speaking World.* New York: Simon and Schuster, 1969.

*———. *Miracles: Poems by Children of the English-Speaking World.* New York: Simon and Schuster, 1966.

McCaslin, Nellie. *Creative Dramatics in the Classroom.* New York: David McKay, 1968.

Mearns, Hughes. *Creative Power: The Education of Youth in the Creative Arts.* Rev. ed. New York: Dover, 1954.

Murray, Ruth L. *Dance in Elementary Education.* New York: Harper and Row, 1963.

*Myers, R. E. and E. Paul Torrance. *Can You Imagine?* Boston: Ginn, 1965.

*———. *Plots, Puzzles and Ploys: Adventures in Self-Expression.* Boston: Ginn, 1966.

Pease, Don. *Creative Writing in the Elementary School.* Jericho, N.Y.: Exposition Press, 1964.

*Petty, Walter T. and Mary Bowen. *Slithery Snakes and Other Aids to Children's Writing.* New York: Appleton-Century-Crofts, 1967.

Reasoner, Charles F. *Releasing Children to Literature*. New York: Dell, 1968.

*Smith, Allen H. *Don't Get Personal with a Chicken*. New York: Permabook, 1959.

*————. *Write Me a Poem Baby*. Boston: Little, Brown, 1956.

Smith, James A. *Creative Teaching of the Language Arts in the Elementary School*. Chapter V. Boston: Allyn and Bacon, 1967.

*Smith, Robert P. *"Where Did You Go?" "Out." "What Did You Do?" "Nothing."* New York: Norton, 1957.

*Tannen, Robert. *I Know A Place*. Books 1-2-3. Boston: City Schools Curriculum, 1969.

Walter, Nina Willis. *Let Them Write Poetry*. New York: Holt, Rinehart and Winston, 1966.

Whitehead, Robert. *Children's Literature: Strategies of Teaching*. Englewood Cliffs, N.J.: Prentice-Hall, 1968.

CHAPTER VII

Creative Teaching
of Handwriting

A Matter of Courtesy

> . . . writing that is to be read to another, both because of
> courtesy and practicability, should be as clear as it can be
> made . . .[1]

TO THE READER

Creative living together calls for courtesy to one another. One
social courtesy that children should be taught is that material
written for others to read should always be legible and attractive.
This chapter explores ways handwriting can be taught as a social
courtesy, and yet, in many instances, taught creatively.

As a teacher or student teacher you will want to set good patterns of handwriting before your students because handwriting is
an eye skill. Turn to page 269 before you read this chapter and
especially the part which describes how Mr. Edwards improved the
handwriting skill of his fifth grade. Try this technique in your
class and note improvements in your own handwriting. Is there
any value in this method over the method used when you were
taught handwriting?

---

1. A. T. Burrows et al., *They All Want To Write* (rev. ed.; Englewood
Cliffs, N.J.: Prentice-Hall, 1962), p. 5.

THE PLACE OF HANDWRITING IN THE ELEMENTARY SCHOOL

Handwriting is a developmental process. It develops in children as an art form. In the scribble stage of art development, children naturally learn the basic strokes required to make manuscript letters. The picture below is a composite of forms taken from children's paintings. It shows how a child's inherent abilities enable him to make, with no instruction, the seven basic strokes required in manuscript writing.

Children are ready to write when these basic strokes appear in their paintings. The first word which most children write is their name; this name usually appears as part of a painting. A child sees his teacher write his name in manuscript on each of his paintings and soon he copies it himself—often with a clumsy tool, the paintbrush. At this point in his development, he does not need to recognize or name letters or sequences of letters; he is only reproducing shapes. In his painting he goes through the manipulative and exploratory stage to the communicative stage. The

FIGURE 7-1. *A composite of basic strokes in manuscript writing as they appear in a child's painting.*

communicative stage occurs when adults can begin to recognize objects and forms in the child's art work. It is at this time that the name begins to appear—or at least parts of it. A careful study of a sequence of any one child's paintings will show a gradual evolution from simple daubings and straight bold strokes into circular strokes and strokes that cross to form crude letters. From this scribbling and daubing, handwriting emerges into the child's life experience as an art form.

From the very beginning, handwriting is a visual skill. A good readiness program allows time for the child to paint letters and to experiment with word and letter forms. Large movements with the brush over large sheets of paper enable a child to experiment and reproduce words without the muscular strain imposed on him when he finally begins to use a primary pencil on lined primary paper. When the young child writes, he is really reproducing forms which he sees; a sharp sense of visual perception must be developed. In the sequence of language development handwriting comes after reading, for a child must have many experiences *seeing* a word before he can reproduce it. The reading readiness program described in Book III, *Creative Teaching of Reading and Literature in the Elementary School,* is also the readiness program necessary for handwriting development. Very soon after children are able to recognize words on their experience charts or in their readings primers, they will want to draw them. Linda, a first grader, gave a story to her teacher one day not long after she had been introduced to the reading primer. Linda selected a picture from the box of pictures which her teacher kept handy for the development of oral expression and visual acuity. Linda announced, "I guess I'll write my story today instead of telling it." She then went to her seat, took out her primer, and laboriously selected the words she needed from the page. These she used, with the words she already had visualized, to write her first story. In terms of our definition of creativity, it was a piece of creative writing, for Linda took parts of her past experiences and assembled them into a new one.

This sort of motivation to handwriting is essential if children are to use it fluently as a tool of communication. Each exciting and new experience in handwriting provided by the teacher at the

FIGURE 7-2. *The seven basic strokes of manuscript writing.*

257

beginning stages of handwriting instruction should be rewarding and satisfying to the child. His attitude toward handwriting will determine the extent to which he will write during his total school experience.

SETTING CONDITIONS FOR THE TEACHING OF HANDWRITING

Certain conditions may be set for the teaching of handwriting, both from the practical and creative viewpoint. They are as follows:

1. Handwriting materials (paints, art paper, large pencils, regular pencils, ball-point pens, and writing paper) should be kept in a place where they are easily accessible to each child so he may write in any form and at any time he likes.

2. The atmosphere of the room must be relaxed, congenial and pleasant. Recent research shows that children do their best handwriting in a comfortable, encouraging atmosphere where some tension is present. Lack of tension tends to create a lackadaisical sort of writing, whereas too much tension creates a tense type of handwriting.

3. An air of expectancy and certain positive tensions (stated above) tend to produce better handwriting in children than no tensions at all.

4. The visual image of the letter or word to be written must be present somewhere. In the beginning stages of the child's handwriting experience these images should be handy in physical form for ready reference in the classroom: on the chalkboard, on charts, on cards above the blackboard or in some simple handwriting book placed before the child. In older children, the image of the shape of the word will be present in his mind and no actual image is necessary.

5. The visual form of the word or letter placed before a child should not be considered as a pattern which he will be expected to reproduce exactly. There are basically two objectives in the teaching of handwriting—legibility and fluency. Because handwriting is personal and maturational, no two children can possibly write alike. In the first place, each starts with different equipment. Children differ in their physical growth. We cannot expect a short fourth grade boy to reach as high as a tall fourth grade boy, nor can we expect children to turn out precise, similar written work. Some children have long fingers, some have short fingers. Thickness of fingers, wrist development and bone structure vary in the

child's hand. With these differing characteristics to begin with, teachers cannot expect children to produce similar products.

6. To a great degree, the teaching of handwriting must remain personal with individualized instruction. Unpleasant writing experiences result for most children when they are forced into reproducing patterns which are too difficult for them. The frustrations which children undergo in an attempt to write in the unnatural and awkward way advocated by certain writing systems cause children to shy away from the handwriting experience. The use of writing scales is also a frustrating experience for many children who simply cannot reproduce the type of writing represented on the scale. On page 271 there are suggestions for a realistic use of handwriting scales.

7. Handwriting instruction must correspond to the pupil's individual growth. Manuscript writing is used at the beginning of instruction because the child's fingers contain muscles that develop later than others in his body. At the age when the child first wants to write, he is capable of making large, definite strokes. Manuscript writing, based on these strokes, provides the quickest way for the child to get into the writing act. As the muscles in his fingers develop and his finger usage is refined, he can easily make other strokes of greater complexity and variety. Little by little he prepares for cursive writing.

Excessive attention has been given in the lower grades to the grade level at which cursive writing should be taught, rather than the time the child is ready to write cursively. Cursive writing should be taught when the child is ready. Some educators feel the teaching of cursive writing is no longer necessary, that our culture demands so much manuscript writing that it would be well to devote our time to perfecting this technique. Manuscript writing can be done as quickly as cursive. However, as long as both types are used in modern living, it is only fair that children should know how to read and write both ways.

When a teacher detects a group of students who are copying the cursive writing patterns from the blackboard or from a chart which she has prepared, she may feel sure that they are ready to put their scribbling into patterns. She can begin to give instruction to this group by permitting them to imitate large samples of cursive writing from the board, or from individual sheets she has prepared. The grade level at which this takes place is unimportant—so long as the children are ready and they are not forced into these complex acts before they are *comfortably* able to perform them.

8. Many *purposes* for writing must be apparent at all times.

Hours of endless, meaningless drill can quickly dull the child's desire to write. At first he enjoys and welcomes the opportunity to reproduce the sample the teacher sets before him, but he soon tires of attempting to refine his work so it looks exactly like the teacher's.

This tiresome and wasteful drill can be avoided. More meaningful writing practice is developed when children write letters, invitations or announcements that are actually sent. At first these may be no more than a copy from the board of a master made by the teacher, which the teacher and pupils have composed together. Later, as the child gains spelling and writing skills, he may create his own letters and invitations. He may compose stories and poems to be read by others from a bulletin board. When the handwriting program is built from a program in creative writing such as described in Chapter VI, children write perpetually to communicate ideas which cannot be expressed orally, because the time or place is inappropriate. In an effective handwriting program, the teacher creates many *purposes* for which the children need to write. The teaching of writing is not necessarily a period set aside to practice meaningless scribblings, but a time in which children enjoy learning another technique which will pave the way to greater fluency in recording their thoughts and ideas.

9. Good attitude should be developed about handwriting practice. Few adults are able to compose and write correctly and beautifully with the original draft of their writing. In like manner, when children are writing for aesthetic values, or for reports to the class, it is unrealistic to expect the original draft or even the first few writings to be in perfect style. All of us have several kinds of handwriting. We write notes differently from the way we write a business letter; we jot a note to a friend more hastily than we write a letter to someone who is not well known to us. The purpose of writing determines its stage of refinement. When all the writing children do is judged by high adult standards, children become discouraged. We should recognize and accept that they write differently for different occasions.

10. The handwriting program must be adjusted to meet the changing times and the needs of children -in everyday living. Children should write in school with the same tools they will use outside of school. From the start, children should have practice with the felt pen and the ball-point pen rather than the obsolete steel point pen. Common sense tells us that no child is ever going to use a steel point pen after he leaves school, and this primitive tool should be eliminated for the use of the more modern one. Felt and fountain pens are easier to use, less messy and more

easily taken care of and should facilitate the teaching of writing. Much of the change in style of accepted handwriting through the ages has been brought about by the invention of a more efficient and more practical handwriting tool.

11. The teacher should continue to recognize and teach handwriting as an art form. Today's children are exposed to all kinds of writing. They see billboards, posters, television commercials, newspapers, magazines, books, advertising, road signs and neon lights and are exposed to mass exploitation of various writing forms at every turn. Because children see so many kinds of handwriting in these forms of communication, they must learn to read many kinds of handwriting and printed script. Some handwriting is obviously used as an art form, such as that which appears in an ad on the subway or in an advertisement in *Vogue* magazine. Children will recognize that some kinds of handwriting are prettier than other kinds. This is a recognition of the art value of the writing. Exposure to many patterns of handwriting makes the job of the teacher less difficult on the one hand and more difficult on the other. Because handwriting is a visual skill, children *see* many forms of handwriting both in and out of school and the image is impressed more readily on their minds. This should make the teaching of handwriting easier and quicker. But because these impressions are not standard, and children often see words and letters represented in *many* forms, the teacher's job is also difficult. She must help children see the purpose behind different forms of handwriting and she must also help them select from the forms those which are most legible and easy for them to use in performing the handwriting act for themselves. The skills of (a) selecting a form to fit a purpose and (b) selecting efficient and legible handwriting forms for common usage, were not a part of the instructional job of the teacher in the past when her own pattern of handwriting was the most constant (and sometimes the only) pattern to which children were exposed. A creative teacher will have children collect many patterns of handwriting in various art forms. These can well be used to build standards in legibility, efficiency of use and beauty as related to purpose.

12. Much nonsense has been published about posture in handwriting. While it is necessary to check to see that children assume the most effective posture while writing, it is ridiculous to assume that all children write their best sitting the same way. The best handwriting is produced when the writer is most comfortable.

Handwriting position is correct only when it produces good handwriting and that will be when the child is released from uncomfortable, unrealistic strains during the act of writing.

13. Finger movement is necessary in developing effective handwriting. The fetish for wrist movement so popular several years ago has subsided to a more realistic understanding that legible, fluent handwriting results when a combination of wrist and finger writing is used. An excessive use of either impedes the communication process, thus guidance should be given at the beginning stages. Moving pictures of excellent writers show that they employ both the wrist and the fingers. The child's fingers are the most useful tools he has in developing written expression. To interfere with the use of these tools is to impede his writing development. Any method used to help a child write is justifiable if it makes handwriting easier, quicker and more legible.

14. In the space age, children use the typewriter at a younger age than ever before. However, the typewriter will replace handwriting only to a certain degree. Note taking, personal writing, editing and other forms of handwriting cannot be replaced by the typewriter. The typewriter has been a help in improving formal communication skills and makes its major contribution in that area. Children will benefit from instruction in typing, but the typewriter will not replace the need for legible handwriting.

THE CREATIVE TEACHING OF HANDWRITING

Can the teaching of handwriting be creative? If the act of handwriting means that we try to help children reproduce letter forms which are as near like a perfected letter form as possible, is not this conformity and imitation in its purest sense? Do we not work in such a situation to destroy the differences in children, to make a common product rather than a different one? If this is so, then how can handwriting or the teaching of it be considered creative in any sense?

Handwriting is noncreative to the degree that conformity to several basic regulations is necessary. In imitating the letter forms supplied by the teacher, the child is indeed noncreative. Handwriting is imitating; it is copying; it is conforming. It is one of the skills used in daily living where conformity and imitation are necessary. But, in any culture there are many times when conformity is necessary and part of the job of the teacher is to help children determine those times when they must abandon individual drives and needs because it is best for the good of everyone concerned.

But though conformity is necessary, there is still room for

individuality. Because people are all different, the *way* they conform is different. In the history of the development of handwriting
in this country there is ample evidence to support the fact that
the practice of teaching any specific method of handwriting has
been successful only to a limited degree. Few adults write according to the method by which they were taught. Though they spent
endless hours in school practicing specific forms of letters, they
abandoned these forms as soon as they were outside the range of
vision of their teacher. If the form being practiced does not come
easily for the writer, he adopts a more efficient, yet still legible
style of handwriting. His personality affects his handwriting and
it becomes different from anyone else's. Handwriting analysts
can often do a skillful job in telling about a person's personality
through his handwriting. In this sense handwriting remains creative in spite of all of our efforts to stereotype it.

The teaching of handwriting can be creative if the teacher will
recognize a few basic guides:

1. Handwriting is a personal thing and no one pattern can be
successfully reproduced by all children. Therefore, the goals of
legibility and efficiency should be stressed above other goals.

2. Different kinds of handwriting are used for different purposes and in different situations. The child's *best* handwriting
should be expected for those papers which are to be shared with
others. Other kinds of handwriting are acceptable when he is
writing for himself, or when he is composing first drafts of material to get his ideas on paper quickly.

3. Handwriting is a tool by which a child communicates. It is
what he writes that is important and should be given priority over
all other considerations. *How* to write correctly and acceptably
comes after ideas are put down in their desired form. Final drafts
of material should be used to develop the best handwriting.

4. There are certain basic principles for all good handwriting.
Instruction in handwriting should stress these basic principles as
much as it stresses the finished product.

5. Handwriting scales and patterns of adult handwriting can
be very frustrating and discouraging to the child because he is not
physically equipped to match them. A realistic handwriting program is based on the improvement of handwriting rather than on
the attainment of some unobtainable goal. If handwriting scales
are to be used to evaluate children's handwriting, they must contain many acceptable forms of handwriting so that each child may
find one enough like his to identify with and work toward it. He

should first have help in analyzing the differences between his own handwriting and the sample on the scale.

A more realistic approach to evaluation of handwriting is to help each child analyze his own specimens according to the basic set of principles mentioned on page 270 and then to use them to improve his own writing. Here the emphasis is creative; it is on improvement and change (a creative concept) rather than on imitation (a noncreative one).

6. Left-handed children need not be handicapped in handwriting performance. If the paper is slanted to the left instead of to the right, the left-handed child can form letters and write exactly the same as his right-handed brothers. However, overhand writing must be discouraged.

Attitude is important here. No ridicule or pressure should be placed on the "southpaw" because of the difference in his method of writing. It will help him to realize that many great men, such as Harry S Truman, Leonardo da Vinci, King George VI, Babe Ruth and Cary Grant, were all left-handed. With a minor adjustment of paper and seating position, handwriting instruction need not be special for the left-handed child.

The teaching of handwriting can be creative when the teacher emphasizes *change, individuality* and *improvement,* rather than imitation and conformity. It can be creative in the ways she sets up a variety of *purposes* which place children in conditions where continual handwriting skills are practiced. It can be creative when it is used as a *tool of communication* for the entire day and not as an isolated, meaningless drill period.

NATURAL, EVERYDAY CONDITIONS FOR DEVELOPING HANDWRITING SKILLS

Setting Purposes: Primary Grades

Miss Martin motivated her first graders to write their names many times, in meaningful situations, by having them:

1. Label their lockers.
2. Make name plates for their books.
3. Label their own chairs and tables.
4. Label napkins for mid-morning lunch.
5. Label their paintings.
6. Make tags to identify their art objects.
7. Sign the dittoed letters sent home to parents.

8. Write their names on cards to be used in primary grades.
9. Write their names on apples cut from construction paper (used each day to check attendance when each child set his apple in a slit in the construction paper apple tree). This technique was varied by using other objects when the group interest was high.
10. Sign their own milk money receipts and bills.

Other opportunities for handwriting in the primary grades are provided through encouraging the children to:

1. Write stories.
2. Write poems.
3. Write simple plays.
4. Write letters—gradually filling in words to the completion of the entire letter.
5. Write simple invitations.
6. Write letters of thanks.
7. Copy and write announcements.
8. Copy and write letters to parents about school events.
9. Print daily school cafeteria menus for the bulletin board.
10. Label exhibits and displays in the classroom.
11. Write simple stories about paintings.
12. Write self-portraits.
13. Write store signs and label prices of objects.
14. Keep weather reports.
15. Write the daily news on the blackboard.
16. Make booklets.
17. Write autobiographies.
18. Plan the daily program for the class and write it on the board.
19. Write captions under pictures.
20. Write greeting cards.

Setting Purposes: Intermediate Grades

Everyday experiences in the intermediate grades which provide purposes for handwriting are:

1. Writing labels.
2. Creative writing experiences.
3. Writing stories.
4. Writing poems.
5. Writing letters.
6. Writing plays.
7. Writing reports for social studies.
8. Writing book reports.

9. Writing invitations.
10. Writing letters of thanks.
11. Writing announcements.
12. Writing for the school newspaper.
13. Writing letters to classmates.
14. Keeping lists or records.
15. Keeping accounts of science experiments, etc.
16. Keeping bills, writing checks, etc.
17. Writing letters to government and other public institutions, to firms, etc., for information, on making arrangements for trips and for materials.
18. Ordering supplies and booklets.
19. Taking minutes of club meetings or school meetings.
20. Keeping reports on the weather.
21. Keeping attendance reports.
22. Keeping reports on book sales, attendance, etc.
23. Writing autobiographies.
24. Making a class directory.
25. Making a book of stories, poems, important social science information, etc.
26. Planning the daily program in the classroom.
27. Making long-term plans.
28. Making book lists.
29. Keeping a vocabulary list of new words.
30. Writing up interviews held with people for information in social studies, science. etc.
31. Taking notes.
32. Making outlines.
33. Organizing materials.
34. Writing plans for assembly programs.
35. Writings captions for pictures and movies.
36. Writing for a school newspaper.
37. Writing stories or sentences dictated by the teacher.

CONTRIVED EXPERIENCES FOR DEVELOPING HANDWRITING SKILLS: PRIMARY GRADES

1. Use large sheets of paper and paint brushes to introduce children to experimentation with word and letter forms. Children can develop basic movements for letter formation by painting them first.

2. Allow children to begin handwriting practice on the blackboard where fat chalk and lack of space does not inhibit the child's attempt to reproduce letters.

3. The dotted line technique can be used to guide children in

the formation of more difficult letters and numbers. Many writing manuals and workbooks contain such exercises.

4. Spread Plasticene in a shallow cookie tray and scratch a letter on the surface of the Plasticene with a stick. The child who is having difficulty with any specific letter may get the feel of making it by pushing the stick into the Plasticene and digging the letter in the soft clay.

5. Allow beginning writers to work with letters and words on large sheets of paper using colored felt pens to get the feel of the letters.

6. Working with a wet paintbrush on a dusty blackboard allows freedom in using large muscles when the child is making the transition from painting to manuscript writing.

7. The formal writing period may begin in this manner:

a. Transfer the writing readiness practice from the chalkboard to large, unlined paper, then to lined paper.
b. Change writing tools from brush, chalk or crayon to large and then smaller pencils.
c. Write all letter forms in manuscript, both capital and small (upper and lower case).
d. Write the first and last names.
e. Write the figures from one to ten.
f. Write sentences, poems, stories and letters from messages dictated by the group, on the chalkboard.

8. Instead of having children write meaningless words out of context, correlate handwriting drill with social studies, science and other subject areas. (Example: make lists of pets or farm animals.)

9. Have each child make a picture dictionary with illustrations.

10. Encourage children to label objects in the room.

11. Encourage children to label bulletin boards and exhibits.

12. Make records of group experiences to be bound in individual reading books. (Examples: "We Make Applesauce," "Our Trip to the A&P Store," "Our Pet Show.")

13. Make titles for books and posters.

14. Use number jingles to create interest in letter or figure formation.

Examples:

> *Big and round and tipped this way*
> *Is the very best way to make an A*
>
> *Round the tree and round the tree*
> *This is how we make a 3*

Tall and straight as it can be
With a cross on top and that's a T.

Across the sky and down from heaven,
That is how we make a 7!

15. Write number rhymes to practice numbers

1, 2
Buckle my shoe
3, 4
Shut the door, etc.
(Children can draw a shoe, a door, etc.)

1, 2, 3, 4, 5
See that airplane dive
6, 7, 8, 9, 10
Up it goes again.

1, 2, 3 little Indians   *(draw)*
4, 5, 6 little Indians
7, 8, 9 little Indians
10 little Indian boys.

a, b, c, d, e, f, g
Tell me what you think of me!

a is for apple
b is for bow
c is for candy
d is for doe
     etc.

16. Write the number of children in a room, in a row, at table, etc.

17. Make up a dittoed address book for each child. Leave room for each child to write his name, address and telephone number. Pass the books around and have each child write in every other book until they are complete.

18. Make calendars on dittoed sheets for practice in number writing. Children can draw pictures to illustrate the calendar.

19. Make number booklets. Have children write a number at the top of the page and then draw pictures to illustrate each number.

20. When practicing letters, help children to know where to begin a stroke by marking this place with an arrow or a colored dot.

21. In transferring from manuscript to cursive writing, use cards which point out the difference in the formation.

22. In transferring from manuscript to cursive, write sentences

or stories on the chalkboard in manuscript and directly below each line write the same story in cursive, using a bright colored chalk. Encourage children to try cursive when they appear to be ready.

23. Study the early history of handwriting. (Examples: Indians using drums and smoke signals, picture signs of early cultures, scrolls made by early writers, handmade books of monks, the invention of the printing press.)

24. Lines to help children write evenly on the chalkboard will last several hours and stand several erasures if they are drawn when the board is wet.

CONTRIVED EXPERIENCES FOR DEVELOPING HANDWRITING SKILLS: INTERMEDIATE GRADES

Analysis of handwriting skills has shown certain basic principles to be consistent in all legible handwriting. Mr. Edwards used the following method to bring into focus those basic principles for his fifth grade group.

Early in the term, he asked each child to write this sentence in his best handwriting:

The boy and the man were excused from the class for the entire day.

He composed this sentence because it contained one type of each letter made by various stroke combinations. It also contained all letters except g, j, k, p, q, v and z.

Each child wrote his sample on a piece of paper. No names were affixed to the papers. The papers were then collected and Mr. Edwards explained to the children that he was going to use the papers to show each child how to improve his handwriting.

Mr. Edwards then selected one very legible sample and one which was not as legible and projected them on a screen before the class by using the opaque projector. The children were asked which of the two samples was easier to read. The most legible sample was identified. Then Mr. Edwards asked the children why.

As the children discovered various reasons, Mr. Edwards wrote them on the chalkboard. Then he used two other sets of the sample papers to further develop an analysis of basic handwriting principles.

From this class, these basic principles evolved.

Handwriting Is Easier To Read When

1. All the letters slant the same way.
2. Tall letters are really tall, and even and low letters are really low and even.
3. The tops of rounded letters are round (such as in the *m*, *n*, and *h*) and not pointed.
4. Oval-shaped letters (such as the *e*, *a*, *o*) are left open, but closed at the top.
5. Words are spaced about two letter *o*'s apart on a line.
6. Each letter has a space after it and does not run into another letter.
7. Looped letters are carefully closed (*e*, *l*, *f*).
8. "Trick" letters cause the most difficulty such as the letters *t* (improperly crossed), *e* (confused with *i*), *a* (left unclosed could be *o* or *u*) and *r* (when not flattened on top confused with *i*, *u*, *e*, etc.), and must be checked carefully.
9. Words rest on the line.
10. Arrangement on the page is carefully made. Margins help to make reading easier.
11. The papers are neat.

Once this set of basic principles was established, Mr. Edwards showed the class some of the other handwriting samples he had collected from the class. These samples were checked against the basic set of principles in terms of legibility. Many children freely identified the samples as their own and noted how they could improve their own handwriting. The rapport between teacher and pupil and between pupil and pupil in Mr. Edwards' classroom was such that children were not afraid to see their own handwriting used for analysis. In classrooms where such rapport does not exist, the teacher may collect handwriting samples from other classes to analyze, thereby removing the threat of criticism.

After the children had practice in analyzing handwriting together, they were asked to write another sentence at the top of a sheet of paper and did a self-analysis of their own handwriting. Using the set of principles on the chalkboard as a guide, each child copied those principles on which he needed to concentrate, under his own writing sample. This became the basis of a series of individualized handwriting lessons during the following weeks.

In order to help each child evaluate his progress in handwriting, Mr. Edwards dictated or wrote on the chalkboard a short paragraph once a week. Each child wrote the paragraph in his best handwriting and gave it to Mr. Edwards. He examined each paper carefully and checked it by writing a series of numbers on the top of the paper. These numbers corresponded to the basic principles for legible handwriting which Mr. Edwards had printed on a chart which now hung before the room. Children checked the numbers with the principles.

Mr. Edwards discovered that some children continued to have difficulty with specific letters. In such cases he made out an individual worksheet or wrote the child a note referring him to a certain page in a workbook or handwriting manual. Children worked on these sheets during the day when other work was finished or whenever they had free time.

Mr. Edwards insured a carry-over from practice to use by using the same code for basic principles when he read reports, stories and other written materials submitted by the children. Each child kept a folder containing his weekly analysis sheet, along with a sample of his best handwriting. These dated sheets helped to show his progress. Often Mr. Edwards used the folder of one child who showed excellent progress, and displayed his papers (written over a period of time) by placing them in the opaque projector. Thus all the children were allowed to see how each other's handwriting had improved.

Occasionally Mr. Edwards used a handwriting scale with an individual child so he could compare his own handwriting to a form accepted by the experts. In such instances, however, Mr. Edwards pointed out the discreet use of basic principles which made the handwriting legible, rather than emphasizing the suggestion that the child should be writing exactly like the sample on the scale.

When creativity is seen as problem solving involving both critical and creative thinking, we can see how Mr. Edwards' approach to handwriting is much more creative than having children compare their writing to someone else's pattern.

Suggestions for Making Handwriting Instruction Enjoyable

1. A joy and pleasure in handwriting may be encouraged if teachers will use Ben Shan's work: Ben Shan, *Love and Joy About Letters* (New York: Grossman Publishers, 1965).

2. When a child is absent from school for a week or more, have the children make get well cards with pictures and messages. Send them all together (in a large envelope) with a child who lives near the absentee. This teaches thoughtfulness for others and makes the absent member feel that he is important to he group.

3. Adopt a merchant marine ship for a year and correspond with the captain and crew. Let them help you plot their trading routes all over the world. You need to apply for the waiting list

if you desire to do this. Write to: Merchant Marine, Battery Park, New York City.

4. Write to children in foreign lands as pen pals.

Addresses to which to write to obtain information on pen pals are: Student Letters Exchange, 821 Elm Avenue, Minneapolis, Minnesota and Executive Secretary, National Council of Social Studies, P.O. Box 413, 1201 16th St. N.W., Washington 6, D.C.

5. Collect various forms of "arty" writing from letters, magazines and newspapers and make a chart or bulletin board display from them.

6. Examine some historical documents to see how styles of handwriting have changed.

7. Collect greeting card saluations from family scrapbooks and records to note the difference in the way writing forms and styles have changed.

8. Try writing with a quill pen and note the differences in the styles of writing which results. Compare the styles to writing with a steel point, a fountain pen and a ball-point pen.

9. With the children, make up check lists to use as self-evaluation devices such as:

Name: _____	Very Good	Good	Fair	Poor
1. Do I keep my letters tall?				
2. Do I leave my oval letters open?				
3. Do I write all my letters with the same slant?				
4. Do I leave attractive margins on my paper?				
5. Do I end my words well?				
6. Do I space my letters well?				
7. Do I space my words well?				
etc.				

FIGURE 7-3.   *A check list for self-evaluation in handwriting.*

10. A teacher may use the following criteria in evaluating handwriting as she attempts to help each child.

a. Slant (parallel).
b. Spacing (of letters *and* words).
c. Size (consistent, legible).
d. Alignment (neat, legible).
e. Loops (open, tall).
f. Stems (tall, closed).
g. Closings (of letters, words).
h. Roundness (to differentiate clearly between i and e, etc.).
i. Retraces (improper or uneconomical formations).

SUMMARY

The teaching of handwriting can be raised from the realm of boring, time-consuming drill if children discover the basic principles necessary to improve their handwriting skills and if they see purposes for using this skill all through the day as a means of communication. Many of the myths associated with handwriting from the past, when the actual nature of handwriting was unknown, must be abolished and replaced by more meaningful practices in handwriting experiences. A legible, attractive hand is an essential social courtesy.

The teaching of handwriting calls for more conformity than most of the language arts skills, but it can be creative in the following senses: (1) it develops judgment and evaluation; (2) new products result from this judgment; (3) it develops an understanding and application of basic principles; (4) it can serve as a tension-relieving agent; (5) the teaching can be open-ended to some degree; (6) it can be individual as well as efficient and legible; (7) certain conditions must be set for good handwriting to develop; (8) it can be success-oriented; (9) knowledge and skills are learned and applied to new situations; (10) it *can* be developed as a problem-solving process; (11) self-learning can be encouraged; (12) ideas and materials can be manipulated and explored; (13) it may be used as a tool for written creative expression; and (14) the results, though somewhat conforming, will also be somewhat individual.

TO THE COLLEGE STUDENT AND THE CLASSROOM TEACHER

1. Send a slip of paper around the room for everyone to sign for attendance. Post it; note the differences in the handwriting.

Does anyone's handwriting particularly reflect his personality. (Example: bold, open, breezy, tight, restricted, large, etc.)

2. Write to some children, your relatives or children in a grade school nearby. Post the letters you receive so you may see individual differences in handwriting at each age level.

3. Invite a handwriting analyst to your classroom and ask her to analyze some of your children's handwriting.

4. Analyze handwriting samples of the students in your class. Can you fit the samples to a handwriting scale? Did the technique used by Mr. Edwards in this chapter help you to improve your children's handwriting? Which technique provided greater motivation?

5. If you are a teacher, study the notes you receive from the parents of your children. Most of the present day elementary school parents were exposed to a formal method of handwriting. How many of them use it in the excuses, notes and reports they send to you? Can you explain why there is so little carry-over in what was taught and what is used?

6. Between the time that this book is written and the time it reaches you, a great deal of knowledge will be added to our understanding of the teaching of handwriting, primarily through the Basic Skills Laboratory at the University of Wisconsin conducted by the National Handwriting Foundation. Much of this research is in mimeograph form. Send for some of it and study it. How does new research free the teacher to increase her creativity?

7. Do you remember your handwriting experiences in elementary school? Did you do "push-pulls" and "compact ovals" during writing classes? What do you suppose was the value in this exercise? Why has it been abandoned in recent years? Select an appropriate book from the bibliography at the end of this chapter and find out what research has to say about these old practices.

8. Do you agree that in the middle school years the transition from manuscript to cursive should be ignored because of the fact that we are required to "print" so much and the time instead should be spent on practicing manuscript?

9. If you are a classroom teacher or a student teacher, how do you evaluate the handwriting of your students? Because of what you read in this chapter, could you add some new techniques of evaluation?

10. Examine the manuals of any currently popular handwriting system and note the rationale behind their system of teaching handwriting. Collect evidence in a school which uses this system as to whether or not goals of the system are being met.

11. Read about the history and evolution of handwriting (see bibliography—Dougherty). There are some interesting things in this article to share with your students.

SELECTED BIBLIOGRAPHY

Burrows, Alvina T., June D. Ferebee, Doris C. Jackson and Dorothy O. Saunders. *They All Want To Write.* Englewood Cliffs, N.J.: Prentice-Hall, 1962.

Dawson, Mildred and Georgianna C. Newman. *Language Teaching in Kindergarten and Early Primary Grades.* New York: Harcourt, Brace and World, 1966.

Dougherty, Mary L. "History of Teaching of Handwriting in America." *Elementary School Journal* 39 (February 1949): 436–38.

Edger, Marlow. "Essentials in Teaching Handwriting." *Education* 86 (1965): 37–65.

Feldt, Leonard S. "The Reliability of Measuring Handwriting Ability." *Journal of Educational Psychology* 53 (December 1962): 288–92.

Greene, Harry A. and Walter T. Petty. "Improving Children's Handwriting." In *Developing Language Skills in the Elementary Schools.* 4th ed. Boston: Allyn and Bacon, 1971.

Handwriting Foundation. *Handwriting and Related Factors. 1890–1960.* Washington, D.C.: Department of Education, 1961.

Hanigan, Levin and Grace Hildebrand. "Handwriting in the Primary Program." In James C. MacCampbell (ed.). *Readings in the Language Arts in the Elementary School.* Boston: D. C. Heath, 1964, pp. 170–78.

Herrick, Virgil E. (ed.). *New Horizons for Research in Handwriting.* Madison: University of Wisconsin Press, 1960.

Horn, Thomas D. (ed.). *Research on Handwriting and Spelling.* Champaign, Ill.: National Council of Teachers of English, 1966.

Myers, Emma. *The Whys and Hows of Handwriting.* Columbus, Ohio: Zaner-Bloser, 1963.

Otto, Wayne and Dan W. Anderson. "Handwriting." In Robert L. Ebel (ed.). *Encyclopedia of Educational Research.* 4th ed. New York: Macmillan, 1969.

Robertson, Wanda. "Creating a Good Environment for Writing." In James C. MacCampbell (ed.). *Readings in the Language Arts in the Elementary School.* Boston: D. C. Heath, 1964, pp. 248–54.

Smith, Lawrence. "Handwriting and Child Development." In James C. MacCampbell (ed.). *Readings in the Language Arts in the Elementary School.* Boston: D. C. Heath, 1964, pp. 167–69.

Templin, Elaine. "Handwriting—the Neglected R." In James C. MacCampbell (ed.). *Readings in the Language Arts in the Elementary School.* Boston: D. C. Heath, 1964, pp. 179–82.

CHAPTER VIII

Creative Teaching of Grammar, Forms, and Word Usage

Echo

On top of old Smoky
  Where everything rhymes
You can hear an echo
  Twenty times.

JIM
Grade 4

Children have an economical way of writing: they get immediately to the point and often waste no words. Witness Jimmy's short poem above about Old Smoky.

Or this letter, sent to me by a second grader after I had visited his classroom in the capacity of an author.

Dear Dr. Smith,

I am sending you this poem that you can read at home.
Sometimes I see Dr. Smith,
Sitting in his room with
His pencil in his hand
And he's feeling very grand.

TIM WILSON
Age 8

TO THE READER

The teachers of Jimmy and Tim are fine, creative teachers. These children have things to say in their own unique way and these teachers have effectively taught them the skills to say it, but in such a way that the boys still enjoy their writing and use it fluently.

In this chapter the author hopes to convince the reader that those boring grammar and word usage drills need not have been boring. Moreover, he hopes to convince the reader that children's feelings are important and that children should feel good about their learnings.

For instance, how did you feel when you were in elementary school when you wrote a composition very carefully and your teacher returned it all marked over with red corrections? Did experiences such as this encourage you to write? How do you feel the mechanics of handwriting should be taught to children? After you discuss this, read parts of this chapter for other ideas. How would you have reacted to these ideas in grammar school?

INTRODUCTION

In a book by Smith, Goodman and Meredith,[1] an excellent summary is made of the research conducted in recent years to test the various assumptions used to justify the teaching of grammar in the elementary school. The authors conclude that school grammar instruction is ineffective. Many children have learned to write effectively while being taught by grammar, but probably more have learned in spite of it rather than because of it.

Inasmuch as grammar in the past has been taught largely through so called traditional teaching and textbook exercises, it is interesting to consider what the results will be when creative teaching is substituted for traditional teaching.

Although capitalization, punctuation, correct word usage and correct forms of written expression are often taught as part of a grammar or English program, a justifiable case could be presented to include them in a handwriting program.

Handwriting is a visual skill, important to the individual only when he wishes to communicate on paper. In developing this skill, his visual perceptions must be refined to a high degree.

Punctuation is also a visual skill; it does not appear in speech. It is used as an attempt to communicate some of the voice quality, voice inflection and natural division of thoughts in oral speech

---

1. Brooks Smith, Kenneth Goodman and Robert Meredith, *Language and Thinking in the Language Arts in the Elementary School* (New York: Holt, Rinehart and Winston, 1970).

into written speech. It only exists on paper. It is logical that it should be taught along with handwriting (or reading), which also exists only on paper.

Like punctuation, capitalization is a visual, written skill.

Many of the problems of correct word usage are problems that appear only when we write them and not when we speak them. When a child says, "I am going to the store," to communicate an idea, it is unnecessary for him to know that there are three spellings for the word *to* and that only one of them is correct. It is only when he begins to write his ideas on paper that this knowledge becomes necessary, or that he confronts the problem of deciding which spelling he must use.

Forms of written expression such as letter writing are also handwriting rather than oral skills; they involve visual perception. A child must learn to visualize his handwritten page before he writes a letter because form is the thing that will "make" the letter.

Forms of written expression include:

1. Various types of sentence structure.
2. Paragraphs.
3. Outlines.
4. Poetry.
5. Forms of correspondence such as business letters, friendly letters, letters of thanks, invitations, announcements, greeting cards and note cards.
6. Alphabetization.
7. Note taking.
8. Script writing.
9. Punctuation.

Like handwriting itself, the mechanics of handwriting require standards of conformity in order to be effective. Teachers may question whether or not the teaching of such skills, already made rigid by common use, can be creative. In the sense that teachers can set conditions which lead children to discover the purpose of writing mechanics, and that children can be helped to apply these standard accepted forms to make their own written communication more creative and more effective, these skill *can* be taught creatively. The creative person is neither compulsively conforming nor compulsively nonconforming, but is free to do either depending either upon his values or upon what is more effective or logical in any situation. Therefore, the creative child will learn the correct use of the forms of written expression and will adapt them to handwriting situations. Like all children, he will learn the forms well if they are taught creatively.

GENERAL CONDITIONS FOR TEACHING THE MECHANICS OF WRITING

Certain overall conditions may be set for the teaching of the mechanics of writing.

1. Because the mechanics of writing and the use of correct word forms and communication forms are *visual* skills, it is important that children "see" these forms. One of the major criticisms which can rightfully be leveled against commercial workbooks is that they often do not differentiate between written and oral skills and try to correct speech problems through written exercises. This is language teaching in reverse of its natural sequence. Correct oral forms are taught on the oral level. Inasmuch as children write the way they speak, the carry-over from speaking to writing will be taken care of. The reverse seldom occurs. Standard use of auxiliary verbs such as "I have finished" and "I had finished" and standard speech forms such as "I haven't any" and "it is I" are oral problems and should be handled in developing correct oral expression.

Correct use of certain words, such as their and there, and uses of punctuation and capitalization are visual or written language problems and can therefore rightfully be taught and corrected on paper. The important principle to be observed in teaching the mechanics of writing is that, as much as possible, emphasis must be placed on *visual* perception of the form.

2. Dealing with punctuation, capitalization, standard word usage and standard written forms is working deeply in the abstract and conceptual forms of communication. Standardized and "correct" communication is farthest away from the best and easiest way to communicate—face to face conversation. For this reason, children need to have extensive concrete experiences with writing and speaking before they are taught the abstract structure and mechanics of language. Slow-learning children may never be able to deal effectively with these abstractions. Normal children will encounter difficulty if the abstractions are not built on several meaningful experiences which gradually lead the children into an understanding of the rules and concepts which build a language. In other words, definitions "grow out" of experiences; they do not precede experiences.

A definition is a concept. It is also a generalization. Generalizations are reached after a series of experiences show us that all these experiences have common elements. In teaching the mechanics of handwriting, many experiences with each of the mechanics is necessary if children are to understand the generalization.

3. The atmosphere of the room must be such that children are not afraid to experiment with punctuation and various word and written forms. The system often called "spoonfeeding" is justifiable in teaching writing skills. Spoonfeeding is that technique, used by some teachers, which almost never allows the child to see incorrect writing forms. In the initial stages of teaching any new skill, the teacher makes certain all children see the form correctly, even if she must show them individually several times on their own papers or on the chalkboard. The children are allowed to use the form only when the teacher is certain it will be used correctly. Inasmuch as forms are visual skills, the purpose in spoonfeeding is to make a correct visual impression on the child's mind, much the same as the teacher does when she builds a sight vocabulary in reading. This technique is in contrast to the one where the teacher teaches a lesson on some handwriting mechanic and then the children are tested by completing a workbook exercise. The danger in the latter system is that, unless the child has learned the mechanic or form in one lesson, he may complete the workbook exercise incorrectly. This tells the teacher that he has not understood the lesson, but it may also distort the visual perception of the mechanic which he is learning. Unless corrected immediately, he may carry this incorrect visual impression in his mind. A sample of spoonfeeding follows.

Miss Farmer was teaching her third grade how to write paragraphs. They were going to write books, and this idea motivated the children. Here are some of the devices Miss Farmer used over a period of a few days:

She had the children look in their reading and story books to to notice how stories are divided into paragraphs.

The children made a list on the chalkboard of things they observed about the paragraph.

a.   The first line is indented.
b.   The sentences are kept apart with capital letters and punctuation marks.
c.   Each sentence tells one more thing about the topic of the paragraph.

Several children were encouraged to name a topic about which a paragraph could be written. These were listed on the board.

On each of the sections of the chalkboard Miss Farmer had drawn lines with yellow chalk giving the usual form of the paragraph (first line indented, the rest of the lines in a neat margin).

Miss Farmer and the children wrote three paragraphs together, using the yellow chalk lines and their rules for writing paragraphs.

Miss Farmer checked the paragraphs with the children; this time she used bright green chalk to go over the punctuation and capitalization used.

Miss Farmer then drew a box around the paragraph, the shape of which accented the indentation. The children discussed the purpose of the indention. Miss Farmer had the children close their eyes and see the box. She pointed out that each time they said or thought of the word "paragraph," this shape should come to their minds.

Miss Farmer asked if anyone in the class thought he could now write a paragraph. She chose one child who volunteered and asked him to go to a clean section of the chalkboard. Miss Farmer then dictated a simple paragraph which the student wrote on the lines she had drawn. The other children watched carefully to check the work.

Miss Farmer introduced a chart on which she had printed a simple paragraph in black ink with the indention in red ink. Miss Farmer said she was going to leave the chart before the room so all might refer to it during the next few days when they were writing their books.

Miss Farmer distributed dittoed papers upon which lines were drawn, with the first line indented. She asked the children to each write the paragraph she was about to dictate. She walked among the children to be sure no one made a mistake, especially with the initial line.

Miss Farmer gave each of the children more copies of the lined dittoed sheet and asked them to write a paragraph on these sheets so they would be sure to do them correctly. She also told the children that if any of them felt they knew how to write paragraphs, they could do so as soon as the sheets were used up.

Miss Farmer then asked the children if they could tell her, in their own words, what a paragraph was. This was the definition arrived at: A paragraph is a group of sentences about *one* thing. You can tell a paragraph because the first line always is farther from the edge of the page than the rest of the lines. At this point Miss Farmer introduced the word "indent," though she did not change the class definition. She printed this definition in colored felt-pen below the sample paragraph on her chart and hung it before the room where everyone could see it.

After each child had written many paragraphs in correct form over a period of several days, Miss Farmer assigned them to some workbook exercises to fix the process.

In this series of experiences, Miss Farmer introduced the visual image of paragraphing a minimum of ten times, each time in a different, interesting and highly motivating way. At no time in all the development of her lessons were the children allowed to see the incorrect form of a paragraph without immediately correcting it. Miss Farmer spoonfed the children until she was sure each had clearly established in his mind correct paragraph shape. From these experiences the children arrived at their own definition.

The teaching of the mechanics of writing and accepted written forms must be kept on an individual level due to the element of intelligence and experiential background which play a large part in each child's readiness. Here is how Miss Farmer carefully allowed for individual differences without placing any undue attention on individuals.

All children were exposed to the initial concept of paragraphing. All children participated in finding paragraphs in the reading books, in pointing out the unique features of a paragraph, in writing paragraphs together, in using the chart as a reference and in visualizing the box form. At this point Miss Farmer knew many of her bright children would have learned the lesson so she allowed for individual differences by:

a. Allowing her children to have as many dittoed sheets as they wished so that bright children could write many paragraphs.
b. Assigning workbook exercises on different levels so each child could work at his level of success.
c. Following up her teaching and working with the slower pupils in groups on the days immediately following these lessons, while those who had learned the concept began to write their stories.

Purposes for the use of writing mechanics and written forms must be apparent at all times. Miss Farmer's children needed to know about paragraphing so they could write books which other people might read. The teaching of handwriting mechanics and written forms may grow out of the child's needs to write letters, to create books, to send invitations, to write social studies reports, to write book reviews and articles for the school newspaper. Once a purpose is established, meaningful teaching and learning can take place.

4. The mechanics and forms of writing should be taught as art forms. Every child will want to make his paper "look nice" and "look pretty." This is the aesthetic value of written compositions.

Comparisons between margins and mounts on the children's art work can be made to show that each accomplishes the same purposes: framing the material, providing a rest space for the eye and creating a focal point in the center of the page. Written composition forms have many correlations with art forms. The beauty of a well-written and well-formed page can be as pleasing to the eye as a well-done painting.

The mechanics of writing and written forms do not, by nature, stem from the child's experience, but they are inherited from the distant past. Some of them do not make sense because they were established at a time when the structure of the language was unsettled and not completely understood. Consequently, the rules of the language are not pure; there are exceptions to all of them. These exceptions exist for no realistic purpose and even interfere with rather than promote communication. They are taught to children by rote memory and regarded as accepted forms.

Handwriting mechanics and writing forms are highly sophisticated skills. The teacher must take the naive child at all levels of his development and contrive experiences which will lead him to an understanding of the purpose and use of language forms. Research has shown that creativity is enhanced when the basic principles underlying an act are understood.

5. Language is not taught in a language period. There should not be a language period in the day—language is the tool of communication used throughout the day. Teachers will take time on certain days to teach specific language skills which grow out of the needs of the class or of individual children. Often such periods will be devoted to a group needing special help rather than to the entire class. When mechanics of writing or speaking and written language forms are used, the effectiveness of the lessons is evaluated by the manner in which this material is put into common practice in relation to the entire curriculum throughout the school day.

SETTING CONDITIONS FOR THE CREATIVE TEACHING OF CAPITALIZATON AND PUNCTUATION: PRIMARY GRADES

Creating a Need or Purpose for Punctuation

An understanding of a need for punctuation may be established by having the teacher read a short story to the children. The story is then written on the board, and the teacher asks the children what they might do to it to make sure a stranger might read it with the intended meaning. Is there some possible way to mark the story so anyone reading it would get an idea about how it was to be read?

In Miss Peters' third grade class the children knew about periods, so they immediately suggested that periods and capital letters be used to break the story into sentences. One child, who did not know about exclamation points, suggested that they write the loud, excited words with big (capital) letters. Another child suggested they draw a line under the quotations to show exactly what the speaker said. Because pitch of the voice goes up with a question mark, one of the children suggested that the word at the end of a question leave the line and go up. A part of their story looked like this:

STOP STOP said the policeman. Where do you think you are go^{ing}.

But John did not stop. He ran into the store and slammed the door. HELP he cried.

Miss Peters told the children she thought people would get the idea very well from the way they had marked the story. "Wouldn't it be easier to read," she asked, "if there was a way to mark it that everyone knew about that would tell them how to read it?" The children agreed, so Miss Peters had them get their story books and discover the way authors wrote stories so they could be read properly. The children could see the need for a common system of punctuation and applied the punctuation marks to their own story.

Miss Cameron used a spoonfeeding technique in her third grade to stress punctuation images with her pupils. She printed a short story (which one of the children had written) on a sheet of heavy tagboard. The story contained most of the punctuation marks which the children had studied. Miss Cameron cut slits in the tagboard with a razor blade at every place where there should be a punctuation mark. The punctuation marks were then placed on strips of cardboard which fit the slits. First the class worked together by putting the correct punctuation marks in the slits. Then the device was used as an independent teaching device—children could try to place the punctuation marks in the strips whenever they had free time and Miss Cameron could check it from wherever she was working in the classroom. Children were helped by the fact that all the strips and cuts were of different sizes and it was almost impossible to make a mistake; this kept the correct image before each child as he worked.

SETTING CONDITIONS FOR THE CREATIVE TEACHING OF CAPITALIZATION AND PUNCTUATION: INTERMEDIATE GRADES

To establish a purpose for punctuation, on the chalkboard write sentences of which the meaning is completely changed when different punctuation is added. After awhile children will enjoy making up their own sentences. Make a collection like this somewhere in the classroom:

> Example: Woman without her man is nothing. *to*
> Woman! Without her, man is nothing!
> Example: The child said the teacher is silly. *to*
> "The child," said the teacher, "is silly."
> Example: The teacher said the girl is pretty. *to*
> "The teacher," said the girl, "is pretty."

Hand out a sheet of paper with as many confusing sentences as can possibly be cleared up by a change of punctuation.

> Pull the blind up John.
> Pull the blind up, John.

> Mary said Joe take out the papers.
> Mary said, "Joe, take out the papers." *or*
> "Mary," said Joe, "take out the papers!"

Proofreading and Punctuation Skills

Five or so children are chosen to be proofreaders for the written material for a day or a week. These children get name cards to wear on their backs such as Period Pete, Sentence Susie, or Capital Charley. Each child checks a set of papers for any mistakes pertaining to his name and each makes his corrections in a different color pencil. You change jobs frequently so that each child gets a chance to do some proofreading and becomes aware of the errors made by himself as well as by others.

Punctuation is a visual skill which requires concentrated thought process in its use. How much easier it would be to remember where to punctuate if we *talked* punctuation. Children will receive a great deal of pleasure in hearing punctuation in Victor Borge's famous punctuation recording.[2] One sixth grade teacher, who could not seem to help her boys remember about punctuation marks, motivated them to writing stories with complicated punc-

---

2. Victor Borge, *Caught in the Act* (Columbia High Fidelity Recording, CL 646).

tuation when she challenged them to read the punctuation as Victor Borge reads it.

Keep a file of folders and label the tabs with the common mistakes in word usage, punctuation and capitalization. In the folders, place sheets torn from workbooks which give help or drill with these problems. Such a file helps develop individualized instruction because a teacher may explain a common error to a child and afford him practice by sending him to the file to select an appropriate work sheet.

Evaluation Games

Here are two activities that may be used after the teacher is certain that the concepts of punctuation are fairly well mastered. They are "polishing up" testing situations.

What's my line? The activity is patterned after the TV program of the same name. Each punctuation mark (a student) appears and is questioned concerning its activities. Students must identify the uses of the punctuation mark.

Beat the tape: The teacher or a student reads a short story into the tape recorder a little slower than usual oral reading speed, but using the correct breathing and grouping to indicate the presence of punctuation marks. The class follows a copy of the story on a ditto sheet and puts in the punctuation marks as the story is read. Children also may put in the capital letters where needed after they have put in the punctuation marks.

Some Punctuation Activities

Hunting for hyphens: When it is time to teach children about dividing words at the ends of lines, turn to a daily newspaper. Newspaper columns are short and contain many hyphenated words. Have the children look for these words. Cut out the columns, circle the hyphen with red crayon and paste them on a chart or bulletin board. Children may analyze the hyphens and come up with generalizations about hyphenated words, or they may use this experience as a practice period after learning the basic principles of hyphens.

Using apostrophes: Apostrophes generally designate the omission of a letter to shorten a word, or a possessive. Noticing the missing letter and the substitution of the apostrophe, or noting the apostrophe used as a possessive, is a skill requiring refined visual perception. There are many ways teachers can help children focus their vision on the particular part of the word where the apostrophe is used:

1. To designate an omission, introduce the concept by using the children's natural speech patterns. Write down on the chalkboard those expressions you have heard during the day which contain shortened words with apostrophes. Develop the principle and then use a series of experiences built on visual presentation.

2. Miss Jones cut several large, red apostrophes from construction paper and fastened them to the chalkboard with a curl of masking tape. Children then placed these in their proper places in phrases written on the board. The large, red apostrophes could be seen from any place in the room. Miss Jones wrote some phrases on the board each morning and chose some children to place the apostrophes. This became an independent activity, which could be done by one or two children and checked by Miss Jones from any place in the room.

3. Colored chalk also helps accomplish the objective of establishing the image of the apostrophe in the child's mind.

4. Miss Wagner invented the following simple device which shows how, when a letter is omitted, an apostrophe must take its place.

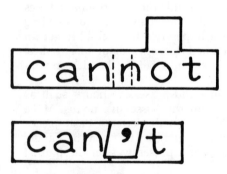

Fold on dotted lines. Then fold tab over. Apostrophe is on rear of tab and comes into view when tab is folded over.

FIGURE 8-1.   *An apostrophe shows an omission.*

5. Colored felt pens on paper help the children become aware of the apostrophe.

6. A chart on the use of the apostrophe at the front of the room, where apostrophes are put in color will serve as a good reference for children.

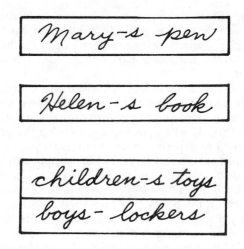

FIGURE 8-2.   *Visualizing apostrophe possessives.*

7. For possessives: The construction paper apostrophes work well here, also. The colored chalk and colored flo-pens mentioned above will help children visualize apostrophes used in the possessive.

Print phrases on strips of cardboard such as in Figure 8-2. Cut a slit in the cardboard where an apostrophe is to be placed. On smaller cardboards make many small apostrophes which fit in the slits. Children can tell where they think the apostrophe belongs and then check by putting it in the slit. This is a spoonfeeding technique which makes it almost impossible for a child to get an incorrect visual impression when he is learning about apostrophes. These cards can be set in a pocket chart before the class for individual use.

Make cards of individual nouns and possessive nouns such as in Figure 8-3. Cut the letter *s* from the possessive nouns. Make several apostrophes to fit before or after the letter *s*. Paste pieces of flannel on all the pieces and play games with them by having the children build singular and plural possessives on the flannel board.

Modern studies in linguistics have contributed a great deal to new concepts about the teaching of grammar and word usage. The structuralists state that the noun is distinctive from other words in that it can be made plural and possessive and that this is a property unique to nouns.

After discovering and using the technique suggested above for checking possessives, children can be asked which words from lists created by themselves can be made possessives. Can these words

Possessive Nouns   Nouns

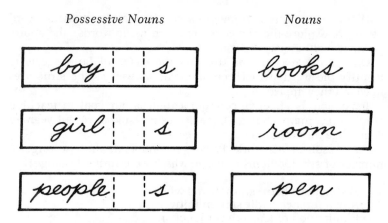

FIGURE 8-3. *Possessives: singular and plural.*

also be made plural? The children have then discovered which words in their lists are nouns.

Quotation marks: On a flannel board write sentences needing quotation marks (use strips of construction paper). Make the necessary marks out of colored paper. Use the strips for initial instruction; games, independent work or drill.

Encourage children to keep individual folders of errors or of papers which have been edited. Date the papers and at least once a month provide a period where children examine the papers in the folders to analyze their own progress. Which mistakes are they still making and which have they eliminated?

WORD USAGE

Objective 2 on page 38 states that each child must acquire necessary communication skills so he may express himself effectively in all media. Three of the skills mentioned in the subheadings which follow are: To learn correct word usage as a social courtesy, to use capitalization and punctuation as a courtesy, and to use word forms correctly.

Correct word usage carries double meaning here. It means he learns how to communicate freely in the environment where he finds himself. Therefore, he will be taught the dialects and the various levels of usage he finds around him as well as the standard English (one level of usage) which will serve him in certain situations much as slang serves him in other situations.

Word usage differs from *grammar* in that in studying word usage we explore the choice we make in using words: the appropriateness of language in context.

One of the reasons for studying the usage of language is to identify the words which communicate as well as the structures in which they appear.

Inasmuch as effective communication is our goal in teaching word usage, many changes have been suggested in recent years to encourage the communication process.

As a result of his work, Pooley[3] recommends that we forget a number of specific items of usage which were formerly taught:

1. Distinctions between shall and will.
2. Any reference to the split infinitive.
3. Elimination of *like* as a conjunction.
4. Objection to the phrase "different than."
5. Objection to "He is one of those boys who *is*."
6. Objection to "the reason . . . is because . . ."
7. Objection to *myself* as a polite substitution for I.
8. Insistence on the possessive case standing before a gerund.

The material which follows has been selected because the children in these classes were motivated to work at improving their own word usage in whatever context they were working.

SETTING CONDITIONS FOR THE CREATIVE TEACHING OF STANDARD WORD USAGE: PRIMARY GRADES

The mistakes which children make in word usage center around a few common errors. Teaching directed toward these few errors will remove the necessity of much boring practice.

It is unlikely that every child needs the same instruction in English usage, and the risk of confusing children who already know grammatical forms can be diminished if as much individual instruction as possible is given. An evaluation of all written work can take place, and the teacher, with the child, can record his difficulties and mistakes on a five by eight card. During the oral expression period in the morning, she may jot down additional notes which show where the child needs help. Children should

---

3. Robert Pooley, "What about Grammar," in James C. MacCampbell (ed.), *Readings in the Language Arts in the Elementary School* (Boston: D. C. Heath, 1964), pp. 210–15.

have access to these cards, so that, with their teachers, they can work out their problems.

To supplement this individual instruction, much group work can be held which is geared to improving language expression. The illustration of the technicolor lesson is a good example of this type of work. (See pages 149–50.) Many teachers now use a tape recorder and permit children to hear themselves and evaluate their own speech. This is an effective way of letting children hear how they sound. This device can also provide opportunity for critical evaluation among a group with speech defects.

Use of the tape recorder affords the teacher the opportunity to make the distinction between those errors which need to be corrected at the oral level and those which may be corrected at the written level.

Some books are written with words which are purposely confusing in order to make the plot more interesting. These books focus the attention of the children upon correct forms. Some of them are:

Which Witch Is Which by Robert Lasson
Ounce, Dice, Trice by Alistair Reid
Way Beyond Zebra by Dr. Seuss
Sparkle and Spin: A Book About Words by Ann and Paul Rand
The First Book of Words: Their Family Histories by Samuel and
    Beryl Epstein

There are also some books which can be used skillfully in teaching grammar. Two such books are: *Grammar Can Be Fun* by Robert Lawson and Monroe Leaf and *Easy in English* by Mauree Applegate.

Antonyms: Find pictures of opposites (example: boy—girl) and paste them at the top of a twelve by eighteen sheet of drawing paper. When children think of a pair of words or find them in reading, they may go and write their words on the sheet.

Teacher says something like:

> Candy is sweet, but pickles are _____.
> The airplane is fast, but a horse is _____.
> The sky is above, the ground _____.
> In the morning the sun rises; at night the sun _____.

Synonym golf: Compile a list of eighteen words representing the eighteen holes of golf. Try to find a synonym for each word. The number of letters in the synonym chosen represents the score for

the word. Score eight for a word for which you can find no synonym. The lowest score wins.

Teakettle: For this game use words that sound alike but have
different meanings, such as *write* and *right.* One player leaves
the room and the rest decide on a double-meaning word. When the
player returns everyone has a chance to use a sentence with the
chosen word. But instead of saying that particular word, you substitute teakettle. For example, "I will teakettle a letter with my
teakettle hand."

Four steps: Objectives: To develop the concept of sequence of
development. To develop imagination.
　　Procedure: Have the children write a sequence of three or more
steps necessary to each of the following activities. It is a greater
challenge to the imagination to act these out before the remainder
of the class.

a.　Washing dishes.
b.　Getting ready for school.
c.　Washing a car.
d.　Cleaning a yard.
e.　Painting a doghouse.
f.　Making a sandwich.
g.　Buying candy or ice cream.
h.　Mailing a letter.

Biographies and autobiographies: One of my student teachers did
an excellent job in showing the difference between an autobiography and a biography to a second grade.
　　She came into the classroom when it was time for her lesson
wearing a George Washington costume and carrying a hatchet.
The children reacted, of course, to the costume. Most of them
knew at once that Miss McGraw was dressed to represent George
Washington.
　　"George" asked the children to listen carefully and he would tell
the class about himself. This the children did and "George" told
a very exciting story of his life in the first person.
　　Then, "George" walked to the opposite side of the room and
asked the children to again listen while he told them another
story about Martha Washington, his wife. The children listened
attentively while "George" told about Martha in the third person.
　　When the stories were finished the children were asked to point
out the differences in the way the two stories were told; one was
told about himself in the first person (autobiography) and one
about someone else in the third person (biography).

The children were then asked to classify books they had read in the room into the two categories. Then each child wrote an auto-biographical riddle about himself and a biographical riddle about a friend in the class. The somewhat difficult concepts were very clear to the children as a result of Miss McGraw's creative lesson.

As a follow up activity to this lesson many children tried their hand at writing biography and autobiography. Some children submitted their autobiographies in poetry form like Stephen's:

> *Me, Myself, and I*
>
> *I like to play,*
> *I like to run.*
> *I like to have*
> *A lot of fun.*
>
> *I like to golf,*
> *I like to swim.*
> *I like to play*
> *With my friend Jim.*
>
> *I like to skate,*
> *I like to ski.*
> *I like to play*
> *Down by the sea.*
>
> STEPHEN CARDAMONE

SETTING CONDITIONS FOR THE CREATIVE TEACHING OF STANDARD WORD USAGE: INTERMEDIATE GRADES

In the elementary grades the major emphasis should be on the actual use of language and the improvement of skills through use, rather than on knowledge about the language itself, and the attention to restrictive rules.

The point has been made that many problems in written expression rise from the errors which appear in oral speech. An analysis of some of these errors will show that many of them are due to the patterns of speech the child mimicked in his growing up. Some are dialects or the regional and illiterate level of folksy talk. Others are the peculiar idiosyncrasies of the home or community. For the child, this language communicates as well as the more acceptable forms. The child should be taught that informal American English (and some colloquialisms) is the goal to work for in daily speech. Emphasis should not be put on standard speech to the degree that the child withdraws from using speech fluently. Rather, he should learn the more acceptable forms of speech just as he should learn two languages, and he will receive help in learning where to apply these acceptable forms (see page 83).

Robert Pooley, in his book *Teaching English Usage*, lists two principles of importance in the approach of usage in the elementary schools:

1. To break bad habits and to achieve more desirable ones mean a set limit on the number of specific items of usage to be attacked in the grades.
2. The items picked for mastery must be taught soundly in accordance with the principles of learning and the psychology of habit breaking.[4]

This means, of course, that certain speech patterns can be altered only at different age levels, as the child matures and through conditioned responses. Children respond well to corrections which are made quietly, politely and with due respect for their feelings. If embarrassment and resentment become associated with correction, the value of the instruction is greatly reduced. A child should not be interrupted when he is speaking, and corrections or suggestions for alterations in his speech patterns should be made individually and privately.

SPECIFIC IDEAS FOR TEACHING WORD USAGE

1. Many children become aware of their speech deficiencies when they are allowed to speak on a tape and then analyze their own voices and speech patterns. One research study showed significant healthy gains were made with the use of a tape recorder.[5] Changes in the writing forms changed significantly with a change of speech patterns.

2. Have each individual keep a folder of his own speech and word errors. Dittoed sheets listing common errors can be clipped inside the folder. Each child uses his corrected papers to diagnose his mistakes and mark the check sheets.

3. Collect cartoons which help children understand grammar usage or the mechanics of writing. (See Figure 8-4.)

---

4. Robert C. Pooley, *Teaching English Usage* (Champaign, Ill.: National Council of Teachers of English), p. 178. Used by permission of the National Council of Teachers of English.
5. Haverly Moyer, "The Effect of Ear Training on Certain Aspects of Children's Usage" (unpublished Ph.D. dissertation, Syracuse University, 1950).

FIGURE 8-4. *Peanuts* (© 1959 United Features Syndicate, Inc.).

4. Attention can often be focused on the good use of writing forms, writing mechanics and word usage by collecting poor samples or mistakes made in newspapers, on television or radio or in magazines and school papers. Make a bulletin board collection of these poor samples of communication. Call it "Boo-Boos" or "Bloopers." For example: "The climate is hottest next to the creator."

5. Focus on effective word usage and the importance of the use of sound word arrangement can often be demonstrated by reading stories and jokes, collected from newspapers, television and magazines, which emphasize misunderstandings due to the improper use of words. Many jokebooks will provide the teacher with such material, such as: Art Linkletter's, *Kids Say the Darndest Things*,[6] and Bennett Cerf's *The Life of the Party*.[7] The teacher must select carefully those items which children will understand. Children will enjoy collecting these excerpts, too.

6. Help pupils realize that words can be assembled in many ways and there are many levels of usage, by collecting examples of levels of usage.

Formal	*Informal*	*Slang*
Do you comprehend my explanation?	Do you understand me?	Dig?
I find him to be unnaturally disinterested and inattentive.	He's not paying attention.	He's spaced out.

Be sure to discuss the place where each of these expressions may be acceptably used.

7. Children may set up their own editing committees. Have each child print his name on a manila folder. Decorate a box big enough to hold the manila folders. Arrange the folders alphabetically in the box. Children will drop their next-to-final drafts of stories, poems and other creative writing in the folders. A committee of children, appointed by the teacher, who are skillful at using punctuation, capitalization and writing mechanics will act as editors. In their spare time they will take a folder and edit the writing of any one child. If the author is working at his seat at the

---

6. Art Linkletter, *Kids Say the Darndest Things* (New York: Pocket Books, 1957).
7. Bennett Cerf, *The Life of the Party* (New York: Doubleday, 1956).

time, the editor can sit with him and go over his work with him. In this way, children learn from each other, and the teacher gets the final draft for final editing. The signatures of both children at the end of the paper will help the teacher to learn those who still need help with certain grammar skills.

8. There are many plays which the teacher might find advantageous. One favorite is "An Adventure on the Planet Grammar" by Kaye M. Howard.

9. Children will enjoy poems which poke fun at grammar, such as the following:

> *The grammar has a rule absurd*
> *Which I would call an outgrown myth.*
> *A preposition is a word*
> *You musn't end a sentence with.*

D. PRALEY

10. Some films help with understanding parts of speech. Examples: *Do Words Ever Fool You?* (11 minutes, black and white, Coronet) and *Grammar: Verbs and Ways We Use Them* (11 minutes, black and white, Young American Films).

11. Certain kinds of individual progress charts or graphs can be utilized by teachers to provide an incentive for children to better their own use of correct written expression forms.

THE LINGUIST AND GRAMMAR

In recent years, the linguists have made contributions to our understanding of the structure of language. A linguist is one who studies the science of speech. He does not as a rule concern himself with the teaching of language. Recently, however, the contributions of linguists have been valuable in helping teachers devise approaches to teaching all aspects of the language arts, especially reading and that area commonly referred to in the past as grammar.

The theories of the linguists have not, as yet, been substantially absorbed in public school methodology. Some progress has been made and teaching the language arts in the future may be greatly affected by new studies in the structure of language. A review of some of the concepts of linguists is essential here.

Modern linguists define grammar as the study of the structure of English speech, the language as it operates: the syntax. In expanding this definition some writers[8] note that grammar is a study of the way a language works encompassing morphology (meaningful forms), syntax (sentence structure), and phonology (sounds).

In studying the structure of English speech, clarification has been made in order to isolate that which is classified as grammar and that which is classified as "word usage." Misconceptions about grammar have been identified and discussed. In some instances, linguists have found it simpler to identify that which *is not* grammar rather than that which is.

Grammar is not usage. It is not that which we have labeled "good English" in the past. Concepts of correctness or incorrectness in language pertain to usage. Consequently, grammar is not "parts of speech." Nor is it the mechanics of composition (punctuation, capitalization, etc.).

Modern grammar is based on structural linguistics and emphasizes learning about grammar by engaging in the work of the linguist—examining the language itself. The student can discover word classes, sentence patterns, kernels, core structures, a nucleus of words and methods of expanding them.

Linguists have invented many labels and many classifications for "grammar" for the English language. These include traditional grammar, historical grammar, structural grammar, generative and transformational grammar.[9]

Types of Grammar

Traditional grammar, according to linguists, is an inaccurate representation of English sentence structure. This is the label given to the type of teaching and learning of the old school. The rules of "proper" and "improper" grammar were based on the rules of Latin.

Linguists have concluded that the teaching of traditional grammar or formal grammar as we used to call it has had a negligible (and even harmful) effect on the improvement of writing.

Historical grammar deals with the origins of English words, the development of the languages and changes in spelling and pronunciation.

---

8. Metropolitan School Study Council, *Structural Linguistics: An Introduction for Teachers and Administrators* (New York: Teachers College Press, 1961).
9. Charles C. Fries, *Linguistics, the Study of Language* (New York: Holt, Rinehart and Winston, 1966).

Structural grammar is a descriptive grammar which separates the structure of language from its meaning, or a study of syntax from semantics. Studies of structural grammar led to new concepts such as phonemes (the sounds of English), morphemes (the meaningful units of language) and phrase structure. The scholars of structural grammar devised a new system of classifying the words in a language, on syntax rather than meaning.

The structuralists discovered that all nouns are distinctive from other words in that a noun can be made plural and possessive. This is a property unique to nouns. The structural linguist is primarily concerned with discovering and describing as concisely as possible the interrelationships and patterns which make up the intricate structure of language.

Transformational grammar extends the concepts of structural grammar to include semantics of language. Linguists identify *obligatory* and *optional* transformations. An obligatory transformation is agreement between a subject and a verb such as: Dinosaurs eat (not eats). An optional transformation is an elaboration of the core sentence such as: The enormous dinosaur eats greedily all day long.

Generative grammar has developed very exact rules for transforming sentences and these rules are usually stated in a formula. The problem of generative grammar is to make general rules explicit.

New concepts of grammar as designed by linguists offer much promise for constructive changes in the teaching of the written language. Because of the newness of the entire field of linguistics, many schools still function under the old concepts of formal grammar. Tiedt and Tiedt[10] express the problem as follows:

> It will be some time before these definitions are assimilated by the teaching profession and even longer until the public understands, for example, that there is a distinction between grammar and usage. When critics of education cry, therefore, for a return to the teaching of grammar so that our young people will gain skill in composition, we can be certain that these representatives of the public really want the classroom teacher to stress the teaching of "correct usage."

Because children come to school *speaking* fluently and using all forms of words and clusters of words, the raw material with which to teach grammar is in the minds and mouths of the children.

---

10. Iris M. Tiedt and Sidney W. Tiedt, *Contemporary English in the Elementary School* (Englewood Cliffs, N.J.: Prentice-Hall, 1962), p. 21.

Tiedt and Tiedt state that a rather wise approach to the study of grammar is to impress the student with his own knowledge of grammar rather than to stress the esoteric, difficult nature of the study on which the class is embarking.

Rather than teaching for "correct" or "incorrect" grammar, linguists recommend that we teach the concept of varied levels of usage. One level of varied usage is standard English, another might be a dialect, another is slang.

About the only logical purpose for examining the structure of English sentences and experimenting with methods of expansion is to foster the student's ability to generate (or create) sentences of his own which are meaningful to him and help him to say well what he wants to say. Exploration of sentence structure should help students develop their own style of writing.

Word Classifications

Structural linguists suggest a new classification for words. Of the eight parts of speech or word classes identified by traditional grammar, structural linguists maintain seven as still useful and identify other function words which appear in English sentences. The first classes: noun, verb, adjective, determiner, intensifier, and adverb are open classes. Open classes are those to which an indefinite number of words can be added. The other classes are called *function* or *structure* words: prepositions, conjunctions, subordinates, auxiliary words and pronouns.

These classifications are defined as follows:

Nouns are words that can be made plural or possessive and may follow the words *the, a,* or *an.*

Verbs are words that can be changed from past to present and usually (except forms of *to be*) add *s* when patterned after *it, she, he.* The morpheme *ing* may be added to a verb.

Adjectives pattern with the word *very*, and the adjective can follow a linking verb.

In the terms of the modern linguist, some words formerly treated as adjectives are identified as *determiners.* They signal that a noun follows. Included in this class are *the, a, an, every, each, this, that, these, those, my, one, two, three, four, most, more, either, neither, our, your, their, his, her, its, no, both, some, much, all, any, several, few.*

Intensifiers pattern with adjectives and adverbs. They include such words as *very, somewhat, rather, quite.*

Prepositions signal that a noun follows, usually a prepositional phrase which serves an adjective or adverb function. Common prepositions include *about, above, across, in, into, up, off,* and the like.

Conjunctions are linking words that signal the joining of equal words or groups of words (*and, but, for, either, or, yet, not only . . . but also*).

Subordinators are linking words that join subordinate subject-predicate word groups (classes) with independent subject-predicate word groups (classes). Included are *who, when, until, unless, that, since, if, what, which,* and others.

Auxiliaries signal that a verb follows. Some auxiliaries may also serve as independent verbs, and only two (*be, have*) pattern with the past form of verbs.

Pronouns do not pattern with determiners, but they substitute for nouns or proper nouns.

One of the most effective ways to introduce children to these word class functions is to use a creative approach where students make discoveries for themselves.

Because the concepts of the linguists are comparatively new, the author has retained the traditional terminology in this volume in places where he feels it is clearer to teachers who have had no training in linguistics concepts. Wherever possible, he has used the new terminology hoping to cause no confusion in the understanding of terms.

GRAMMAR

Ideas for Teaching Parts of Speech

1. To build a speaking vocabulary in referring to word classification, Mrs. Felshaw gave the children many experiences with nouns, verbs, intensifiers, pronouns, etc., from which the children arrived at definitions. The names for classes of speech were printed on long strips of tagboard with the definitions after them. The names were cut apart from the definitions with an unusual cut of the scissors. Not only did the children have fun matching the definitions with the names, but any student who did not remember the definition could match the cut in the tagboard much like putting a puzzle together.

2. *Word classification game:* Give pupils cards that have a noun, verb, adjective, etc., on them. All pupils who have cards that name something exchange seats. All pupils who have cards that express action change places. All pupils who have cards that describe may change places, etc. If one seat is removed, one child will be left standing each time and he may call for the next exchange.

3. *Prepositions:* Play a preposition game. Place a box on a table. Put an object in, under, beside, below, above or on the box. List the words which describe where the object is and label them as prepositions.

After one group of children discussed what prepositions were, they collected lists of them.

One day in Miss Stone's sixth grade the children painted prepositions for art. Some beautiful abstractions resulted where children painted their ideas of: *across, under* and *around.* (See Fig. 8-5.)

4. *Consequences:* Equipment: A long slip of paper and a pencil for each player. The leader holds the following list of descriptions:

FIGURE 8-5. *The painting of a preposition.*

a. An *adjective* to describe a man.
b. A man's name (proper noun).
c. An *adjective* to describe a girl.
d. A girl's name (proper noun).
e. Where they met (prepositional phrase).
f. What he wore (noun).
g. What she wore (noun).
h. What he said (quotation).
i. What she said (quotation).
j. What the world said (quotation).
k. The consequence (sentence).

Each player writes the first statement, which is read, at the top of his slip, then folds the slip down and passes it to the right. The second statement is written beneath the first, folded down, and passed on. When the list is completed, each slip is passed once more, and the players all read the complete stories they hold.

5. *Adjectives and adverbs:* Take small, short sentences lacking in descriptive words and have the children build them into longer, more exciting sentences.

Miss Aaron's fourth grade class changed a sentence as follows:

> The birthday cake sat on the table.
>   *to*
> The snowy, white, delectable, three-layer
> birthday cake sat proudly on the gaily
> decorated party table.

6. *How I feel:*

Objective: To teach adjectives and vocabulary dealing with texture.

Procedure: Keep in the room a box of miscellaneous materials of contrasting textures. Examples: fur, felt, cellophane of different colors, oil cloth, aluminum foil, sandpaper, wood shavings, dried split peas, velvet, satin, terry cloth, corrugated cardboard, textured wallpaper, rubber, cotton, manila rope, yarn, sawdust, etc.

Let each pupil select 4 or 5 of these making sure to get contrasting textures and staple or glue them to cardboard to make a collage design. Then they can draw black outlines around them and fill in the spaces between them by using crayons or water colors.

From discussion of the different pictures build texture words.

7. *Hands and feet:*

Objective: To develop the concept of adjectives (or adverbs).

Procedure: Have the children trace their hands (and feet) on construction paper and then using as many adjectives (or adverbs) as possible, describe them. (Wrinkled, soft, rough, and flexible, tightly, loosely, etc.)

8. *Adjective shorts:*

a. As a class draw or cut out and paste a whole chart full of faces. Write the adjectives that best describe each face.
b. Reverse the above process. List the adjectives on the board, then find or draw a picture to match each word.
c. Near Christmas, cut out pictures of presents you'd like to have, and find adjectives for each one.
d. Pick a bouquet of the twelve most appropriate adjectives and nouns they describe from the story you read in reading in the morning or from your favorite library story.
e. Keep a personal adjective book in which you copy well-used and different adjectives and their nouns for later use.
f. Shut your eyes and recall something interesting you saw today. Describe it in one good sentence. How many adjectives did you use?
g. Choose a favorite television or movie star and find the two best adjectives to describe him or her.
h. Gather lists of adjective pairs (nouns and adjectives) that you use in arithmetic, science and social studies classes.
i. Have an adjective search of a page in the reading or literature book. See who can find the largest number.
j. Have the students spell all the adjectives in the week's spelling list.
k. Make a collection of advertisements that use adjectives to make the product attractive.
l. Put a picture on the bulletin board. Let each child add one adjective that might be used in telling about the picture.

9. *Adverb research:* Students may do a bit of scientific research to find out what percentage of adverbs end in *ly*.

10. *Adverb chart:* Have an empty chart ready and divided into four columns headed by *When? Where? How? How Much?* Students think of common adverbs that might fit under each heading. Put the finished chart in a conspicuous place for the class to use for reference.

11. *Quotation marks:* Have the children write stories in dialogue. One way to start is to write imaginary telephone calls, morning greeting, requests to go to a movie or to buy a coveted toy. Soon children will be writing creative dialogue.

Set up a press conference to help children distinguish between direct and indirect quotations. Let some take turns acting as president, vice-president, or other figures in the news, while others assume the role of reporters for newspapers and news services.

Holding unrehearsed conferences the reporters take careful and accurate notes. When the study is in this framework, it doesn't take long for boys and girls to learn the difference between the gist of a statement and the statement itself. Combine the role-playing with finding examples of official statements and reports about the statement that appears in the daily papers.

12. *Nouns:* It is in the intermediate grades that singular and plural nouns are introduced to children. In most cases these are spoken skills, but the exceptions to the general rule are written skills. The plural for scroll is scrolls, for boy, boys. But the exceptions require memorization of the visual image. After studying nouns which follow this general rule, a chart of the exceptions should be made and kept in the classroom where children may go to it for easy reference. Such a chart might look like this:

Exceptional Plurals

inches	shelves
children	men
deer	women
sheep	halves
feet	geese

13. *Some games to play with nouns:*

Geographic tennis—One side calls out a common noun such as "city" and the other side must bat back with "Philadelphia" or any city in the geographical area within bounds named before the game begins. Then serve with another category such as "river" which might call for the St. Lawrence. No scoring is done until one side misses, then the opposite side scores.

Noun password—Played like the TV game except the words used are nouns.

"*I have a word secret*"—Each side takes turns asking questions of one who is "It." "It" announces "I have a secret word! It's a proper noun, the name of a person who is connected with the government." Then each side takes turns asking such questions as: "Does he live in our own state?" etc. You can play the noun game under such categories as winter sports, music, books, or television characters.

14. "*Septain*" *poetry:*

Objective: To build new words meaningfully into the child's vocabulary: nouns, adjectives, adverbs, antonyms.

Procedure: Give the children a dittoed sheet with lines drawn on it as shown below. Tell them to put a word on the top line and its opposite on the last line such as big and little. On line 2 write two words that describe line 1. On line 6 write two words that describe line 7. On line 3 write three characteristics or verbs describing line 1. On line 5 write three characteristics or verbs that go with line 7. Line 4 is the transition line where words, a sentence or a phrase must be written to get the reader logically from one word to its opposite.

One of my students wrote the following from the opposites, conformity and creativity.

Conformity

Rigid   Destructive

Crushing   Ego-Killing   Deadening

Convergency   Divergency   Imagination   Openness

Releasing   Rejuvenating   Resurrecting

Insightful   Joyous

Creativity

15. *Fun games with verbs:* Loban[11] has stated that problems with the use of verbs prove to be the most frequent kind of deviation from conventional usage in the elementary school. Lack of agreement between subject and predicate, particularly in the third person singular, proves to be a major difficulty in the use of verbs. Consistency of verb tense is another difficulty.

If such is the case it would seem that instruction in these problems should be made more exciting, effective and interesting to children.

Verb magnetism—Write sentences involving the use of any troublesome verb form leaving blanks where the verbs should be. Spread small word cards with tiny magnets glued to the back on a nearby table. Divide the class into two teams. Members of each team take turns placing the correct form of the verb over the blank space left in the written sentences. Keep an on-going score for each team. (Curls of masking tape may be used on a regular chalkboard to hold the cards in place if no magnetic chalkboard is available.)

Employment agency—All except three children are given a verb card such as *seem, draw, flown, swim.* The children holding these verb cards are the "employers." The three other children (the "employees") hold the card with a helping verb such as *has, have,*

---

11. Walter Loban, *The Language of Elementary School Children* (Champaign, Ill.: National Council of Teachers of English, 1963), pp. 81–89.

or *had*. Each employer in turn holds his word card in front of the group and says "Do I need help? Does anyone want a job?" If the word on his card needs a helping word, one of the three helpers who raised his hand may be chosen to stand beside him. The teacher chooses another child to use the word(s) in a sentence.

Verb pantomime—One student performs an action before the group and the class is to guess the action. They must use the action word in a sentence to describe the person acting and the action.

16. *Tenses*—Most common of all errors of tenses in the elementary grades are the following.[12]

> *come* for *came*
> *seen* for *saw*
> *have did* for *have done*
> *has went* for *has gone*
> *run* for *ran*
> *done* for *did*
> *rung* for *rang*
> *give* for *gave*
> *ask* for *asked*
> *have rode* for *have ridden*
> *have took* for *have taken*

17. *Diagramobile:* A study of sentence structure can be dramatized through the use of a diagramobile, which is made from wires or sticks suspended from the ceiling by thread. The subject and the predicate are pasted on cards and form the main cross bar of the diagramobile. From the subject are hung such modifiers as the articles, adjectives and modifying phrases. Similarly, adverbs and phrases are suspended from the predicate. The more complex the sentence, the more fascinating is the mobile. Added color gives additional interest—adjectives in red, adverbs in blue, etc. The structure of the mobile appeals to the visual image and helps children remember the proper placement of parts of speech.

SETTING CONDITIONS FOR THE CREATIVE TEACHING OF SENTENCE STRUCTURE: PRIMARY GRADES

The first language form to which a child is exposed is the simple sentence. Prerequisite to the writing of sentences is the speaking or telling of stories, poems and daily events in sentence form. Oral

---

12. Harry A. Greene and Walter T. Petty, *Developing Language Skills in the Elementary Schools* (Boston: Allyn and Bacon, 1959), p. 138.

expression periods, such as the show and tell period described on pages 147–48 help the children to speak using one idea or a related group of ideas in sentences.

As soon as the child is capable of speaking simple sentences, the teacher takes advantage of this skill and forms first reading experience charts. The short, simple sentences with proper punctuation used on these charts help the child see the correct written form for simple sentences.

Many children attempt to copy reading charts. The teacher can make sure each child uses the correct punctuation for the sentence during these first attempts at copying.

The image of the correct form for a simple sentence is reenforced when children begin to read in their preprimers and primers. Being exposed to correct form, children reproduce it if they are given careful guidance while making the transition from reading to writing visual images on paper.

As soon as handwriting begins, children should write for a purpose at all times. Even when they can only write a few words, they can be written in sentence form.

The teacher can capitalize very quickly on the few words the child can write by thinking of ways he can use these few words in simple sentences. She may print a note or a letter on ditto paper for a variety of purposes for the child to take home. All the child does in this instance is to sign his name, but he is seeing sentences and is, at the same time, being introduced to the accepted, standard forms of writing. Samples:

An Invitation Form

Broad Street School
April 4, 1963

Dear Mother and Dad,

We will have a play. It is on Wednesday. Please come to see it.

Love,

_____

A Note Form

Dear Mother,

I need 60 cents for milk.

Love,

_____

Sentences can also appear on planning charts, programs, get-well notes to sick classmates, greeting cards, the daily news, science experiments and in all other written classroom experiences. Very soon children will be using these forms in their own creative writing. Many of the ideas mentioned in Book III can be used at the early primary level to invite children to write in complete sentence form.

The question mark is generally introduced to young children as a sentence form. Often teachers explain the use of the question mark and then use it in:

1. Writing questions on the board for children to answer.
2. Labeling lost and found articles: Am I yours?
3. Labeling science materials: What am I? What can I do?
4. Using surprise items: What is in the box?
5. Writing personal notes to the children which include questions like, "How old are you?"
6. Using questions on charts such as, "Who are our workers?"
7. Using games: Where is the ball?
8. Using questions on reading charts: "Who will go?"

Seeing a form used correctly gives the child a correct visual image. When he begins to include questions in his stories, he will use the correct form from the beginning, because he is imitating the form to which he has been exposed.

The exclamation point can be introduced early in the child's reading program. Reading charts provide a logical place to introduce it. In exploring punctuation marks (see page 284) the teacher can bring the purpose of exclamation points to the attention of the children. She will find many ways of using it, such as those suggested in the section on reading (see Book III, *The Creative Teaching of Reading and Literature in the Elementary School*).

> Surprise! Today we have a surprise!
> Look! What is in the box?
> Help! I need help! (Safety poster)
> Stop! (At the street crossing)
> Close me! (On the lid of the clay box)

Many first and second graders are able to use complete simple declarative, interrogative, exclamatory and imperative sentences from the very beginning of their writing attempts, because they are *imitating* the *correct* forms used in their classroom.

The compound and complex sentence is introduced in a parallel manner to the introduction of other sentence forms—in the first readers or story books. Once again it is important to find creative ways of keeping the correct forms of the sentences before the children. The continued use of reading charts, designed at this point to fulfill many purposes, will help to give children easy reference material and will keep correct sentence forms before them. Compound and complex sentences can appear in letters, invitations, notes, greeting cards and on bulletin boards.

In the primary grades no attempt is made to teach the forms of sentences, as such, to children. They learn about sentences through continual use of them. Children speak in simple, compound and complex sentences long before they come to school, so the primary teacher is concerned with helping children have the best start possible in getting their speech forms translated into correct written form.

Fun with Sentences

1. Collect magazine pictures and mount them. Use each picture for inspiration to write a statement, a question, an exclamation or a command sentence. If children write on strips of paper, they may display their sentences by tacking them under each picture on the bulletin board.

2. Put a sentence on the board such as:

> "The man walked down the road," *or* "The boy drew a picture."

Give the children crayon and paper and have them draw as many versions of the sentence as they wish. The sentence is to be copied at the bottom of each drawing. The drawings are stapled together into a small book. All sorts of interpretations will come of the sentences as children translate their experiences into drawings.

3. Ask children to try their hand at writing three-sentence stories. Each story must contain a question, a statement and an exclamation. This can be used at many grade levels.

From Miss Farrell's second grade came this story:

Run Away

Oh! Oh! Spot ran away. Did you see him go?

From Mr. Brinker's sixth grade came this story:

A Tragedy at Sea

"Help! Help!" he cried! "Will no one save me?" "I am drowning."

4. Take a small sentence, such as "Mary went." This is a sentence, but not lively. Add a word or words to tell when.

Yesterday Mary went.

Add a word to tell where.

Yesterday Mary went visiting.

Or, "John bought something." Add a word to tell what.

John bought a pencil.

Add a color word.

John bought a yellow pencil.

Add a word to tell where, then a word to tell when.

John bought a yellow pencil today at the book store, etc.

5. Children enjoy poems about punctuation. Read some to focus attention on the punctuation mark being studied. Also, encourage the children to make up their own.

SETTING CONDITIONS FOR THE CREATIVE TEACHING OF SENTENCE STRUCTURE: INTERMEDIATE GRADES

In the intermediate grades sentence sense has been well established if the children have had a sound foundation of experience in the primary grades. A nomenclature regarding sentences should be established so the children can make a study of sentences in relation to their own creative writing. The words *statement, question* and *command* can be replaced with *declarative, interrogative, exclamatory* and *imperative*. In the upper grades such concepts as compound and complex may be used to label sentences, but this should not be mandatory. Many children like to learn sentence labels and should be encouraged to do so but the stress should be on the accepted usage and not on the structure or the nomenclature of the sentence.

Suggestions for Developing Sentence Skills

Many of the suggestions given for developing sentence usage in the primary grades can be modified for use in the intermediate grades, especially for groups of slow-learning children.

1. In the intermediate grades children should be doing a great deal of creative writing. An analysis of this writing will provide the teacher with the clues to the kinds of sentence structure she needs to teach. Application of the children's learning should come in writing stories, poems, book reports, invitations, letters, puppet shows, dramatizations, roll movie scripts, television and radio scripts, character sketches, social studies reports, science reports and scripts for shadow plays.

Intermediate grade children can begin to learn the basic structure of sentences. Most intermediate grade teachers help the children identify the subject and predicate of a sentence (both the complete and single subject and predicate). Children will enjoy looking for subjects and predicates in the stories they read.

2. Many of the social courtesies of living together can be learned if each classroom teacher has a host and a hostess each week assigned to meet guests to the classroom and make introductions to the teacher and the children. In planning these introductions together, careful attention can be given to sentence structure.

3. Children can also dramatize many social courtesies connected with fifth and sixth grade classroom activities. These dramatizations may be written and studied for sentence structure after they have been dramatized. Some such instances may be:

a. Helping boys learn how to ask girls for a dance.
b. Showing boys how to serve girls from the refreshment table at classroom parties.
c. Showing children how to introduce their parents to the teacher at the school open house or at a school play.
d. Helping children in making announcements over the school public address system.
e. Preparing for oral reports, radio and television shows.
f. Making announcements to other classrooms (cafeteria menu, coming events, etc.).

4. One film which will help children understand sentence structure is *Making Sense with Sentences* (Coronet).

Paragraphing

1. In the account of Miss Farmer's classroom on pages 280–82 she demonstrated a meaningful way to build the concept of paragraphing. The teacher at any level can encourage the writing of paragraphs through many devices once a good sentence sense has been established and the child has a clear picture in his mind of the paragraph form.

2. Mr. Kaplenoff reports the following activity carried on in his fourth grade which helped children distinguish between a paragraph and a sentence.

He took this sentence: "He couldn't quite hang onto it." The class wrote, and then read stories using the sentence in one of the paragraphs. Although a complete thought, the sentence meaning was dependent on the context of the paragraph within the scope of the individual story.

3. One film which will help the children in learning about paragraphing is *Building Better Paragraphs* (10 minutes, Coronet).

Outlining

Outlining is largely a way of organizing and classifying a body of material to be used later as a reference for some particular purpose. The basic concepts of outlining begin when kindergarten children group things in order or by topic for any special purpose. After many experiences with organizing and classifying materials, children are ready to outline.

Some samples of readiness experiences which prepare children for organizing and classifying are:

1. Putting doll furniture into the correct rooms in the doll house.
2. Putting materials back in their proper place after use in the classroom.
3. Setting up the tables in the room for the midmorning lunch.
4. Planning periods, with the teacher, during the school day.

With these diverse and varied activities as a background, the teacher may select experiences which help children to classify words according to topics, the knowledge of which is essential in outlining.

Mrs. Henderson, in the second grade, made a simple, attractive bulletin board about buildings (made from big envelopes) and a street. She included a grocery store, a gas station, a fruit market, a dairy, a filling station and a house. The children were given cards with a word printed on each card. They were told to slip the card into the top of the building where that particular word would be found.

Regardless of the children's grade level, the ability to classify and organize material in this manner is essential before meaningful outlining can take place. Any teacher may begin to teach outlining with devices such as this.

In a fourth grade classroom, Mr. Eagan felt that his pupils did not understand basic outlining concepts, so he planned a series of experiences aimed at teaching these concepts to the children.

Through talking with the children he learned that some of the girls had kept their doll houses and still played with them on occasion. He also found that some of the boys had received toy forts and toy villages for Christmas gifts. He asked a few children if they could bring these toys to school. Some did and the teacher used these toys to teach outlining.

He placed the doll house at the front of the room where all the children could see it. Then he took all the furniture and placed it in a box in the middle of the room. He let Janet tell about the doll house because she had brought it to school. Then he asked the class what they had been talking about. He then printed the words, "The Doll House" in big letters on the chalkboard.

Next he asked the children if they would name the rooms in the doll house for him. As they named the rooms, he wrote them on the board in this fashion:

The Doll House

    I.   Rooms in a doll house
        A.   Living Room
            1.
            2.
            3.
            4.
            5.
        B.   Master Bedroom
            1.
            2.
            3.
            4.
            5.
        C.   Kitchen
            1.
            2.

D. Attic
   1.
   2.
   3.
   4.
   5.
       etc.

Then Mr. Eagan divided the class into eight groups. Each group was assigned to a room in the doll house. A chairman was to go to the box in the middle of the room and bring back all the furniture that belonged to the room to which his committee was assigned.

After this was done, Mr. Eagan asked one child from each group to go to the chalkboard and list under his topic all the furniture found in that particular room.

Mr. Eagan then asked the children about the miniature dolls Janet had brought to place in the doll house. Janet showed the dolls and Mr. Eagan added roman numeral II to the chalkboard, followed by this topic: "II. Dolls in the Doll House." He then listed the dolls as the children named them.

Later the children were allowed to set up the doll house. Mr. Eagan asked the class, "Now, let's look at the chalkboard. What have we done?"

"We've told about my doll house," said Janet.

"Yes," said Mr. Eagan, "but we didn't write a story about it, or a poem about it, or draw a picture. This is a new way of telling about something. It is called outlining. An outline is like a skeleton or frame. It gives us the main parts but we have to fill in the details."

Mr. Eagan then took Billy's toy village and asked the children to help him outline its story. He now drew attention to the *form* of the outline and again allowed the children to make an outline from their direct experience.

After this was done, the children together explored the ways they could use an outline. Someone pointed out that the form they had used in planning trips was really an outline, to which Mr. Eagan agreed.

Their list looked like this:

When We Can Use Outlines

1. In planning trips.
2. In planning parties.
3. In planning stories and poems.
4. For planning our social studies reports.
5. For getting an idea about what is coming in our books.

6. In taking notes during radio and television programs.
7. In doing our science experiments.

Later Mr. Eagan helped the children outline a report together. He printed the form of the outline on a chart which he put before the class for reference. He helped each child make out an outline by giving dittoed sheets to the class, lined and lettered with correct outline forms. Soon children were outlining material from encyclopedias, almanacs and supplementary reading materials for their social studies reports. Later Mr. Eagan helped the children learn how to use an outline to study.

Some suggested methods of teaching outlining skills follow.
1. Children can classify many kinds of words in preparing for more advanced experiences in outlining. Capitalize on the flowers they bring in. Classify words regarding the *feel* of the flower (soft, silky, satiny, damp), the *looks* of the flower (bright, gay, pretty, droopy, beautiful), the *smell* of the flower (sickish, sweet, fragrant, delightful, etc.).
2. Some books help children learn to classify.
3. Take roll call by using different topics—when the child's name is called he must respond with a word in the predetermined category. Some categories might be: names of cars, words in French, types of shoes, names of songs, names of games, words correlated with units, etc.

POETRY FORMS: PRIMARY GRADES

Most children write their first poems in story form; this is a natural consequence of the instruction they have received in writing stories. In the primary grades, poems generally begin to appear on an individual basis as some children, aware of the concepts of rhyming, make attempts to rhyme their stories. Often these first poems are dictated to the teacher.

The teacher can establish written forms for poetry writing as soon as their children are able to read. Learning poetry forms is a visual skill. Children should see the complete form of a poem as it will appear on a sheet of paper, before they begin to write it. This calls for a sensitivity to the art form or shape of the poem as well as to the wording of it.

There are many acceptable forms for poetry writing. The child must become familiar with many such forms and then be encouraged to choose his own. He must also be informed of the different types of poetry such as free verse, blank verse and rhyming verse so that he may choose a form which suits his purposes. Often a simple piece of written prose is beautiful enough to be written as free verse. The teacher can be alert to the signals of her children's readiness to write poetry and can capitalize on these signals by using them to introduce poetry forms. A rich background of experiences with poetry will make her instructional task meaningful (see Book III, *Creative Teaching of Reading and Literature in the Elementary School*).

Suggestions for Helping Children to Write Poetry Forms

1. Put simple poems on reading charts as soon as the children are able to read them. Often simple nursery rhymes which the children know may be used this way. Draw attention to the fact that the beginning lines are capitalized and that a period ends each idea, but that the beginning lines are not always directly under each other as in an experience chart.

2. As soon as a child creates a poem, use it to make a reading chart. Explain that one way people can tell whether the material they are about to read is a poem or a story is by the shape of it on the page. Read the poem which was submitted and print it on a reading chart, using a form which is different from the straight margins usually used in a reading chart. Note the contrast in form. Accent the shape of the indentations of the beginning lines of poetry by drawing a jagged margin with a brightly colored felt pen.

3. Miss Fleming, a second grade teacher, printed simple poems which her children liked, and poems which they had written, on colored construction paper. She cut out the poems, accenting the pattern of the first lines of the poem by following jagged margins. When mounted on regular tagboard, the shape of the poem was easily seen from any place in the classroom and provided an easy reference for the children. One of Miss Fleming's charts looked like Figure 8-6.

4. Poems with iambic pentameter may be printed on pieces of cardboard in two-line sections and distributed to the children. They then read the poem and assemble it in a pocket chart at the front of the room, thus drawing attention to the alternate indenta-

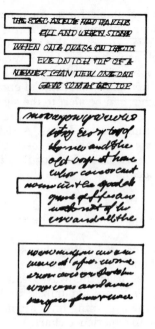

FIGURE 8-6.   *Ways to write poems.*

tion of the lines of this type of poetry and providing the teacher with a method of checking the children's ability to match rhyming lines.

POETRY FORMS: INTERMEDIATE GRADES

Many of the suggestions given for the development of the visual and art form of poetry in the primary grades may be adapted to the instructional program of the intermediate grades. In fact, it will be necessary to develop form consciousness through steps similar to those taken by Miss Fleming if the intermediate grade children have not developed sensitivity to poetry forms.

However, the stress for writing poetry should be on the *content* of the poem and not the form. Much of the instruction for developing poetry forms will be done on an individual basis as the teacher helps each child edit his draft work for final display or publication in the classroom. See Book III for suggestions on teaching poetry.

FORMS OF CORRESPONDENCE

Letter Writing

The need to write letters arises almost immediately with the child's school experience. For the first time in his life he is removed from the presence of people with whom he has had close contact. Direct communication with those people is now impossible. The child will feel a need to communicate in written form if the teacher capitalizes on the situation and helps him develop skills to fulfill this need.

Among the most common forms of letter writing which a child needs early in his school experience are:

1. Friendly letters.
2. Letters of request.
3. Letters of thanks.
4. Letters of invitation.

Situations arising in the classroom for which these forms are needed are many.

Friendly Letters

1. Writing to friends in others schools.
2. Writing to relatives.
3. Writing to pen pals in other communities, states or nations.
4. Writing to teachers other than the classroom teacher.

Letters of Request

1. Writing to parents for money for supplementary materials or textbooks.
2. Writing letters for the teacher for materials to be brought from home (book drives, materials for costumes, props for plays).
3. Writing for permission to take a field trip to a farm, a dairy, or a museum.
4. Writing to travel agencies and commercial firms for free materials.
5. Writing to authors or consultants.
6. Writing letters to the school principal requesting equipment.
7. Writing to Santa Claus.

Letters of Thanks

1. Writing to thank lay people and commercial enterprises for allowing the class to take a field trip.

2. Letters to the principal for new books or materials.
3. Letters to the Board of Education for certain granted privileges or gifts to the class.
4. Letters of thanks to consultants who visited the class to show the children various materials, films or filmstrips.
5. Letters to another grade thanking them for invitations to assemblies and exhibits.
6. Letters to parents and relatives for gifts received at Christmas, holidays and birthdays.
7. Letters to the policeman or another community helper who may have helped the class on a particular trip.

Letters of Invitation

1. Invitations to parents to parties, assemblies, exhibits, and class programs.
2. Invitations to parents to visit the classroom.
3. Invitations to other groups to attend assemblies and exhibits.
4. Invitations to the Safety Patrol to accompany the children on a trip.
5. Invitations to a policeman or postman to visit the class.

At an early age in the child's school experience he adds another written expression form to his needs—the business letter. Experiences which prompt the use of the business letter are:

Business Letters

1. Writing to commercial companies for free materials.
2. Writing to travel agencies for posters.
3. Writing to museums, historical societies and libraries for information.
4. Writing letters of inquiry.
5. Writing letters to order classroom supplies.
6. Writing to gather material for special reports (such as writing to a college of education to find out how teachers are trained).
7. Writing to make arrangements for trips.
8. Writing letters for the purpose of sponsoring exhibits.
9. Making arrangements for consultants.
10. Gathering information for making decisions on bargain prices, quality materials, etc.

As in other forms of written expression, the visual image of the letter form must become clear in the child's mind before he can actually write a letter. Stress should be put on the shape of the letter, and from the very beginning of instruction the child should see the complete form of the business or friendly letter. When he is unable to write, but can read, letters which are to go home can be run off on a duplicator, with a line drawn in the place where the child is to print his name. As he learns new words, he can write more and more of the letter, but the form should be complete each time.

Some newer exercise books introduce written expression forms at an early stage in the child's growth by having him cut printed words from the printed page and paste them in appropriate blanks on the simple but correct letter form. As soon as he is able, the child prints the word in the blank instead of pasting it in. Little by little the printed words are omitted, and only lines, drawn so the child still maintains the pattern of the letter, remain. He now copies his leters from the chalkboard, where he has helped his classmates compose it. Room is left for his own creative endeavors by making certain he will substitute his own ideas whenever he has them, in place of the ideas used on the chalkboard. Before long each child is writing his own letters on paper, lined by the teacher in a way that aids in the retention of correct form. As soon as the form is fixed in his mind, the child can use his skill on regular lined paper.

The accent in such exercises is placed correctly, upon the visual form of the letter. The child does not write incorrect letter forms because he does not see them. The instruction in punctuation and capitalization which he has been receiving is applied to letter writing from the beginning.

Many children write their own creative letters at an early age. These letters are often made more creative when they are illustrated or decorated.

In the intermediate grades, the parts of a letter may be studied and a nomenclature for referral developed. This should come only after the child has written many letters in correct form.

Suggestions for Developing the Correct Use of Letter Forms

Use many of the ideas previously mentioned under the development of paragraphing, outlining and building poetry forms, especially the following:

1. Use a felt pen to outline the shape of a business or friendly letter.
2. Use construction paper cutouts to show form and shape.
3. Use dittoed work sheets (or workbook sheets), lined so the child keeps correct form in mind.
4. Keep collections of letters which show various forms.

5. Use a flannel board or pocket chart to construct letters to-
    gether, arranging in proper form the strips of paper on which
    the letter has been previously printed.
6. Use colored chalk to emphasize the shape of letters.

Children in the intermediate grades will be able to analyze letters for quality of content, interest value and correctness of form
by using the opaque projector technique used on page 269 to
analyze handwriting. From this analysis would come a basic set
of principles for letter writing. Through the use of the opaque
projector and the overhead projector, children can learn to contrast various letter forms and make lists of the differences between friendly letters and business letters.

Alphabetization

This necessary skill for language usage may be developed as soon
as children have learned the alphabet. This generally occurs soon
after they have learned to read and are beginning to study
phonetic sounds.

Alphabetization is a memory and visual skill. Children must
remember the *order* of the letters and recognize their *shapes* in
order to be able to alphabetize.

The alphabet serves two purposes: that of making words which
do communicate, and that of providing a system of organizing material—a system known as alphabetization. A knowledge of the
sounds of the letters may unlock the pronunciation of a new
word; a knowledge of their order will unlock the system by which
written material is classified.

Note Taking

The ability to take notes is important in a society which is subjected to much verbalism and produces much printed material.
Children will need to know how to take notes for these purposes:

1. To keep records of science experiments.
2. To make records from encyclopedias and other reference ma-
    terials in order to make reports in social studies.
3. To report to the class on certain radio and television program
    assignments.
4. To be able to organize material from several resources into
    one composite report.

5. To grasp the main ideas of a speaker's presentation.
6. To be able to organize and classify material.
7. To be able to glean ideas from textbooks and newspapers.

Prerequisite to note taking are many experiences in classifying and outlining similar to those described on previous pages. Outlining is one form of note taking and suggestions for teaching outlining meaningfully and creatively appear on pages 314–16. Other forms of note taking may be taught to children so they may master the technique of making accurate and interesting oral and written reports.

Note taking has its beginnings in the early grades when children learn the value of jotting down ideas for future use.

In a first grade room the children listed the questions they were to ask on a trip to the airport. After the questions were listed, each child copied one question on a five by eight card. This was a note to remind him of the question for which he was responsible. When the class returned to the schoolroom, each child wrote the answer on the back of his card. These cards and answers were saved in a file box as a future reference source.

In another first grade the children were asked to copy three words from a list on the board. The words were to tell about the circus, the farm, etc.

Experiences such as these are the basis for note taking. In the primary grades, children can begin to use cards or a notebook to take simple notes: answers to specific questions, records of daily events, plans for coming events or names of books they have read.

Early in the intermediate grades, note taking will be very important to children when they collect material for making science and social studies reports. At this point conditions can be set for developing this skill effectively through a variety of activities.

1. Show them notes from which a speech has been made or a manuscript written.

2. Make a list of all the instances in the classroom where note taking will be necessary.

3. Make a list of all the possible ways notes may be taken (example: cards, "idiot" cards on television, notebooks, outlines) and all the permissible shortcuts used in note taking (abbreviations, types of shorthand, etc.).

4. Take a question from those the children ask and use it as a demonstration on how to take notes. For example, Tom brought a rock to school. The children asked what kind of rock it was. Mr. Metz, Tom's teacher, used this situation to show the children how to take notes. On the board, he wrote this question: "What types of rocks are there?" Then he wrote the following on a large card.

Kinds of Rocks

(*Children's Encyclopedia,* Vol. 13, p. 235)

I.   Igneous
     —once molten, now cooled
     —granite, basalt
II. Metamorphic
     —"changed" rocks
     —slate, marble, micaschist
III. Sedimentary
     —deposits subjected to great heat and pressure
     —shale

Mr. Metz read the children the article from which he had copied his information.

The children then took two other questions from their list of questions on the chalkboard: "What kinds of homes do people live in in China?" and "How are oranges raised?" Mr. Metz divided the class in half. Part of the children gathered material from textbooks and encyclopedias to answer question one and the rest gathered material to answer question two. Group one was called on to read material pertaining to the first question. On the chalkboard, the children made notes with Mr. Metz's guidance. Then question two was handled in the same manner. After the notes were edited, the class took question one and together wrote a report, from the notes on the chalkboard. Then they each wrote a report individually, from the notes on question two. These reports were shared and suggestions were made for their improvement.

From this experience, Mr. Metz and the children were able to make the following chart.

Suggestions for Taking Notes

a.   Always put the reference at the top of your notes.
b.   Read the paragraph, page or article carefully and look for facts to answer your question.
c.   Pick out the main ideas from the article or paragraph and write them down as main topics.
d.   Add any subtopics which will help you to remember important facts.
e.   Group facts under your topics.
f.   Record facts accurately.
g.   Read your notes over to see if you have all the information you need to make a good report.
h.   Work out a plan for note taking that best suits you.

5. Have all the children take notes to answer one question, using a common textbook as a resource. Make note cards and use

an opaque projector to project them on a screen before the class. Evaluate the notes and check them against a chart of suggestions, such as those mentioned above.

6. Give children many interesting assignments, other than social studies reports which will require note taking. Oral reports can be made from these notes in class. Examples:

a.   Listen to the president's press conference tonight on television and select the five main topics on which he spoke.
b.   Watch a certain television program and list the answers to a group of questions prepared by the teacher.

Scripts: Radio, Play and Television

In the primary grades dramatic play is free and planned on the spot. From this spontaneous form of creative play emerges an organized, yet still creative, type of dramatization. Organized dramatization can be used for many purposes in the primary grades (see Book III, *Creative Teaching of Reading and Literature in the Elementary School*).

In the intermediate grades children will want to dramatize rather freely, but they will also want to write plays. They will need to know the correct written forms for scripts, dramatizations, puppet shows, shadow plays, and television shows.

A group of children, for instance, may decide they want to write a play. They may have written stories before, but not plays. The problem then arises, What is the proper way to write a play? If the ideas for the play have already been suggested, it is wise to get these ideas down on paper or on the board. Then, because it is a new experience for the class, the correct way to write plays can become a group lesson. A search through English books will disclose valuable suggestions for playwriting; the library corner may contain some plays written for children, which may be studied for form. Reading books often have short plays which may be used. Then, from the various forms of material collected, the class reads some plays. They learn how plays are written, the importance of stage directions, lists of characters, scene descriptions and the like. They list new words like *exit, enter, upstage, downstage, climax* and *plot* on their vocabulary chart. They may write the first scene collectively on the board to apply what they have learned.

After everyone understands how plays are written, the class can divide into committees to write the other scenes, reporting to the whole class frequently. A series of good reference charts may result as the play develops. Criteria for a good play may be listed on one to help keep the committees conscious of the factors necessary to make scenes interesting. The scenes need to be outlined from the original plot so each committee knows exactly what part of the plot it must cover. Then, after each scene is read, evaluated, rewritten and finally accepted, the play is typed in proper form so each child has his own copy. Good reading experiences follow in tryouts for the parts, in chart making for cast of characters, committees, jobs, etc. Written invitations to other classrooms and to parents, posters for advertising, hand made props and scenery all constitute good opportunities for developing oral, written and creative expression.

Teachers often use the writing of scripts as a springboard for teaching predominant types of punctuation, such as the colon (used after the name of each character who is speaking), the parenthesis (used to set off stage directions) and the semicolon (often used to show sudden changes in thought). As in other forms of written expression, the script has a unique appearance and children must learn to recognize its design and to have it in mind before they write their own plays.

USING REFERENCE MATERIALS

A teacher paves the way to discovery by providing children with skills which enable them to find things for themselves. Discovery is an essential element of the creative act. When children are able to use the dictionary, the encyclopedia, almanacs, glossaries, indices and the school library to satisfy their needs, new worlds, awaiting their discovery, are opened to them.

Reference charts made by the children are often the first stage in the development of the concept that one may go to a specific source (other than the teacher) for help. One of the first sources children use after the reference chart is the picture dictionary. From this usable resource it is but one step to the use of other reference works.

Using the Dictionary

In teaching dictionary usage, the teacher should keep several objectives in mind.

1. To give the children resources so they can develop independent language skills.
2. To teach the arrangement of the alphabet letters.
3. To develop an understanding of the purpose of the dictionary.
4. To learn how to find words in the dictionary quickly and efficiently.
5. To learn how to arrange work alphabetically.
6. To learn what information can be found in the dictionary.
7. To learn the difference between an abridged and an unabridged dictionary.
8. To learn of the many kinds of dictionaries.
9. To make a careful study of the pronunciation of words.
10. To develop an understanding of homonyms, antonyms, and synonyms.

In order for children to be prepared to use the dictionary effectively, they must first be able to alphabetize. Simple picture dictionaries can be effectively used as early as the first grade by children who are interested in words. Often a keen interest in picture dictionaries on the part of the children is the cue for the teacher to begin dictionary work. Many children will look things up in the dictionary on a trial and error basis even before they have learned to aphabetize.

Contrary to popular belief, the dictionary is not used by children as a primary means to check spelling. A child must know how to spell a word before he can look it up in a dictionary. At least he must have a substantial visual image of the word in his mind, or the dictionary is of little help to him. Words which are looked up in the dictionary are those whose meaning we question or for which we need more meaning than our experience produces. The dictionary communicates to children only if it has been carefully chosen so the definitions in it are within the realm of the children's experience.

Once aphabetization is mastered, children can be encouraged to use the dictionary to help them in their creative work. Inasmuch as phonics are generally introduced in the reading program before the alphabet is learned, the simple dictionary can be used to help children find new words in their reading, or help them in sounding out unfamiliar words.·

Some suggested methods of teaching dictionary skills follow:

1. Have each child make an individual dictionary box. Use the drawer of an ordinary matchbox in which are kept one by two and

one-half inch cards of oaktag. Children keep boxes handy on their desks. When a child needs a word spelled, the teacher writes it on a card. The child uses it for his immediate need and files it in the box. Misspelled words from spelling tests are added to these. The child uses his words for further reference as well as gaining practice in alphabetization.

2. Choose a word with several meanings; set up sentences using this word. Example:

Stalk

a.   The plant has a little stalk.
b.   The tiger stalks his prey.
c.   He stalked haughtily down the street.

3. Dictionary fun—What is it? (develops divergent thinking). Can you tell what the following really are?

a.   A titmouse is not a mouse.
b.   A prairie dog is not a dog.
c.   A peanut is not actually a nut.
d.   Beggar lice do not crawl.
e.   A jack rabbit is not a rabbit.
f.   A Belgian hare is not a hare.
g.   A lady bird is not a bird.
h.   Sea lilies are not lilies.

4. Dictionary fun—Information (develops convergent thinking skills). Dictionaries tell us many things:

a.   How many feet in a mile?
b.   How does the python kill its prey?
c.   Who were the minutemen?
d.   Is the bat a bird or an animal?
e.   What are two animals whose names begin with Z?
f.   What is coral?
g.   Where does a bighorn live?
h.   What makes a rattlesnake rattle?

5. Give children sentences containing words with unusual meanings. Ask them to use their dictionaries to see if the word is properly used, and if so, to take notes on the new meaning of the word.

Examples:

a.   The girl had a good *purchase* on the rope.
b.   The barnacles will *cleave* to the side of the boat.

c.   She wore a pretty *print* to the party.
d.   They punished the old *scold* by ducking her in a pond.
e.   She wore a *stole* to the summerhouse.

6. Give the children lists of words you are sure they do not know but for which they know synonyms, and ask them to find their pronunication and meaning, and to use each word in a sentence. Sample list: heft, swab, abbey, abbot, platypus, Ionic, tartar, zephyr, yokel and chorister.

7. Give the children a story with one word repeated many times. Have them substitute synonyms by using the dictionary to find new words. For example:

The Place

There is a wonderful place *which I like to visit every winter. This* place *is high in the mountains. It is a beautiful* place, *nestled in a little* place *near the water. In the summer this* place *is visited by tourists from many* places. *In the winter, it is a lonely* place. *Old John stays there and old John knows his* place. *He keeps the* place *going and it is then that I like to go there in* place *of the time when people are at the* place.

Encourage children to write creative stories such as the one above for their classmates to work on.

Using the Encyclopedia

Children will experience the joy of discovery as soon as they are able to use resource materials to find information to help them in answering their problems. In recent years the publication of simple picture encyclopedias and picture dictionaries has made it possible for teachers to teach the skills of using reference books as early as the kindergarten and the first grade.

Reference work on the elementary level is the basis of research techniques which the child will use most of his life. Children do not need to know all the answers to the many questions which will cross their minds but it would be unfortunate if they did not know where to find the answers.

In the unit teaching, this simple skill of looking up factual material and reporting on the findings is essential. Children will need to know (1) where they may find answers and (2) *how* to use the resources which contain their answers. Time must be taken in the child's school years to teach the use of the dictionary (see above), the table of contents, an index, a glossary, an almanac, the encyclopedia and other children's reference books (such as *The Children's Periodical Guide, Informaton Please,* the telephone book, and various atlases and reader's guides).

A child is motivated to seek information when he is curious or interested in a problem to which no one has a ready answer. He must know (1) where he can go for an answer, (2) how to find the material, (3) how to locate the specific answer, (4) how to be able to take notes on the material and (5) how to be able to report back to a group (if his motivation came from a group problem).

All through elementary school the teacher should take time to introduce resources available for seeking out materials at each level of the child's development. At the beginning of each unit children can list available resources in which they may find their answers (see Book V, *Creative Teaching of the Social Studies in the Elementary School*). The teacher or the school librarian can take time to explain the use of all the textbooks and reference resources available to the children and demonstrate any unique feature in using them. Then the teacher will need to check to be sure children have been instructed in how to use the material properly.

Basic to research work at this level is an automatic use of alphabetization. The child must also know how to take notes (see page 322) and to outline (see page 313). He should have had experience in using simple references such as the dictionary (see page 326), an index and a table of contents. Each of these skills can be introduced simply at any place where materials on the children's level are available. Any teacher who discovers that her pupils have not acquired these skills should teach them as soon as possible. Children who cannot perform these skills are handicapped in their ability to work independently and to fulfill the objectives of unit teaching (see Book V).

Children need also to be taught study skills and effective ways to use textbooks (see Book V). They need to be taught map, graph and chart skills, skills of discussion, listening and sharing and skills of evaluation.

Using the School Library

Children should be introduced to the school library soon after they arrive in school. From an early age they should have happy library experiences, rich in discovering new materials and new ideas. There are books to explore; files to use; card catalogues to utilize;

posters, films and charts to take out and a series of planned library experiences with the children and the school librarian.

The role of the school librarian in such a program cannot be minimized. Her major objective is to *encourage* children to use the library. Proper use of the library and accepted library behavior are important for children to learn. The library should be theirs so that they can explore it on their own and enjoy sharing its books. Well-planned library periods can do much to encourage good library experiences. In planning trips to the library, teacher and children should ask the librarian to sit in so she knows what each particular class requires and what her role is to be.

If a school library is not available, the need for skillful teaching of library usage is even greater. Lack of a school library is unfortunate in a sense, yet fortunate in another sense. Ideally, the best kind of library is one housed in the same room with the children. All teachers should create a library corner in their rooms; books may be borrowed from state libraries, town libraries or from the children. Children often will bring a few books a week to school and then share a few more the following week. When many children do this, much joy can be obtained through sharing and through the remotivation which a constantly changing bookshelf affords. Some teachers have utilized a language arts period to have the children write letters to their parents explaining their plight and asking for books for the school. Such book drives often produce much good material.

A good library corner should have interesting bulletin board displays, a file where children learn to alphabetize and keep materials and reference materials such as globes, maps and charts. It can be supplemented by trips to the town library or the nearest branch library. If no library is available in a school district, it would be well for the teachers to join forces to attempt to secure a Bookmobile.

SUMMARY

"In silence I rested my eyes on the view outside the window and visibly meditated the question, 'Grammar?' I spoke my thoughts. 'I don't know . . . I never use it myself.' (A quick laugh from the group, but I went on unmoved.) 'I have studied it of course, and I have taught it, and enjoy teaching it. But I don't know what good it ever did me . . . Really, I don't . . . I speak and write the language I have heard, in my family and among my friends. It is important, of course, to have the right kind of family and the right kind of friends . . . My speech is probably full of blunders; I don't know; it doesn't seem to bother anybody. They laughed at me up in New England, where I went to school, because I said thawt for t-h-o-u-g-h-t, instead of thot, but they didn't like me or respect me any the less for that. I know that my written language is far from what it should be, for I can't write a page that does not need revision; and even after I have done my best work upon something that I want to publish, the copyreader in the editorial rooms makes corrections. And this same story is told by everybody who writes for print, not excluding teachers. Grammar? I suppose it is like good manners, or friendliness, or unselfishness, or sportsmanship; it's something one lives and therefore cannot get satisfactorily out of a book.' "[13]

The mechanics of handwriting can be taught. They are the tools which free children to be more creative. Knowing the correct use of grammar, of word usage, of language forms and skills for organizing materials gives them certain psychological security which will make possible the use of the language tools in creative projects and reports.

TO THE COLLEGE STUDENT AND THE CLASSROOM TEACHER

1. Questions for Discussion:
a. This chapter met the goal stated by the instruction on page 277 and I agree (disagree) that instruction in grammar and word usage could have been much more fun in school than it was.
b. Discuss Hughes Mearns' quote above. Do you agree or disagree? You will enjoy Mearns' books on the teaching of grammar (see bibliography below).
c. What is a good system for grading children's papers in the skill areas of the language arts?
d. See Smith, Goodman and Meredith comment on page 277. Do you agree that school grammar instruction need be ineffective? Do you suppose the children studied had teachers who used creative approaches to teaching grammar or traditional approaches?
e. Many students of the English language feel strongly that language should be taught in its pure form while other stu-

13. Hughes Mearns, *Creative Power: The Education of Youth in the Creative Arts* (New York: Dover, 1958), p. 17.

dents believe it should be taught in its functional form to promote effective social communication. Assign some class members to gather material on both sides of this issue and debate it in class.

f. Go to the college library for the purpose of examining some original manuscripts. Notice how famous authors write and rewrite before they are satisfied with the end result. Franklin Roosevelt wrote one fifteen-minute fireside chat twenty-four times before he was satisfied with it. In light of these observations, how realistic are we in demanding that children submit a perfectly written paper as the result of one lesson? Discuss this concept with your classmates or colleagues.

2. Make a collection of some of the grammar rules which you learned as a child and which have stayed with you over the years. You know, this sort of thing:

> *I before e*
> *Except after c*
> *And when sounded as ā*
> *As in neighbor and weigh.*

Now list all the exceptions to the rules that you can find. Do we have a pure language? Do rhymes of this nature help or confuse children?

3. One of the most enlightening articles on grammar to be published appeared in *The Reading Teacher*.[14] It was written by a linguist who made a study of the number of times each of the so-called rules of grammar which we teach children, actually applies. Read the article; you are in for some surprises. Can we honestly say many of these statements are really rules? What constitutes a rule?

4. If you are a teacher who is following a textbook for your language program, evaluate its use. Have the children in your room write something they want to write—completely unsupervised and unstructured. Collect the papers and make out a diagnostic chart of the language problems the children are having. How much effect has the material you have covered in their textbook had on their written language skills? From your chart select areas which show definite class or small group weaknesses. Plan some creative lessons around these needs. Think of creative ways you may use the textbook.

If you are a student make a study of a current language arts textbook and evaluate the material in it—and its presentation.

---

14. Theodore Clymer, "The Utility of Phonic Generalizations in the Primary Grades," *The Reading Teacher* 16, no. 4 (January, 1963).

5. Some games for teaching correct word usage are so complicated the children often lose sight of the purpose of the game. Find such games and discuss their value, if any.

6. Recent studies have shown that adults tend to improve in English usage when the incorrect visual image is immediately replaced by a corrected image. Read some of these studies and discuss their significance to teaching the mechanics of handwriting.

7. Creative teaching was previously described as open-ended teaching, that is, the motivation for learning is presented by the teacher and then the child feels his way to a logical solution to the problem presented in that motivation. Much of language teaching is actually teaching the child to follow predetermined patterns to which he must conform, according to accepted social courtesy. Check through the suggestions for teaching in this chapter and classify them under these two headings: (a) creative teaching (open-ended, leading to discovery and invention) and (b) creative ways to teach children to conform.

8. For many exciting, creative ideas for teaching grammar, see Mauree Applegate's book *Easy in English.* It is listed in the bibliography which follows this chapter.

9. Two good books for teaching proper library usage are *A Guidebook for Teaching Library Skills*, Books I and II, by Margaret V. Beck and Vera M. Pace (Minneapolis: T. S. Denison, 1965).

10. Play Victor Borge's record (*Caught in the Act*) to your colleagues and note their reactions to the phonetic punctuation section. Brainstorm other ways you might effectively use this record.

11. Brainstorm all the written language skills which might be taught by having the children present a daily weather forecast.

12. Many schools do not present parts of speech as part of their curriculum until junior high school. How do you feel about this? Does knowledge of parts of speech improve the child's correct, effective use of written expression? Note all the creative writing written by children in this book before they learned parts of speech and then ask yourself what is the purpose of teaching parts of speech?

13. There are many excellent recordings about listening and countless hundreds of good listening records. A few (from Educational Record Sales) that you might use in class as examples are listed below:

a. *Let's Listen* (Grades 1–3): ear training in good listening habits.

b. *What Is Listening?* a program of training skills for young children.

c. *Young Listener's Library*: a musical anthology designed to give the youngest listener an introduction to classical music.

d. *Listening Time*: stories emphasizing ear training.

SELECTED BIBLIOGRAPHY

Applegate, Mauree. *Easy in English*. New York: Harper and Row, 1963.

————. *Helping Childen Write*. New York: Harper and Row, 1964.

Bach, Emmon. *An Introduction to Transformational Grammars*. New York: Holt, Rinehart and Winston, 1964.

Braddock, Richard, et al. *Research in Written Composition*. Champaign, Ill.: National Council of Teachers of English, 1963.

Chomsky, Noam. *Aspects of the Theory of Syntax*. Cambridge, Mass.: M.I.T. Press, 1965.

————. *Current Issues in Linguistic Theory*. The Hague: Mouton, 1964.

————. *Topics in the Theory of Generative Grammar*. The Hague: Mouton, 1966.

Cobb, Stanwood. *The Importance of Creativity*. New York: Scarecrow Press, 1968.

DeLancey, Robert. *Linguistics and Teaching: A Manual of Classroom Practices*. Rochester, N.Y.: State English Council, 1965.

Dixon, Robert M. *Linguistic Science and Logic*. The Hague: Mouton, 1963.

Evertts, Eldonna. *What's New in Language Arts: Composition*. Washington, D.C.: American Association of Elementary-Kindergarten-Nursery Educators, N.E.A. Center, 1968.

Fries, Charles C. *Linguistics, the Study of Language*. New York: Holt, Rinehart and Winston, 1964.

Gleason, H. A., Jr. *Linguistics and English Grammar*. New York: Holt, Rinehart and Winston, 1965.

Haider, Norman. *Haider's Guide for Structural Linguistics*. Cedar Grove, N.J.: Phillips-Campbell, 1964.

Hook, J. N., Paul H. Jacobs and Raymond D. Crisp. *What Every English Teacher Should Know*. Champaign, Ill.: National Council of Teachers of English, 1970.

Joos, Martin. *Readings in Linguistics*. Committee on Language Programs of the American Council of Learned Societies. 4th ed. Chicago: University of Chicago Press, 1966.

MacCampbell, James C. (ed.). *Readings in the Language Arts in the Elementary School*. Part VI: "Written Composition," 230–82; "Grammar in Language Teaching," 216–28; "Toward a New Perspective in Grammar," 200–9; "Evaluating Children's Composition," 263–77. Boston: D. C. Heath, 1964.

Mearns, Hughes. *Creative Power: The Education of Youth in the Creative Arts*. New York: Dover, 1958.

Newman, Harold. ("Toward a New Perspective of Grammar and Composition." In James C. MacCampbell (ed.). *Readings in Language Arts in the Elementary School.* Boston: D. C. Heath, 1964, pp. 200–9.

Platts, Mary E., Sr. Rose Marguerite and Esther Shumaker. *Spice: Suggested Activities to Motivate the Teaching of the Language Arts.* Benton Harbor, Mich.: Educational Service, 1960.

Powell, Brian. *English Through Poetry Writing.* Itasca, Ill.: F. E. Peacock, 1968.

Sanders, Richard (ed.). *New Directions in English.* A linguistic program in language and composition grades 1–8. New York: Harper and Row, 1969.

Shane, Harold Gray. *Linguistics and the Classroom Teacher.* Washington, D.C.: Association for Supervision and Curriculum Development, 1967.

Shuy, Roger W., Alva L. Davis and Robert F. Hogan. *Social Dialects and Language Learning.* Champaign, Ill.: National Council of Teachers of English, 1964.

Strickland, Ruth. *The Contribution of Structural Linguistics to the Teaching of Reading, Writing and Grammar.* Bloomington: School of Education, Indiana University, Bureau Educational Studies and Testing, 1963.

Sturtevant, E. H. *An Introduction to Linguistic Science.* New Haven: Yale University Press, 1947.

Tiedt, Iris M. and Sidney W. Tiedt. *Contemporary English in the Elementary School.* Englewood Cliffs, N.J.: Prentice-Hall, 1967.

————. *Readings on Contemporary English in the Elementary School.* Englewood Cliffs, N.J.: Prentice-Hall, 1967.

Waismann, Friedrich. *The Principles of Linguistic Philosophy,* R. Harre (ed.). New York: St. Martin's Press, 1965.

CHAPTER IX

Creative Teaching of Spelling

A Crazy Subject

Spelling is really very queer.
You spell a word both dear and deer
And both are right. I just can't see
Why sometimes "i" comes before "e"
And why does "ar" say "ar" and "er"?
And even ē I'm never sure
Which one to use in spelling "herds."
Spelling's a pain—it's for the birds!

KEVIN K.
Grade 6

TO THE READER

The purpose of this chapter is to answer some of the current problems in the teaching of spelling in terms of the most recent thinking among educators. Questions to be tackled are:

1. What part does phonics play in the teaching of spelling?
2. From where should class spelling lists be derived?
3. What methods for teaching spelling seem to work most effectively?
4. Can spelling be taught creatively?
5. What are the objectives for teaching spelling in the elementary school?
6. Does writing a misspelled word ten times *really* help the child to learn it?

7. Are spelling rules of any real value in helping the child to spell?
8. Under what classroom conditions is spelling best learned?

INTRODUCTION

Spelling is basically a visual skill. What makes a child a good speller? Primarily it is when he has stamped on his memory a visual image of each word which he can reproduce on paper. All of the mechanics of teaching spelling may help a child a great deal in his spelling ability. Phonics will help him guess at the spelling of new words. Rules for spelling (such as the *i* before *e* rule) help him in remembering unique features about troublesome words. But, in the long run, in order for him to spell correctly, the word he writes must match the perception of that word which he has stamped on the marvelous mechanism of the brain.

When our image of a word is fuzzy or incomplete, we are not sure that it is spelled correctly. We sit to write a letter to a friend. We write, "We gave our school play tonight. It was a big success." We are not sure of the spelling of the word success so we turn to someone in the room and we say, "How do you spell success?" The someone says, "s-u-c-c-e-s-s" and we promptly answer. "That's what I have but it doesn't *look* right!" What we mean is that the word we have written does not conform to the shape and image in our memory, or our memorized image is fuzzy and we want to check it.

Words which do not follow the rules of ordinary spelling can only be memorized as nonphonetic words must be memorized in reading. Research shows a high correlation between reading and spelling ability. A good reader sees many words over and over in many situations, and the images of these words become clearly imprinted on his mind. It is easier for him to reproduce these words on paper than it is for the child who has not seen the word as many times in print.

Our chart of language development (see page 87) shows us that spelling is far down in the sequence of language development. It is a sophisticated skill in many ways. There is a correlation between spelling ability and intelligence. Slow learning children may never master an adequate spelling vocabulary.

Spelling is a polishing-up technique—one of the refinements that comes after the basic concepts of speech and recorded communication have been established. In a culture where sounds have been borrowed from many other cultures and words have a multitude of meanings, spelling is a difficult process at best.

When children do not have a clear visual image of a word, they resort to auditory perceptions, using the phonetic rules they have learned which they try to apply. In this case misspellings are often the result of incorrect auditory reception. A child spells "I don't wanna go" because he hears "want to" that way. He spells "encyclopedia" as "ensighklopeedia" because he has never noticed the spelling of the word before, nor has he been called on to spell it and he applies phonetic spellings he already knows.

The basic emphases in the teaching of spelling, then, should be on seeing the word and hearing it correctly. Most misspellings are due to a deficiency in these two areas.

The child's ability to apply phonics is well demonstrated in the following spelling taken from one group of papers. Unfortunately, because the English language is nonphonetic to a great degree, these spellings are incorrect.

parashoot	parachute
caus	because
pepple	people
trubble	trouble
no	know
site	sight
upbrela	umbrella
bowkay	bouquet
prezent	present
decerashion	decoration
micerfone	microphone

Phonetic spelling is widened in Colleen's hilarious story below. Colleen is in the second grade.

> I got in truble one day. With a grait big giant that was after me. But I ran and ran as fast as I can. I saw a bottle so I jumped in to it. Then the giant saw me! But what should I do! I must run out agann so I did! I was drunk so I fall down why did I fall down. Then the giant put me in the bottle and he drank me all up! That was the end of me. But my hole family was crying! But I can't help that! Cuse I am sopost to be Dead! And my family went to Church!
> The End

In a rural sixth grade classroom Martin Peters, a pupil, submitted this story: (see pages 83–84).

A Sattidy Morning

One Sattidy morning I got up before anyone else. I went to the refrigeador and got some eggs and milk and made my own breffast. Then I took my new rifle and went hunting.

Over the fields I went until I came to the woods. Just inside the woods was a small pond. As I got near the pond I heard a noise. There on a log sat a stoopid ole bullfrog. I aimed my rifle and fired. But I missed him. What do you think that ole bullfrog did? He was so stoopid he just sat right there croaking. I diden have the heart to shoot him again.

A careful look at this story shows misspellings of the following words:

> *Sattidy* for *Saturday.*
> *Refrigeador* for *refrigerator.*
> *Breffast* for *breakfast.*
> *Stoopid* for *stupid.*
> *Ole* for *old.*
> *Diden* for *didn't.*

Martin's teacher was concerned over his spelling disabilities. She arranged her class schedule so she could work with him individually for ten minutes a day. During that ten minutes she gave him drill in phonics. But Martin does not need phonics drill. His phonics ability is excellent. His problems in spelling stem from improper auditory reception and lack of correct visual perception.

If Martin's teacher knew his parents well, she would know them to be plain, comfortable country folk who own a successful apple farm. Martin's parents never went past the fourth grade, but their lives have been rich with many interesting experiences and they are solid, happy, American stock. New words have crept into their vocabularies in a subtle and roundabout way. They pronounce the word *Saturday* as *Sattidy*, the word *refrigerator* as *refrigeador* and the word *breakfast* as *breffast.* In all the years when Martin was forming his speaking vocabulary, he heard only his mother and father speaking, and, being quite isolated from other people, he picked up their pronunciations. So strong is the influence of the early years that other pronunciations, which Martin has heard in school for six years, do not replace the ones he still hears at home.

The misspellings of the words *stupid, old* and *didn't* are also auditory problems. Sloppy pronunication or slovenly listening habits may be the cause of his problem in this case.

Martin's teacher needs to help him *say* and *see* the words themselves. In the case of *Saturday, refrigerator* and *breakfast,* he needs to listen carefully while looking at the word. An individual card file with each word that he misspells would help Martin a great deal. Careful pronunciation of the word should be made as he visualizes it. At no time should the teacher make Martin ashamed of his own speech. To do this would mean that he may become ashamed or critical of his parents' speech. For years these people have communicated by use of these symbols and it is not the job of the teacher to destroy this communication system which is so well established. What Martin's teacher must do is to help him accept two different levels of language and help him to understand that informal language is often different from written language. She can also show him that correct written language requires that he know the formal level of language and that he will need to spell correctly in order to be socially courteous.

The misspelling on Martin's paper of the word *stupid* is a common mistake; the *u* and *oo* sounds are alike. Again, the visual image is important. Martin needs to *see* this word repeatedly in order to imprint the correct form on his memory.

Poor listening habits account for the misspelling of the word *old.* The teacher can work to help Martin listen to *all* parts of the word, especially its ending. This skill will also help him with misspellings of words like *didn't.* Printed cards of these words will help him to visualize their endings.

Actually Martin is being very creative in his approach to spelling. He is taking facts he knows (or thinks he knows) and putting them into new patterns. By the creative teaching of spelling is not meant that we will help Martin to spell words in new ways. It means we will resort to gimmicks, devices and other motivational techniques so Martin will be able to visualize and remember standard spellings. Knowing the correct spellings of words will leave Martin free to create with more security, inasmuch as his work will not be subjected to social disapproval. Spelling correctly means conforming in the most rigid sense. But, the teaching of spelling can be, to some degree, creative and stimulating.

OBJECTIVES IN TEACHING SPELLING

Objectives for teaching spelling in the elementary school are rather obvious and may be stated simply as a sensible, modern philosophy for strategies in teaching.

1. Spelling is taught to help each child to learn to spell correctly those words which he speaks and wishes to put on paper for others to read.

2. In order for others to read his thoughts, these words must follow the arbitrary form accepted by the society in general. Thus, a child learns correct spelling as a *social courtesy* to others who read his writing.

3. Spelling is taught in the elementary school so children may develop a *positive attitude* toward correct spelling and the need for it, and a pride in being able to spell correctly.

4. Spelling is taught to help each child *develop good study habits* and the ability to work with auxiliary materials well enough so he has resources for solving his spelling problems throughout life.

The great amount of research in the area of spelling has helped us to understand more clearly how spelling should be taught to attain these goals. Conditions can be set for more efficient learning of the spelling words if we keep some of these basic principles in mind.

1. *The source of word lists must be considered carefully.* A reference to the language sequence chart (see page 87) shows us that spelling becomes essential to children only after they begin to write. Children write those words which they use in their oral vocabulary, and oral vocabulary is a verbalization of their own experiences. Words which are not drawn from their experience are meaningless to children and only tend to clutter up their organized vocabulary resources, or confuse the spelling of words they already use. The teaching of spelling is more realistic and brings better results when it is based on actual experience. The teacher who takes the children on a trip to the dairy, or who helps her class live through the experience of producing a play, has little difficulty in teaching the multitude of words that arise from such an experience. Children need these words for their charts, scripts, poems and stories, and they learn them best by using them. If a vocabulary chart is kept in the room and new words are added daily, a long list soon results. From this list of fifty or sixty new words each week, the class can choose twenty which they must learn how to spell. This should be the spelling lesson for the week —composed of words which the children understand, know and need.

In Chapter II of this book, reference was made to Loban's research. Loban[1] found that the correlation between spelling and the other symbol skills, reading and handwriting, is indeed very high. We can accept the truth that children learn best to spell the words they read and write and not words imposed on them weekly from a textbook.

Textbooks in recent years have greatly improved in the presentation of word lists. These lists are now derived from the vocabularies of children rather than those of adults. They are compilations of the words most commonly used by children. As such they serve as a check to the average teacher or as a resource for her in planning spelling lists for her own class. She can introduce many words at the oral level of communication, if she feels a need for the children to know words which are common to most children.

One thing the textbook does not do is teach words which children need at a special time, or to teach words which are newly coined and used constantly by children. In the first category fall such words as *robin* and *mumps*. Where adults probably use the word *robin* a great deal in the spring as they look for signs of spring, the child uses it often during the year because he is always interested in birds. An epidemic of mumps creates the need for the knowledge of the spelling of the word so children may send letters to the afflicted persons, and can use the words in writing the daily news, poems and stories in school.

Local and regional words which are of great importance to children cannot be put into textbooks. A child who lives in an industrial area has many words such as *mill, factory, steel, boss, strike* and *machine,* in his oral vocabulary, while a child living in a suburb may have different words such as *station wagon, airport, ranch house, picture window, school bus,* and *cafeteria* in his spoken vocabulary. The teaching of these words in each case should come at different times—but, in each case, at a time when they are most needed by children in their written communcation.

In the second category fall such words as *rocket, missile, astronaut, dragstrip, orlon, megaton* and words which have been created or which have come into common use since the textbook was published or since the word list studies were conducted. Children are not only exposed to the sound of these words on television, radio and daily conversation, but also *see* them on bus advertisements, on television or in the newspaper. They are a vital

---

1. Walter Loban, *The Language of Elementary School Children* (Champaign, Ill.: National Council of Teachers of English, 1963), pp. 87–89.

part of a child's written communication and must be utilized in a realistic communication program.

Words foreign to the child's experience have no place in his communication system. They are an added attraction, remote from his regular experience, an imposed task to be mastered, and often a boring chore. Attitudes toward spelling and an insight and desire to spell are not fostered by sterile lessons learning such words. Even the most skillful teacher has difficulty teaching such words so removed from meaningful content, and many of our teachers, lacking this skill, become slaves to the book which tells them so precisely what to do. In the most extreme cases, where we have midyear promotions, many teachers teach the lessons in sequence and have the children learning Christmas words at Easter.

Some of the words used in school will not need to be memorized; their life use is too infrequent. They should be copied from the dictionary when needed. Children should not be forced to learn to spell words which they will seldom if ever use in life situations. Constant use of the dictionary should be encouraged for the proper spelling of unusual and rarely used words. If, with a basic vocabulary well learned, the habit of consulting the dictionary when in doubt is established, the child will be well equipped to meet his ordinary spelling needs if he has some idea of the spelling of the word.

2. *An understanding of phonetics and word structure should be meaningful and should rise from the child's experience.* Good listening habits are necessary in teaching children to spell phonetically. The many suggestions offered in Chapter IV to develop good listening habits and those suggested in Book III, *Creative Teaching of Reading and Literature in the Elementary School,* to develop audio perception have as much bearing on the learning of spelling as they do on learning to read. The phonics practices and the work in structural analysis suggested in Book III also develop spelling abilities in children. There is a high correlation between reading and spelling ability and the ability to read, with all its related skills, is the best readiness program for learning to spell.

3. *Spelling is basically a visual skill and more emphasis should be placed on the "look" of the word than was formerly placed on the sound of it.* Children learn to identify things by shapes: people, dogs, tables. The shape of the total word is the way the child first sees it. This visual image is the pattern impressed on his mind. Any distortion of this pattern is likely to cause misspelling.

When the child is asked to write a word ten times to learn to spell it, we may be asking him to learn it the hardest way for him.

He is not hearing the word, and unless carefully supervised, he may be seeing each letter separately and missing the total word pattern. The value of this type of learning is dubious.

The way a word *looks* is as important in teaching spelling as the way it sounds. And we do not mean the way the letters look, letter by letter. Rather it is how the total word looks, each letter in its proper place and related to the others. Good teaching accepts as its first responsibility the idea that the child see and hear the word correctly. He closes his eyes and attempts to see the word; he checks his visual image with the board or a book; he again shuts his eyes to see it and says it *softly;* then he checks by trying to write it and comparing it to the model. When he is able to reproduce the word correctly, he goes on to study the next word.

4. *Spelling rules, like all definitions, must grow out of experience and should not precede it.* Exceptions to rules must be understood. Primary children write their first words simply by the reproduction of shapes. As they become phonics and structure conscious, they gain techniques to attack new words in reading and to write new words (or spell them). Exceptions to phonetic and word structure rules may be noted when the child first comes upon them and notices that an application of the rule does not work. Children may begin to make charts of these exceptions until they have enough evidence to formulate a rule. If the exceptions and the generalizations grow out of the children's experience and are kept on charts or in a class-made book, they will understand these exceptions using the charts and books as a ready reference when solving spelling problems.

Miss Watson's third grade noticed that when two vowels appeared together in a word, only one was heard. Miss Watson suggested that the children collect such words from their reading books and from their experience. She printed these words on a chart over a period of a few days. She made two separate lists as the words were suggested. Her lists looked like this:

1	2
boat	pear
beat	tear
meat	bread
leak	book
mean	took
tear	about
oar	would
feel	our
peach	ready
cheer	chief

read	brief
your	break
seen	heard
each	does
please	goose
sheep	
tail	

After the list was large enough to show a rule *and* some exceptions, Miss Watson used it for a lesson. She asked the children to look at the double vowels in each word in list one. They pronounced the words together. Miss Watson reminded them that they had collected these words because only one vowel was heard in each, the other was silent. The children went through the list and found which vowel was silent. They noted that in each case it was the second vowel.

Miss Watson then drew their attention to the first vowel in each word by circling it with a red felt pen. She asked the children to read the sound of each vowel she had circled. Then they were asked which sound of the vowel was used in each case. They identified the long sound.

"Do you suppose we could make up a rule about double vowels when they appear in a word that will help us to know how to read and spell that word?" asked Miss Watson.

The definition suggested was as follows: when there are two vowels in a word, the first one often says its own name and the second is silent. Miss Watson printed this definition on the bottom of the chart. Then she introduced this list of new words, taken from the children's reading books.

coat	bean
peel	dear
reach	hear
steam	neat
poet	

The children applied the rule to each word to see if it would work.

Miss Watson then introduced list number two. She asked the children to read the words. The principle was then applied to each word; they could see that it did not work. Miss Watson asked if they could use their rule in all instances. The children agreed they could not. Billy suggested they print at the top of the list, "except these words." The children were then ecouraged to watch for words which did not follow the rule and print them on the chart.

The first rule was later applied when Miss Watson gave the

children a series of drill exercises with words to spell, such as *rear, foam, goal, reel, gear, toad.* In each case the children had to memorize the silent vowel which made the first vowel *"say its own name."* An understanding of spelling rules and their exceptions results when the rules grow out of the experiences of the children and are not imposed on them.

5. *Conditions should be set to develop efficient study habits in spelling.* Good study habits are basic, and the children and teachers should work out a *plan* for studying their spelling words. Different children learn in different ways, and the plan for study need not be the same for all children. Children can study independently by making up a plan which suits their needs. Independent study removes boredom on the part of the student and is often time saving for the teacher.

A plan for learning the weekly spelling list is important and many good spelling texts tell of such plans. The teacher can work out with the children one which works best for her group or for individuals in her group. A sample of one such plan employed by one teacher follows, not to serve as a pattern, but rather to provide an idea of how the actual mastery of the words may be obtained, while considering group and individual needs and interests.

In this particular grade, on Monday the teacher and the children went through the vocabulary chart from the previous week's work and underlined in red twenty words they felt they should learn. Knowing that some children had already learned many of them, the teacher gave a pretest so that each child could make a list of the words he would study for the week. Before this test, the words were discussed and their meanings associated with the occasion that prompted their appearance on the chart. Other meanings for the words were discussed, the words were used in other ways, small words within large ones were discussed and word derivations were sometimes brought out; for example, *lawyer* contained the word *law,* etc.

The test was then given. After the test each child checked his own paper by comparing it with the teacher's master copy on the board. He made out a new list of the words that he misspelled. These were the words to study for the week. The teacher checked each list to be sure every child had the spelling of each word copied correctly on his paper. Notebooks were sometimes used to keep a running record of troublesome words.

On Tuesday, those who had all words correct were dismissed to do other things. The children who missed words brought their lists to the teacher and met in a group. The words were discussed, put on the board and explained carefully.

The whole list was pronounced with each child saying the pronunciation aloud. Then each child was told to look at his first misspelled word and to try to see the entire word. He then shut his eyes and tried to see the word. Then he checked with the writing on his paper. Then he looked at the word and spelled it to himself, and next closed his eyes and tried to *see* each letter and spell the word. He tried to write it on a piece of paper and checked it again with the original. If he wrote it correctly, he studied his next word. If not, he repeated the entire process for the word which he missed.

In this way, each child studied different words under teacher guidance, and good study skills were developed. When a child finished his list (as those who missed only a few did), he helped the next one to finish by hearing him spell his words aloud or by dictating them to the child so he might try writing them all again.

On Wednesday, everyone joined in some games with words. Then the teacher dictated the entire list and the children took the test again. This helped to check up on any pupils who had merely guessed correctly on Monday. After the test the words were checked by the children and new lists of words were made out for study. Only the few who had real spelling difficulty were left with misspelled words.

Thursday's period was left for those who had such lists. The other children worked at other jobs and the teacher worked with those children who needed more help than any others. Again the words were studied as on Tuesday. Dictionary work and word analysis skills were developed. More games and drill work were employed to help those students. Generally a careful check was made at the end of the lesson of each pupil by the teacher.

On Friday the test was again given. Any words missed at this time were placed on a five by eight card or in the spelling notebook and studied at odd times by the children. Words missed weekly and added to the card gave the child an account of all the words he had missed during the year. On short weeks (when vacations occupied part of the school days), the teacher and children restudied their cards for their review spelling lessons.

The teacher may judge the effect of her teaching by the manner in which the children use the words they have learned in their written classwork. If the words appear and are spelled correctly, she is giving her children additional tools for communication and is fulfilling the objectives for teaching spelling. She is also giving them a tool which they can employ for creative communication purposes.

6. *As in handwriting and grammar skills, a permissive atmosphere must prevail in the classroom so that children will feel free*

to explore words and to question their structure. Vocabulary charts, word games, a typewriter, certain kinds of textbooks, word files and other devices which give the children the chance to explore and enjoy learning to spell help develop the attitude toward spelling which makes correct spelling important to them. Success experiences are essential to every child. These successes come in the practical application of the words to his daily work, in praise and congratulations from the teacher when he spells correctly and when he contributes new words which aid in the group communicative process.

7. *Spelling is a maturational as well as a learning process.* All children are not ready to spell as many words or the same kinds of words at the same time. Provision must be made to meet individual differences in the spelling program.

8. *All children do not need the same spelling instruction.* The basis for the effective and creative teaching of spelling, like handwriting, lies in the teacher's ability to diagnose each child's spelling problems and to give him the individual instruction which will remedy these problems. The main problems in spelling generally revolve around the following causes: improper visual image of the word, inability of the child to syllabicate, inability of the child to use phonetic sounds, utilization of words which have no meaning to the child, difficulty with exceptions to common spelling words and difficulty with parts of words such as reversals or nonphonetic words.

Children must be motivated to *want* to spell correctly. This is accomplished through the same devices which make him want to write legibly (see Chapter VII). Spelling is another refinement of the handwriting act. From the time that children begin to write their own words, stories or poems, diagnosis for cause of misspelling can take place on an individual basis. Teachers can group children who have common problems or use techniques to help individuals who have unique problems.

INDIVIDUALIZING SPELLING

1. Some children are natural spellers. They see a word a few times, and it seems to be photographed in their minds to be reproduced easily. These children need not spend much time on spelling drill. They can benefit from a plan such as that described on page 347, known as the test-study-test method. If they know the words for the week, they are excused for other work, or they are given more complex words.

2. For children who need instruction in spelling, the study plan

described on page 348 allows the teacher to spend most of her time with the children who need her most.

3. The teacher may use the stories, poems and articles which children write to diagnose their spelling problems. If a series of charts with spelling rules is left in the room after children have constructed the rules, the teacher may number the chart and then edit the child's papers by placing a number over the misspelled word which tells the child where to look for help.

4. A five by eight card for each pupil can be used to list the basic spelling principles with which he is having trouble. These cards can be used as a basis for grouping children with similar problems or for individualized instruction.

5. Spelling scales can be used to help teachers determine individual difficulties (Gates, Dolch, Horn, Betts).

6. Standardized tests will help diagnose children's spelling difficulties.

7. Some teaching machines help children to progress at their own rate in spelling ability.

8. Poor spellers can be assigned fewer words to learn during the week, with the understanding that as soon as the list is learned, they may have more words to learn.

9. Instill in children a purpose and desire to be good spellers by trying to:

a.   Impress upon students that spelling errors make a poor impression in letters and other written work, causing them trouble in such matters as applying for jobs.

b.   Show students that the words they are learning in their spelling lessons are those which they can and do use now and will continue to use in the future.

c.   Teach an efficient method for studying their spelling lessons.

d.   Convince students that they can improve their spelling ability by providing definite evidence of progress-comparison of scores on first and final tests of the week-progress charts, etc.

e.   Allow children to assume responsibility for learning to spell by setting up their own goals and taking the responsibility for reaching them.

f.   Give many opportunities for writing, so students will feel a need for spelling.

g.   Lead children to take pride in correct spelling in all written work and to proofread for spelling errors.

h.   Emphasize mutual helpfulness rather than competition in the classroom. Games, contests, devices and working for marks should be used to supplement the more basic appeals listed above, not substituted for them.

i.   The teacher must be interested in spelling herself! Enthusiasm and sympathetic understanding of the needs of individuals will go a long way toward obtaining desired results. A little praise for small improvements made by poor spellers may bring about greater improvements.

10. *Individualized evaluation:* Some teachers develop a knack for getting children to write creative stories using as many of their spelling words for the week as possible. Here is an unusually successful one, by a fifth grader. The spelling words are underlined.

A Story—The Boy That Got the 4th of July and Halloween Mixed Up.

Once upon a time there lived a little boy who was only 6 years old. One day when he was shoping with his mother he herd someone say that she couldn't wait until Halloween. Then he herd a boy reply I can't wait untill the forth of July. On the way home from the store the little boy asked what Halloween was. His mother said it was a Haladay, when you go trick-or-treating. Then he asked What's The 4th of July? Its a Haladay when you by firecrackers. The next day he wanted to earn some firecrackers for the 4th of July. He asked the storekeeper if he could have a job. The storekeeper asked if he had any experience. He said yes; He immediately began. He quit before the forth of July. He said to himself what is the 4th of July? Its when you go trick-or-treating. So he asked his mother when is the 4th of July. His mother said July 4th. On the 4th of July he made a costume. He was supposed to be a hero. He had a handkerchief with his name on it. He put the firecrackers away for Halloween. On the way down the street he tripped over some hardware. Then he herd someone say who are you? He turned on his flashlight to see who asked. I'm John! I'm going to the 4th of July party. In that? Yea. Wheres your firecrackers? I put them away for Halloween. The boy said costumes are for Halloween. Firecrackers are for the 4th of July. John was so embarrested that he suddenly felt heat and stayed hidden the rest of the day. The next year His mother said don't forget—but John interuppted I won't forget I'm grown up now.

LINDA BRISTOL

CONTRIVED EXPERIENCES THAT SET CONDITIONS FOR TEACHING SPELLING: GAMES

Spelling lends itself well to games and games serve as motivators to teaching. A few precautions must be exercised in using spelling games, however.

The purpose of the game should always be to teach the spelling words. Many games become so involved that the purpose is lost in the development of the game and it contributes little to the learning of the word. Games should be kept simple, with emphasis always on the correct spelling.

Visual impressions are important. In introducing spelling words, games should not be used which distort the image of the word. Games such as scramble, where words are listed on the board with the letters in incorrect sequence for the children to un-scramble, are inappropriate because they often confuse the child more than they help him. Games used at the onset of the spelling teaching experience should not distort words. After the words are learned, games such as scramble may serve as testing devices, but only when the teacher is certain children have a visual impression of the word firmly established in their minds.

Games should include every member of the class or group and at no time should any of the children be eliminated completely. The fallacy of the old type spelling bee was that the children who were poor spellers were eliminated almost at once, leaving those to practice who needed it least. Poorer spellers need to participate *more* than good spellers—and their participation must be active. The visual form of the word must appear many times during the course of the game. Some provision must be made for all students to participate, even when the game calls for some to drop out. The dropouts then become checkers or help in the playing of the game.

Some commercial games and aids are excellent for teaching spelling. These include such games as:

spelling lotto
anagrams
spelling wheels
the typewriter
word cards
word building cards
self-instructing teaching machines

Games: Primary Grades

Inasmuch as success in spelling is due largely to the child's ability to visualize a word, spelling words can be written or printed on cards with a flo-pen and placed on a flannel board where they can be moved about for a variety of reasons. As words are mastered, they can be easily removed, leaving before the children only those which are more difficult. Some children may have the card with the word on it on their own desk over a period of time where they see it repeatedly. Words on cards can be filed alphabetically, after they are mastered, and may be used frequently on the flannel board for review, or used in the file as a check by any child who is not sure of the spelling.

1. Miss Ashforth helped her primary children develop visual images of their spelling words by making three small houses from cardboard boxes which she placed at the front of the room. Each was labeled with a sign: "Sally's Playhouse," "Dick's Ranch House" and "The Gingerbread House." Large pieces of gray paper were cut to represent stones. Words from the spelling lesson were lettered on these stones and they were placed a few feet apart, leading to each house. The children were placed in three groups. One child started at the opposite end of the room and walked to the house by stepping lightly on each stone and naming and spelling the word as he did so. If he failed to recognize a word, another child picked him up. A record was kept of the child's progress inside the house in an envelope. Eventually all reached their goal, then new stones were substituted.

2. The teacher selects words, in the spelling lesson, which can be pictured. She prints eight words on the board and numbers them. The children fold a sheet of paper into eight folds and number the blocks made by the folds. Then they copy the word from the board in the top of the block and illustrate the word. It is important that the teacher check each paper to be sure the child has copied the word correctly at the time he is copying it. Later these papers may be cut apart and the illustrated words used for study or for playing other spelling games.

3. Use clever devices to motivate children to good spelling. Mrs. Bickel made a large Christmas tree out of poster paper. Each week from Thanksgiving to Christmas the words for the week appeared in the colored balls on the Christmas tree. When the test was given on Friday, the children wrote their words on a dittoed sheet on which was drawn a Christmas tree with circles which were left plain. The children wrote the words in the circles. If the word was correct each child was allowed to color a design in his circle making a Christmas tree ball. This left the misspelled (but corrected) words exposed to be colored as quickly as the child learned the word. Variations of this idea can be used throughout the year, for example:

a. Draw on the board circles to represent snowballs. If a child spells his word correctly, let him write it in one of the snowballs.

b. Cut out bells or stockings for children to write words on Christmas week. Booklets can be made from the week's spelling papers.

c. Have him write his Easter words on eggs and all can be placed in a basket on the bulletin board.

d. September words can be written in leaves dittoed on a page. October words can be written in pumpkins lined up on a fence. For November use a row of turkeys or pilgrim hats. January can be snowflakes; February may be hearts; March could be shamrocks; April, umbrellas; May, flowers. Other ideas might be balls, pitchers' mitts, houses or any form appropriate to a social studies unit.

4. Use a round-robin drill with the spelling words. One child says a word he remembers and spells it, the next one repeats that word and adds one of his own, a third child repeats both and adds another, etc. This goes on until one child misses and then it begins again. The missed words are always written on the chalkboard.

5. Disappearing words: a child takes a word he would like the rest of the class to guess such as *grown*. He might say, "Change one letter and the word disappears. A new word takes it place." (*drown* for *grown*)

6. Each child will choose a partner and act out any words in the spelling lesson. The children watching guess the word and write it down.

7. The Owl Game: Individuals or small groups working together with paper have fun figuring this out. In this Owl Game we give you definitions of words which you must supply. They all end, owl.

A noise from a canine in distress	(howl or yowl)
To rove about stealthily	(prowl)
A feathered friend	(fowl)
To make a fierce noise	(growl)
A monk's hood	(cowl)
To make a distorted face	(scowl)
The lower part of the face	(jowl)
A concave vessel, hemispheric	(bowl)

Other ending sounds can be used. Children can work this game in reverse by dividing into groups, making up their own definitions and trying them on each other.

Games: Intermediate Grades

1. There is an old game which can be used very effectively in the intermediate grades to draw attention to the specific arrange-

ment of letters in a word if the teacher has children who need this sort of practice. Give the children the poem below and tell them that one four-letter word can be used to fill each blank, but each time it is used the letters are rearranged to make a different word.

A ———— old lady	(vile)
On ———— bent,	(evil)
Put on her ————	(veil)
And away she went;	
"————, my son"	(Levi)
She was heard to say,	
"What shall we do to ———— today?"	(live)

The creative aspect of this game comes when the teacher challenges the children to find words which can be used in this way, and to make up poems for the rest of the class. Stephen, grade five, submitted the following:

Mother stopped scrubbing her ————	(pots)
Dirty from cooking the roast	
And said, "———— playing with	
your ————	(stop, tops)
And take this letter to ————.	(post)

Johnny, grade four, wrote this poem:

———— said to me	(Eta)
"I've nothing to ———— but ————"	(eat, tea)
"Well I'll drink it," I said	
But she ———— it ahead of me.	(ate)

Some starters for fun are:

stone (notes, tones, onset)
time (mite, emit, item)
tears (stare, rates)
rats (arts, star, tars)
mile (Emil, lime)
pat (tap, apt)
meat (team, mates)
tires (tiers, rites)
arms (mars, rams)
ropes (pores, spore)

2. Write a long word on the board. Then have the children try to make a list of as many different words as they can find in the long word.

Example:	extraordinary	
Words:	extra	ordinary
	or	din

Later, after they have learned the long words, they try to make as many different words as they can from the letters in the long word.

3. Individual progress charts or individual graphs can be kept by each student to record his own growth in spelling. These graphs and charts provide for self-incentive and maintain comfortable learning conditions in the classroom.

Word Derivations

Children enjoy the origin of words and knowing these origins sometimes helps them to understand their spelling. A fourth grader always wrote brekfast until I explained to him that the word came from the biblical concept of breaking the fast of the night—"break fast." He never misspelled it again. Some other word derivations of interest to children might be these:

1. *neighbor:* A neighbor once was a nearby farmer.

   neigh—near

   bor—farmer

   Now it means "anyone who lives nearby."
2. *August:* The Romans honored Julius Caesar by naming a month, July, after him. Later, when the Romans wanted to honor Augustus Caesar, the nephew of Julius Caesar, they decided to name a month after him also. Before the English took the name August from the Latin, this month was called "Wead-Monath," or "weed month."
3. *alphabet:* The word alphabet comes from the words Alpha and Beta, the first two words of the Greek alphabet.

SUMMARY

Creativity cannot be developed through the teaching of spelling. In order for spelling to communicate, conformity to accepted forms is necessary and there is no allowance made for individuality in these forms. But, spelling can be taught creatively to some degree and in such a manner that it is interesting and exciting to children.

The real measure of a child's spelling progress is how well he carries over this learning into his writing. Guides for this kind of evaluation include the following questions:

1. Does the child spell commonly used words correctly in all his written work?
2. Does he keep a list of the words he misspells?
3. Can he study independently?
4. Can he apply simple generalizations?
5. Does he use the dictionary and other auxiliary aids comfortably?

When the child develops a positive attitude toward spelling, when he can write the most common words with ease and accuracy, when he feels secure in his ability to face new words and use a variety of approaches with them, when he takes pride in his written work and feels satisfaction in it as a means of personal expression of his feelings, thoughts and ideas, then, it is realistic to expect that he senses its value as a way of sharing his information. He has developed a tool which helps him to be more creative in his writing.

TO THE COLLEGE STUDENT AND THE CLASSROOM TEACHER

1. In the poem at the opening of this chapter, Kevin has expressed a few of the frustrations of a child when he encounters his spelling lists. Can you project your thoughts into those of a child and imagine other rules and inconsistencies in current spellings which must frustrate him?

2. Examine some spelling books and the teacher's manuals which accompany them to note the recommended method of study in each. Do they all seem to be based on the knowledge and reasoning presented in this chapter? Which ones appear to be sound methods with respect to the material presented here?

3. Have everyone in the class write up an observation report of a child at play, or of an observation in an elementary classroom. They need not put names on their papers. Appoint a committee to read the papers and keep a record of the misspelled words. Put these words on the chalkboard before the class. Analyze the words and make a list of basic principles being violated or the causes of spelling errors.

4. How much does the personality of a college student enter into his spelling ability? You will be interested in having someone report on a research study done in this area. (Jack Holmes. *Personality and Spelling Ability*. University of California Publications in Education. Berkeley and Los Angeles: University of California Press, 1959.)

5. Make a file of all the interesting and creative ways you can teach spelling to any given age level: collect gimmicks, devices, games and techniques other than those mentioned in this chapter.

6. Did this chapter adequately answer the questions listed at the beginning?

7. Discuss this statement: Spelling *can* be made interesting and fun, but it is actually one time when children must conform in order to communicate well. Therefore, it cannot really be taught creatively.

8. If you are a teacher, identify your poorest spellers. If you are a college student, ask a teacher in a school where you are working to help you identify poor spellers. Collect sample papers from them. Make a diagnostic chart of their spelling difficulties. In evaluating the teaching can you determine whether or not the teacher is giving suitable remediation? Think of all the ways you could go about remotivating these children toward spelling and helping them improve their spelling skills.

9. Try one idea from this chapter each day over a period of days and note the reaction of the children. Then, get ideas from them as to ways they can improve their spelling. Be sure to try many ideas of your own.

10. Take a spelling workbook and for one hour go from page to page filling out the blanks and following the exercises. Are the activities meaningful to you? Are you aware of the objective behind each activitiy? Would children be aware of these objectives? Would the material you covered be motivating and helpful to you if you were a child?

11. A linguist is interested in the structure of spoken words. How would a linguist approach the teaching of spelling? Some spelling series have been designed by linguists. Examine them and note any differences in approach from other texts.

12. Ask someone to dictate the following words to you:

kimono	pneumonia
grammar	penicillin
currency	bridle
mayonnaise	questionnaire
carburetor	valuable
organdy	picnicking
battalion	hallelujah
hippopotamus	sacrilegious
rhinoceros	supersede
maneuver	penitentiary
concede	parallel
homogeneous	liquefy

Correct them. Rarely do all people taking this test receive a perfect score. Why? The words are not uncommon. You know phonetic sounds and many spelling words. Why did you not receive a perfect paper? Can you tell now that you have read this chapter?

SELECTED BIBLIOGRAPHY

Blake, Howard. "Studying Spelling Independently." In James C. MacCampbell (ed.). *Readings in Language Arts in the Elementary School.* Boston: D. C. Heath, 1964, pp. 183–87.

Dawson, Mildred A. and Georgianna Collis Newman. *Language Teaching in Kindergarten and the Early Primary Grades.* New York: Harcourt, Brace and World, 1966.

Fitzgerald, James A. "Spelling: Diagnosis and Remediation." In James C. MacCampbell (ed.). *Readings in Language Arts in the Elementary School.* Boston: D. C. Heath, 1964, pp. 188–94.

Greene, Harry, A. and Walter T. Petty. "The Teaching of Spelling." In *Developing Language Skills in the Elementary Schools.* 4th ed. Boston: Allyn and Bacon, 1971, pp. 391–428.

Groff, Patrick. "Research on Spelling and Phonetics." *Education* (November 1968): 132–35.

Hahn, William P. "Phonics: A Boon to Spelling." *Elementary School Journal* (April 1964): 383–84.

Hodges, Richard E. *What's New in Language Arts?: Spelling.* Washington, D.C.: American Association of Elementary-Kindergarten-Nursery Educators, N.E.A. Center, 1970.

Horn, Thomas. "Spelling." In Robert L. Ebel, ed. *Encyclopedia of Educational Research.* 4th ed. London: Macmillan, 1969, pp. 1282–94.

Horn, Ernest. *What Research Says to the Teacher: Teaching Spelling.* Department of Classroom Teachers and American Educational Research Association. Washington, D.C.: National Educational Association, 1967.

Horn, Ernest (ed.). *Research on Handwriting and Spelling.* Published for the National Conference on Research in English. Champaign, Ill.: National Council of Teachers of English, 1966.

Petty, Walter T. *Improving Your Spelling Program.* San Francisco: Chandler, 1959.

Shane, Harold, Mary E. Redden and Margaret C. Gillespie. *Beginning Language Arts Instruction with Children.* Chapter VI. Columbus, Ohio: Charles E. Merrill, 1961.

Yee, Albert H. "The Generalization Controversy on Spelling Instruction." *Elementary English* (February 1966): 154–61.

CHAPTER X

Conclusion

Our Walk

The autumn leaves
Hang on the trees

Red
Gold
Yellow
and Rusty

The autumn leaves
Hang on the trees

Dangling
Trembling
Trembling and
Falling

The autumn leaves
Fall from the trees

And children
Bring them to school
All gold, And yellow, and Rusty

PHYLLIS

The above poem was written in this form and with the spellings as you see them by a bright second grade child. How many of these words appear in a second grade speller? Not many. Phyllis was able to spell these words because she was in Miss Crane's classroom (previously described on pages 147–49) and was introduced to the words first in a meaningful experience and then in printed symbol form. The words were left on charts before the class so Phyllis could see them all day and use them as a reference when she needed them.

How did the public school go so far astray from creative, exciting teaching as I have described in this book? Can it be that in our search for truth we have left the truth behind (along with the children)? The entire process of building and using words can be very exciting, very creative and, when results such as we have seen here are obtained, very effective!

It is the sincere hope of the author that he has shown teachers how to meet the objectives of teaching the language arts in the elementary school in a stimulating and effective manner. What were those objectives? The key phrases as stated on pages 37–39 are as follows:

1. Each child needs to experience language. In every chapter I have tried to show how all language skills are most effective when built on natural or contrived experiences.

2. Each child must acquire necessary communication skills (listening, speaking, reading, spelling, writing, word usage, capitalization, punctuation, grammar, word forms and the use of reference material), so he may express himself effectively in all media. I have devoted whole chapters to the development of these themes.

3. Each child needs to come to appreciate the beauty of the language itself. Chapter VI is devoted exclusively to this although other chapters also demonstrate how this objective might be met.

4. Each child will develop his own communication even when away from the influence of the teacher. Ideas to help children to love to write and to learn to write run throughout the book.

It was the author's hope that he would show how all these objectives might be accomplished in a creative manner.

The teaching of the language arts appears to be one of the most versatile means for developing creativity in children. All teachers have creative power within them. There is no time like the present to set it free!

INDEX

DATE DUE

FE 13 '82			
NO 23 '82			
NOV 16			
FEB 16 '86			
MAR 4 '87			
APR 22 '87			
MAR 5 '88			
APR 28 '88			
MAY 1 '88			